How to Help Your Missionary

A Guide for Parents of Missionaries, Including Messages
of Inspiration and Encouragement

How to Help Your Missionary

A Guide for Parents of Missionaries, Including Messages
of Inspiration and Encouragement

By Raymond E. Beckham

CFI
Springville, Utah

ISBN 13: 978-1-55517-966-5
ISBN 10: 1-55517-967-3

Published by CFI, an imprint of Cedar Fort, Inc., 925 N. Main, Springville, UT, 84663
Distributed by Cedar Fort, Inc. www.cedarfort.com

LIBRARY OF CONGRESS CATALOGING-IN-PUBLICATION DATA

Beckham, Raymond E.
   A guide for parents of missionaries, including messages of inspiration and encouragement /
by Raymond E. Beckham.
      p. cm.
   ISBN 1-55517-966-5
   1. Church of Jesus Christ of Latter-day Saints--Missions. 2. Mormon Church--Missions. 3.
Mormon missionaries--Family relationships. I. Title.

   BX8661.B43 2006
   266'.9332--dc22

                                          2006019042

Cover design by Nicole Williams
Cover design © 2006 by Lyle Mortimer
Printed in the United States of America

10   9   8   7   6   5   4   3   2   1

Printed on acid-free paper

Dedication

To Ida Lee, the best missionary companion and eternal companion anyone could hope for.

Table of Contents

Introduction

To be the president of a mission in The Church of Jesus Christ of Latter-day Saints is a once-in-a-lifetime opportunity. I was serving as a scoutmaster at the time of our call, and someone told me that being a mission president was something like taking three hundred boy scouts on a two-year overnight hike.

Nothing could be further from the truth.

Missionaries are not boy scouts. They are young men and women on the brink of adulthood trying on the mantle of spiritual discipleship for the first time. Also, this scoutmaster had a wonderful companion to share the joys and happiness of missionary service. Third, few experiences in this life are equal to serving the Lord Jesus Christ full time in helping a few of God's children find peace and happiness in the restored gospel.

Our service with more than seven hundred young, dedicated missionaries during our three years in the Canada Calgary Mission was the highlight of our lives. I enjoyed being a scoutmaster; I loved being a mission president!

This book came from our constant admonition to our missionaries to "be the kind of missionary your parents think you are." This statement gave most of our missionaries pause for thought. It helped them focus on the work.

Sister Beckham was a great inspiration to the missionaries. When they said, "Do we have to do that?" Ida Lee would answer, "No, you *get* to do it!" She helped them learn how to cook, how to memorize their discussions, how to get along with their companions, how to conduct perfect family home evenings. And she was the perfect mother for the three of our five children who accompanied us to Canada. Such a companion is absolutely essential to the success of a mission.

We often talked about putting together some thoughts to help parents with their missionary sons and daughters. We saw firsthand the struggles of our missionaries and how important it was to have family support and help. We also saw the unfortunate consequences of mistakes made by parents despite of all their good intentions.

Ida Lee suggested the title for this book: *How to Help Your Missionary Be the Missionary You Think He Is.* Unfortunately, we put off the project too long. She passed away suddenly in 1994.

Pass this book along to girlfriends, siblings, boyfriends, and other family members. Its contents could be helpful to them as they write to your missionary.

As we talk about "he" and "him," please know that we are also talking about sister missionaries. It became too burdensome to always be saying he/she and him/her.

chapter one

A Brief History of Missionaries in the Church

Missionary work has been at the heart of the Savior's Church since He was on the earth. Just before the end of His ministry, He said to his disciples, "Go ye therefore, and teach all nations" (Matthew 28:19). Mark recorded this as a command to "go ye into all the world, and preach the gospel to every creature. He that believeth and is baptized shall be saved; but he that believeth not shall be damned" (Mark 16:15–16). Jesus was even more direct after His resurrection when He told the apostles to be "witnesses unto me both in Jerusalem, and in all Judaea, and in Samaria, and unto the uttermost part of the earth" (Acts 1:8). Christianity went forth throughout the ancient world because those who heard the message carried the word to others. Without those Christian missionaries, many of whom gave their lives for their religious convictions, the message of Christ could have been silenced for hundreds of years.

The gospel has been restored in all its fulness in these days, and with it comes the same admonition to its members: "to stand as witnesses of God at all times, and in all things, and in all places that ye may be in, even unto death" (Mosiah 18:9). Christ also said, "Go ye into all the world, preach the gospel to every creature, acting in the authority which I have given you, baptizing in the name of the Father, and of the Son, and of the Holy Ghost" (D&C 68:8). To missionaries, he added, "Serve him with all your heart, might, mind and strength, that ye may stand blameless before

God at the last day. . . . For behold the field is white already to harvest" (D&C 4:2, 4).

The process of spreading the word of the Restoration began while Joseph Smith was translating the Book of Mormon in 1829. Then it expanded after the Church was organized in 1830. The Prophet's brother Samuel H. Smith took the newly published book and began circulating it in upstate New York in April 1830. Four men were called that fall to take the message to American Indians in what are now the states of New York, Ohio, and Missouri (James B. Allen and Glen M. Leonard, *The Story of the Latter-day Saints* (Salt Lake City: Deseret Book, 1976, 58). Samuel Smith traveled more than fifteen thousand miles in serving fourteen short-term missions in many states and in Canada (William E. Barrett, *The Restored Church* (Salt Lake City: Deseret Book, 1969, 76). Erastus Snow described his departure for a mission to Pennsylvania: "I left Kirtland on foot and alone, with a small suitcase containing a few Church works and a pair of socks, with five cents in my pocket, being all my worldly wealth" (in Milton V. Backman Jr., *Heavens Resound: A History of the Latter-day Saints in Ohio, 1830–1838* [Salt Lake City: Deseret Book, 1983], 119–20).

In 1835, all members of the Quorum of the Twelve were called on missions to the Eastern states, the only time all twelve members of the Quorum undertook missions at the same time.

Additional missionaries were called to other states and to Canada, and in 1837 Heber C. Kimball was called "to go to England and proclaim [the] gospel, and open the door of salvation to that nation." Elder Kimball's reaction was probably very close to what today's missionaries may feel when they open the envelope containing their call:

"O, Lord, I am a man of stammering tongue, and altogether unfit for such a work; how can I go to preach in that land, which is so famed throughout Christendom for learning, knowledge and piety; the nursery of religion; and to a people whose intelligence is proverbial" (Joseph Smith, *History of The Church of Jesus Christ of Latter-day Saints*, ed. B. H. Roberts, 2d ed. rev., 7 vols. [Salt Lake City: The Church of Jesus Christ of Latter-day Saints, 1932–51], 2:490).

Like many missionaries today, Brother Kimball put aside his uncertainties, exercised faith, and accepted the call.

"However, all these considerations did not deter me from the path of duty; the moment I understood the will of my Heavenly Father, I felt a determination to go at all hazards, believing that He would support me by His almighty power, and endow me with every qualification that I needed; and although my family was dear to me, and I should have to leave them almost destitute, I felt that the cause of truth, the gospel of Christ, outweighed every other consideration" (Orson F. Whitney, *Life of Heber C. Kimball* (Salt Lake City: Bookcraft, 1973), 104).

Less than eight months later, hundreds of converts had joined the Church in England because of Elder Kimball and other missionaries, and many branches had begun to be organized.

By 1839, seven of the twelve apostles were in the British Isles. Two others joined them the next year—this at a time when the Church had been driven out of Missouri and was laboring to build a city in the swamplands of Nauvoo. By 1841, there were 5,864 members in England (out of 16,865 worldwide in 1840), and many others had left to join the Saints in Illinois. During the Nauvoo period, missionaries were called right up to the Prophet's death in 1844 and continued to be called under the leadership of Brigham Young.

The Prophet Joseph Smith was killed on June 27, 1844. Most of the following month was filled with uncertainty as apostles and others returned to Nauvoo. Early in August, Brigham Young and the Twelve were sustained to lead the Church. Within a week, Wilford Woodruff and others were on their way to England and other countries to preach the message of the gospel.

The calling of missionaries continued through the Nauvoo period and the movement of the Saints to the Salt Lake Valley. After settlement in the Great Basin, families were sent to organize towns and settlements throughout the West. Missionaries were called as early as 1849 to go to Scandinavia, France, Italy, Germany, and the South Pacific. By the end of 1850—after a decade of unprecedented hardship, including persecution, the martyrdom of the Prophet, and the exodus of the Saints from Nauvoo—the number of Church members had grown to 51,839. Missionaries were in India as early as 1850, in Constantinople by 1884, and in other Middle Eastern countries early in the twentieth century.

At a special conference in 1852, when 106 missionaries were called to go to South America, China, India, Spain, Australia, Hawaii, and the South Pacific, George A. Smith said, "The missions we will call for during this conference, are, generally, not to be very long ones; probably from three to seven years will be as long as any man will be absent from his family" (as cited in Robert L. Backman, "Faith in Every Footstep," *Ensign*, January 1997, 7–8).

SISTER MISSIONARIES

Those earlier missionaries were usually married men with families, but women were also involved in the work. Hyrum Smith, Lucy Mack Smith, and Lucy's niece, Almira, went to Michigan in 1831. The wives of Wilford Woodruff, Parley P. Pratt, Erastus Snow, Willard Richards, John Page, David W. Patten, and others traveled with their husbands to be wives first and missionaries second. The calling of women during the 1830s and 1840s was not recommended and was not very common. In 1850, Heber C. Kimball said men should "leave families at home, and then their minds will be more free to serve the Lord" (in *Journal of The Church of Jesus Christ of Latter-day Saints*, 28 August 1852, 1).

By 1865 women began being set apart for missionary work—mostly with their husbands and mostly to do genealogical work. The first women to be called independent of their husbands took place in 1873, but the numbers were few during the years that followed. In the October 1890 issue of *Young Women's Journal,* women were reminded that their missions were in the home.

About two hundred women were called as missionaries between the organization of the Church in 1830 and 1898—two years after Utah achieved statehood. Most of these women served in nearby Western states, as well as Hawaii, England, and New York. Women were "certified" as missionaries in 1898, which marked the first time that sister missionaries' calls were considered equal to those of elders. In the early years of the twentieth century, however, Church leaders talked of sister missionaries being called "on occasion," "under some circumstances," "occasionally," and "as conditions require," but regular calls have been continued since that time.

DIFFICULTIES OF EARLY MISSIONARIES

Early missionaries went forth without purse or scrip. This often meant depending upon others for food, lodging, and clothing. Untold hardships, discomfort, pain, loneliness, ridicule, and great danger were a few of the many obstacles missionaries faced in the nineteenth and early twentieth centuries.

One of the most successful missionaries in the history of the Church was Wilford Woodruff. One of his early journals reflects some of the difficulties faced by those early missionaries:

> We dared not go to houses and get food, so we picked and ate raw corn, and slept on the ground. . . . We had walked all day with nothing to eat, and were very hungry and tired. Neither the minister nor his wife would give us anything to eat, not let us stay overnight, because we were "Mormons," and the only chance we had was to go twelve miles farther down the river to an Osage Indian Trading Post kept by a Frenchman named Jereu. And this wicked priest, who would not give us a piece of bread, lied to us about the road, and sent us across the swamp, and we wallowed knee deep in mud and water till ten o'clock at night trying to follow this crooked river. We then left the swamp, and put out into the prairie, to lie in the grass for the night. . . . We arose in the morning, after a good night's rest. I was somewhat lame, from wading in the swamp the night before. . . . We crossed the river and started on our day's journey of sixty miles without a morsel of food of any kind . . . so we had great difficulty to keep the road. Soon a large drove of wolves gathered around and followed us. They came very close, and at times it seemed as though they would eat us up. . . . We lay on the bare floor, and slept through a long, rainy night, which was pretty hard after walking sixty miles without anything to eat. That was the hardest day's work of my life. . . . We got up in the morning and walked in the rain twelve miles. . . . Word was sent through all the settlements that two "Mormon" preachers were in the place. A mob was soon raised, and warning sent to us to leave immediately or we would be tarred and feathered, ridden on a rail, and hanged . . . my companion wanted to leave, I told him no . . . we walked forty miles a day through mud and water knee deep, a distance of 175 miles. ("Wilford Woodruff's First Mission—by Himself," in Preston Nibley, *Missionary Experiences* [Salt Lake City: Deseret News, 1942], 37–41)

Many journals of missionaries reflect the sacrifices and challenges of taking the message of the restored gospel to people in many lands. The one above from Wilford Woodruff is reflective of others that have suffered abuse and threats along with hunger and cold and danger.

From its earliest days, the Church has sent missionaries two by two, following the admonition of Christ: "And ye shall go forth in the power of my spirit, preaching my gospel, two by two, in my name, lifting up your voices as with the sound of a trump, declaring my word like unto angels of God" (D&C 42:6).

The Savior had earlier given similar instructions to his disciples in Mark 6:7 and in Luke 10:1.

AGES OF MISSIONARIES

Most of those called in the early years of the Church were mature men with families. This continued through the nineteenth century and has at times been implemented when shortages of young men created a need. During the Korean War in the early 1950s, for example, many married men with families were called to serve full-time missions. For most of the nineteenth and early twentieth centuries, there was not a specific age for those to be called. For example, Joseph F. Smith was called to go to Hawaii when he was fifteen. At some point in the early 1900s the minimum age for young men was standardized at twenty-one, later modified to nineteen-and-a-half by World War II, and then changed to nineteen in the 1950s. For young women, the age was twenty-three during most of the first half of the century and then changed to twenty-one when young men's ages were changed to nineteen. For a few years in the 1990s, couples could not be called after age seventy, but today the health of the couple is the determining factor for missionary service.

SENIOR MISSIONARY COUPLES

Senior missionary couples play a vital role in the world as they perform a variety of essential services. In addition to those who serve as missionaries in proselytizing activities, many are called to serve in public affairs, humanitarian services, visitors centers, family history, office work, reactivation assignments, leadership assignments in small branches, teaching in seminaries and institutes, and in many other ways to serve full time in fulfilling the needs of the Church.

Senior missionary couples have served missions almost from the beginning of the Church, but it was not until the middle of the twentieth century that they began serving in a major way. Even then, these couples were called to be missionaries in every sense of the word. They maintained a daily missionary routine and schedule, memorized the discussions, and were expected to proselyte full time. Gradually, senior couples and senior sisters began filling specific functions in the mission field that young men and women could not do. These assignments grew to include hundreds of necessary tasks that can be performed only by those with a lifetime of experience and training. Today senior couples are as much a part of the Church's total mission as are the younger missionaries, even though the vast majority of missionaries are young men and women who follow Paul's admonition to Timothy to "let no man despise thy youth" (1 Timothy 4:12).

METHODS OF TEACHING

Over the years the methods of presenting the restored gospel has evolved to a missionary book known today as *Preach My Gospel.* This guide to missionary service includes five lessons that are to be taught to investigators:

1. The message of the restoration of the gospel of Jesus Christ.
2. The plan of salvation.
3. The gospel of Jesus Christ.
4. The commandments.
5. Laws and ordinances.

Each lesson contains several principles and doctrines, including baptismal interview questions, commitments, and doctrines to be taught. Although missionaries should totally learn the concepts in each lesson, they should not teach by a memorized recitation but should feel free to use their own words as directed by the Spirit.

The missionaries teach the first four lessons to investigators before they are baptized, with help, if needed, from ward missionaries and other members. After baptism, the first four lessons are taught again to new members, plus the fifth lesson. Local leaders determine how long the full-time missionaries are involved with the new members after baptism.

Preach My Gospel also includes many helpful hints for missionaries and is an invaluable addition to any home's library. Today it is the primary source for all missionary service and is accompanied by a Missionary Daily Planner to help missionaries plan their day and week. Its central theme, as outlined by the First Presidency, is "intended to help you be a better-prepared, more spiritually mature missionary and a more persuasive teacher. We urge you to use it daily in your personal and companion preparation, and in your district meetings and zone conferences. Study the referenced scriptures and learn the doctrines and principles."

Missionaries should become familiar enough with the teaching lessons to the point that they can teach by the Spirit because they have a full knowledge of the lessons and their accompanying scriptures. Missionaries are free to teach the concepts and the lessons in any order, as the Spirit directs.

By contrast, early missionaries relied heavily on the Bible, with heavy emphasis on the Book of Mormon and the restoration of heavenly authority. Most proselytizing was done door to door or in small groups. In 1844, Hyrum Smith said to the departing missionaries:

"Preach the first principles of the gospel—preach them over and over again . . . you will then be able to make them plainly understood by those you teach, so that you meet scarcely any honest man who will not obey them, and none who can oppose. Adduce sufficient reason to prove all things, and you can convert every honest man in the world" (Joseph Smith, *History of the Church*, 6:322–23).

In the first half of the twentieth century, the most popular method was tracting—leaving a religious tract at every home and hoping for a follow-up discussion if the family had any questions. If questions came up, there was no organized way for the missionary to present the scope of the Church to the investigator. Each missionary was left to his own methods, knowledge, and experience. In the early 1900s, a six-month missionary preparation course at Brigham Young Academy included as its core James E. Talmage's *Articles of Faith,* along with subjects on the Book of Mormon, Church history, and biblical history. Many General Authorities wrote books and pamphlets about a variety of subjects for the missionaries to use in their tracting.

Many mission presidents prepared materials for their own missionaries. The most lasting was a series of twenty-four weekly topics assembled by Elder LeGrand Richards in the 1930s, at the time serving as president of the Southern States Mission. It was titled *The Message of Mormonism.* Elder Richards later enlarged his material and published it in book form as *A Marvelous Work and a Wonder.* Many other tracts and booklets were published up to the end of World War II, but a missing ingredient in all of them was a challenge to the investigator to be baptized.

The first organized, systematic mission plan that included a baptismal challenge was the Anderson Plan. Developed by a young missionary, Richard L. Anderson, in the Northwestern States Mission in 1947, *A Plan for Effective Missionary Work* included in its fourteen discussions the Book of Mormon and the restoration of the original Church as its central theme. It emphasized a logical analysis of relevant scriptures and involved the investigator in a point-by-point discussion of each topic. It was such an immediate success that the Church in 1952 developed its own plan, *A Systematic Program for Teaching the Gospel,* built around seven discussions and encouraging missionaries to rely on the Spirit as they taught the gospel. Subsequent revisions were made in 1961, 1973, 1985, 1994, and 2001, and all of them stressed the following to the missionaries:

Your goal is to help investigators become converted by the Spirit and be baptized into the kingdom of God. To do this, you must help them feel and recognize the influence of the Spirit (see D&C 50:14–22). As they feel the Spirit, you will be able to help them make and keep the commitments that lead to conversion and baptism. These discussions are based on a simple pattern for helping investigators make and keep the basic commitments (see *Ensign,* September 1973, 90–91).

Today's missionary lessons were introduced in 2004 in *Preach My Gospel.* It counsels missionaries to "prepare investigators to feel the Spirit, for conversion to the gospel comes through the Spirit." *Preach My Gospel* states that the purpose of the missionary is to "invite others to come unto Christ by helping them receive the restored gospel through faith in Jesus Christ and His Atonement, repentance, baptism, receiving the gift of the Holy Ghost, and enduring to the end."

LENGTH OF SERVICE

The length of missionary service has varied since the early days of the Church when missionaries were called for indefinite periods of time. The standard twenty-four-month mission term for young men and the eighteen-month term for women evolved during the early part of the twentieth century, but those who were to learn a foreign language served an extra six months. In 1969, the extra six months were eliminated and all young men and women were called to serve twenty-four and eighteen months, respectively.

In 1982, terms for elders were reduced to eighteen months because of economic conditions, but the twenty-four-month term was reinstituted at the end of 1984. Couples have had the opportunity to serve for six, twelve, or eighteen months. The length of calls for mission presidents was standardized to three years in the 1960s. Before that time the term of service could be from one year to a dozen or more. Some mission presidents had served as long as twenty years. In June 1961, the first official training seminar was held for mission presidents. It was at that time that President David O. McKay outlined his concept of "every member a missionary" and urged members to become more involved by bringing at least one new member into the Church each year.

MISSIONARY PREPARATION

As the number of missionaries grew, so did the number of missions worldwide. Very little missionary preparation was initially available for missionaries, and it was left to the mission presidents to do whatever training was necessary. Brigham Young University had a missionary preparation class for those planning to go on missions, but no formal training was given to missionaries until they arrived in the mission field.

This changed in 1925 when the mission home in Salt Lake City was dedicated by President Heber J. Grant. About a hundred missionaries were trained at a time. The training lasted from three to six days. Church procedures, proper manners, missionary methods, and a review of Church doctrines were given to missionaries from the United States and Canada. Only a few missionaries were being called from other countries, and they were sent to their missions without going to the mission home. For fifty years the mission home experience was the beginning of a missionary's calling.

The Missionary Training Institute was organized on the BYU campus in 1961 to teach Spanish. Missionaries would still go to the mission home in Salt Lake City, but those assigned to certain Spanish-speaking missions were sent to Provo for two additional months while waiting for visas. By 1963, the name was changed to the Language Training Mission, and from 1968 to 1975, other Church schools in Idaho and Hawaii also had Language Training Missions, which by this time offered training in most languages. Finally, in 1978, the Mission Home in Salt Lake City was closed and all missionaries were sent to the new Missionary Training Center in Provo for four weeks of missionary training and an additional eight weeks for language training. By the end of the century, fifteen MTCs in Europe, South America, Asia, and the Pacific taught and trained missionaries.

Church members too were being prepared to help the missionary effort. The proposal by President McKay, "every member a missionary," was expanded and enlarged by succeeding Church leaders. The October 1977 issue of the *Ensign* was devoted exclusively to helping members learn how to assist missionaries. In 1982, each member participated in a six-lesson Sunday School class that encouraged members to become more involved and taught specific ways of doing so. President Spencer W. Kimball's goal was to have members do the finding and missionaries do the teaching. The September 2005 *Ensign* introduced the *Preach My Gospel* handbook and continued to stress the importance of members in missionary efforts.

FINANCIAL ARRANGEMENTS

As mentioned previously, most of the early missionaries of the Church—beginning with the Prophet's brother Samuel in 1829—went without purse or scrip. This meant that they had little or no money and were totally dependent upon others to help them with food, lodging, and the necessities of life. This continued well into the twentieth century, although many families and priesthood quorums were contributing to a missionary's expenses during those years.

Young men were and are encouraged to help with their missionary expenses by working and earning money to save for their missions. Thousands of young men and women have borne the entire expenses of their missions, and families have contributed large sums of money to help their sons and daughters serve missions. Local wards and stakes often receive contributions from members to assist with specific missionaries from their neighborhoods. In addition, many Saints throughout the world contribute regularly to the Church missionary fund to assist missionaries from developing countries.

Until 1994, the expenses of serving missions in the world varied from mission to mission. Some missions were two or three times (or more) as expensive as others. How much a family would pay depended on the mission to which their son or daughter was called. Today all families and individuals pay the same amount into a central missionary fund, and these funds are then distributed through mission presidents to individual missionaries. Because of this system, young missionaries and their families know in advance the cost of a mission and can better prepare for it. Missionary couples are not part of this system and must be responsible for their total expenses. The Church pays the travel costs of missionary couples if they stay in their assigned missions for at least twelve months.

THE WORK CONTINUES

Elder M. Russell Ballard of the Quorum of the Twelve discussed the need for the "greatest generation of missionaries" in his October 2002 general conference address. "What we need now," he said, "is the greatest generation of missionaries in the history of the Church. We need worthy, qualified, spiritually energized missionaries who, like Helaman's two thousand stripling warriors, are 'exceedingly valiant for courage and also for strength and activity' and who are 'true at all times in whatsoever thing they [are] entrusted' (Alma 53:20)." He continued, "Please understand this: the bar that is the standard for missionary service is being raised ("The Greatest Generation of Missionaries," *Ensign*, November 2002, 47, 48)."

President Gordon B. Hinckley said in 2003, "The time has come when we must raise the standards of those who are called . . . as ambassadors of the Lord Jesus Christ to the world" (in M. Russell Ballard, "One More," *Ensign*, April 2005, 69).

Since that time, every effort has been made to call missionaries who are obedient and faithful, hardworking and dedicated, morally clean and honest, and who have sincere testimonies of the gospel of Jesus Christ because they have been better prepared.

The number of missionaries serving in the world varies from 50,000 to 60,000. They have been "called of God, by prophecy, and by the laying on of hands by those who are in authority" (Articles of Faith 1:5). In Old Testament times, the prophet Daniel looked forward to the time when God's kingdom would roll forth and fill the whole earth (see Daniel 2:26–45). The Lord Jesus Christ, in a latter-day revelation, referred to Daniel's prophecy. We must so work "that his kingdom may go forth upon the earth, that the inhabitants thereof may receive it, and be prepared for the days to come, in which the Son of Man shall come down from heaven, clothed in the brightness of glory" (D&C 65:5). The work of today's missionary is the same as it was in the days of the Savior, in the days of Joseph Smith, and in the succeeding generations since the gospel was restored to the earth.

Elder Ballard's comment, "What we need now is the greatest generation of missionaries in the history of the Church," is becoming a reality. Today's missionaries are fulfilling that role.

chapter two

A Mission Is a Family Affair

For most families, the process of a mission call begins early in life. Family home evenings, Primary, friends, Sunday School, family discussions, scripture reading, Church meetings, and returned missionaries all play a part in shaping and developing a young man's testimony of the gospel and desire to serve a mission. For others, it might be more of a last-minute decision. Either way, the entire extended family—parents, siblings, grandparents, cousins, and others—is a part of the missionary's mission and can play a role in its success.

President Gordon B. Hinckley said, "There is not a home from which missionaries come that will not be enriched and blessed because of their service in the cause of the Lord. What a wonderful thing this great program is. How grateful every father and mother ought to be who has a missionary in the field. What a wonderful service it is" ("Excerpts from Recent Addresses of President Gordon B. Hinckley," *Ensign*, October 1996, 73).

WHY MISSIONARIES GO ON MISSIONS

Some have said that a missionary should not go on a mission unless he wants to go. This is not true. Sometimes we do things we don't want to do because they are the right things to do. President Spencer W. Kimball said that every worthy young man should go on a mission. He did not say that every young man who wants to go on a mission should go on a mission. A mission is a sacrifice in which we give part of our life to the Lord. Along with the missionary's sacrifice come the sacrifices of his family—the loss of a loved one for a period of time, financial contributions, and other challenges.

Some young men do not want to go. We had one young man who didn't want to leave his 4-H cow that he had raised from a calf; another couldn't stand to leave his new pickup truck; another couldn't bear to leave his newborn little sister; still others couldn't stand the thought of leaving girlfriends or parents or sports. We found that many resist simply because it is expected of them.

Young men go on missions for a variety of reasons. One missionary came to the mission field because he had made a promise to a dying mother. Another came to escape an embarrassing situation at home. Another came because he couldn't figure out how to get out of it. One came because he couldn't get into college and didn't want to find a job. Some came because it was the thing to do. Some came because of pressure from their parents. Whatever their reasons for coming, and whatever their reasons for not wanting to be there, we found that within three months, they were all there for the same reason—they wanted to serve the Lord.

Some have also said that certain young men, because of lazy habits or similar weaknesses, should not be imposed upon some unsuspecting mission president. This is not true. Most missionaries, once they get the spirit of their missions, rise to the opportunities and challenges of a mission and overcome many weaknesses, doubts, and misgivings.

A MISSION IS A PARTNERSHIP

A mission is a partnership among the missionary, the Lord, and the family. A loving, supporting family is a crucial part of that partnership. Many missionaries, especially new converts, do not have their families' support. They can be successful even without one of the partners—the family—but the bond between the missionary and Lord must be even stronger. The missionary with strong family ties and support is fortunate indeed.

From the time of filling out mission papers to the time the missionary enters the Missionary Training Center, the entire family senses the excitement of the pending call. Interviews with the bishop and stake president, medical and dental examinations, guessing where and when the mission will be, waiting for the letter from the president of the Church, picking out clothing, going to the temple, intense studying and preparing—all are shared by members of the family as they watch the beginning of a transformation take shape in the life of the prospective missionary.

These are exciting times for the family as they join with the missionary in sharing the joys, fears, doubts, and anticipation of a mission. This is a time for sharing and praying together and for discussing the family's involvement in support of the missionary. It is a time for bringing the family closer together.

Members of the family might be asked to participate in the missionary's final preparations. The bishopric often assigns topics to those who might be speaking in the same sacrament meeting as the missionary, and sometimes members of the family might be asked to speak or pray. In preparing for the program, the family should pray together for the missionary's preparation. This is a time for family involvement.

The setting apart of the missionary by the stake president is another opportunity for the family to participate in the mission. This can be a time of sharing, encouraging, testimony bearing, and reminiscing about earlier times together and the missionary's growing-up years. Before or after the setting apart meeting with the stake president, the family might consider a family program, a family dinner, an ice cream social, or an evening of being together.

Then comes the time for entering the Missionary Training Center with its powerful, concentrated learning and spiritual experiences. Parents are permitted to accompany the missionary to an orientation meeting if they wish, but sometimes distance and work schedules do not permit the parents to do this. Saying farewell is a time for encouragement, love, reassurance, and support. This last time together will be something the missionary will remember throughout his mission—especially at critical, discouraging, and lonely moments. Make it a special, spiritual moment—one that can become memorable for the missionary.

Letters home from the MTC will sometimes make the family wonder who is writing the letter. They know it can't be the person they dropped off just a few short weeks before! It *is* the same person, but he is much more spiritual and much more in tune with God. I have often said that if a missionary changed as much on the outside as he changes on the inside, his family and friends wouldn't recognize him when he came home.

BE AWARE OF MOODS AND NEEDS OF YOUR MISSIONARY

Missionaries have their emotional highs and lows like everyone else, but for several reasons, they are more intense than others.

Missionaries are far away from their homes and loved ones. They are often battling feelings of loneliness and isolation. They are living different lives from those they have experienced in the past. They are working under pressures of intense study, long hours, rejections and approvals, unfamiliar food, less sleep, and many other frustrations of missionary work. Lack of experience in the work sometimes brings about more extreme emotions— higher highs and lower lows—than would normally be expected.

Successes and failures have a more pronounced effect on a young man or young woman than they do on more mature and seasoned adults. Younger people are still learning to deal with a wide range of emotions and feelings. And Satan is always there to influence them the wrong way.

Among the many obstacles placed in the path of a missionary's success are such things as homesickness, rebelliousness to missionary discipline, poor companions, rejection, lack of cooperation on the part of Church members, work that seems too hard, discouraging letters from home (such as a "Dear John" letter from a sweetheart), weather extremes, concerns for loved ones at home (illness, death, family contention), poor diet, discouraging results, and a general lack of the Spirit brought about because of a combination of these and other problems.

Families can make a big difference in how a missionary overcomes these obstacles. Your letters are important. Your prayers are important. This book has been written to give you not only an understanding of the challenges facing your missionary but also ways in which you can help him overcome them.

WORKING WITH THE MISSION PRESIDENT

Mission presidents are busy, but their special calling is to see to the well-being of their missionaries. It is therefore important that he know about special problems or challenges of each of his missionaries.

If there are problems at home such as death or serious illness in the family, parents should feel free to contact the mission president immediately. It is better for the mission president to personally inform the missionary about serious problems than for him to read about it in a letter or to receive a direct telephone call. The mission president is in a better position to evaluate the effects of such news on the missionary, and he can make decisions concerning the immediate needs of the missionary.

If parents have serious doubts or concerns about the mental attitude of their missionary, these feelings should also be conveyed to the mission president. Most problems like this can usually be worked out in correspondence between the parents and the missionary, with help from his district or zone leaders and his companion. If such difficulties continue, parents should feel free to contact the mission president. My experience is that it is better to be safe than sorry in such circumstances, but it is also good to allow enough time to let things work out for themselves.

PRAYING FOR YOUR MISSIONARY

Families can be of great help in the missionary's emotional battle. Nothing helps more than an encouraging letter from home or the knowledge of prayers being offered in his behalf.

President Joseph F. Smith was one of the youngest missionaries ever sent to a faraway mission—to Hawaii at the age of fifteen in 1853. As president of the Church in 1899, he said to the Saints:

> I never pray to the Lord without remembering His servants who are in the nations of the earth preaching the gospel. The burden of my prayer is, 'O, God, keep them pure and unspotted from the world; help them to maintain their integrity, that they may not fall into the hands of their enemies and be overcome; lead them to the honest in heart.' This has been my prayer ever since I was in the mission field, and I will continue to pray thus as long as I live. (Discourse by President Joseph F. Smith, *Millennial Star,* 1 November 1906, 691–92)

In one of his letters to his son, Joseph Fielding Smith, he wrote of his prayers:

> O! God, my Father, bless, comfort, sustain and make efficient my sons, and all thy servants in the mission field. When doors are shut in their faces, give them grace, forbearance and forgiving hearts. When coldly spurned by scornful men, warm them by thy precious love. When cruelly treated and persecuted, be Thou present to shield them by thy power. Make thy servants to know Thou art God, and to feel thy presence. Feed them with spiritual life and with perfect love which casteth out all fear, and may

17

all their bodily needs be supplied. Help them to store their minds with useful knowledge, and their memories to retain thy truth as a well filled treasure. May they be humble before Thee and meek and lowly as thy glorious Son. Put their trust in Thee, in thy word, and in thy gracious promises. And may wisdom and judgment, prudence and presence of mind, discretion and charity, truth and purity, and honor and dignity characterise their ministry and clothe them as with holy garments. O, God, bless abundantly thy young servants with every needed gift and grace and holy thought, and power to become thy sons in very deed! (Joseph F. Smith to Joseph Fielding Smith, 18 July 1899, in Joseph F. Smith letter press copybooks, 1875–1917, LDS Church Archives, 389)

Families should know that similar prayers are being offered throughout the world for those in missionary service. The First Presidency, the Quorum of the Twelve, the Quorums of the Seventy, and other Church leaders pray every day for our missionaries. Most Church meetings invite others to help the missionaries. Prayers are said over the altars of the temples for their well-being.

The prayers of parents and siblings and other members of the missionary's extended family are very important in sustaining and supporting him while he is serving the Lord full time. As you pray for your missionary, keep in mind the highlights of President Smith's prayer. As a missionary, apostle, and prophet, he prayed from his experience to know the needs and challenges of a missionary.

I don't know who wrote the following poem, but it might help the family to better understand the heart and mind of a missionary as he passes through the phases of a mission experience. Think about his shifting emotions as you read this description from an unknown missionary.

Today I am frightened.
My heart is beating a silent fury.
Before me are my family and friends
I love so much and must leave behind.
Pray that I might have courage.

Today I am studying.
With all my intellect I am diligently preparing.
Preparing for the days ahead,
That I might be an effective tool in the hands of God.
Pray that my mind might be clear and alert.

Today I am homesick.
The memories of fun, school, family crowd my mind.
I almost long to return to the carefree days of my youth.
Pray that I might feel the spirit of love.

Today I am successful.
The doors of those seeking truth open to me.
They are receptive to the word.
They will be baptized!
Pray that I might be humble.

Today I am discouraged.
Lowly I trudge home through the rain.
Pondering the slammed door,
The cruel hasty words, the laughing jeers.
Pray that I might have faith.

Today I am happy.
The light shines in my eyes.
From within me I have found joy.
Today I have lived close to the spirit.
Pray that I might always find this joy.

Today I am sad.
Reluctantly and with tears in my eyes
I must someday leave this country and the people
I have taken into my heart and loved.
Pray that I might always remember.

Today I am full of love.
Love for the Lord who called me on this mission.
Love for my family who supports me.
Love for the friends who installed the desire within.
Love for those who had faith in me.
Love for those who prayed for me.
But remember today, today,
I miss you. I love you. I need you.
Pray for me always.
I am your missionary.

chapter three

The Rules and Procedures of Missionary Work

Missionaries have always been expected to live according to very high standards of personal conduct. As the world was divided into geographical missions, mission presidents developed their own guides for missionary conduct. As early as 1906, the Eastern States Mission had published its *Elders Reference* as a guide containing rules and regulations of missionary life. The First Presidency issued the *Elders Manual* in 1918 that contained "a number of helpful suggestions and instructions." The *Missionary Handbook* was published in 1937 under the direction of the First Presidency to "supersede all other previous publications of a similar nature." The *Missionary Handbook* continues to be published today. It is a small, white book that can be carried in an elder's white shirt pocket. Your missionary will be given a copy of it.

CHURCH STANDARDS AND MISSIONARY RULES

From the earliest times, missionaries have been expected to: (1) keep their thoughts, words, and actions in harmony with the message of the gospel; (2) dress neatly, bathe frequently, polish shoes, and keep clothes clean, mended, and wrinkle free; (3) never be alone with anyone of the opposite sex or to participate in dating or flirtation; (4) obey mission rules, civil regulations, visa requirements, and laws of the land where they serve;

(5) never become involved in political or commercial activities; and (6) respect the customs and culture of those whom they serve, including their religious beliefs, practices, and sacred rites. It is taken for granted that missionaries will live by Church standards and the covenants they have made in the temple. Today's *Missionary Handbook* reflects those guidelines and principles. It also briefly discusses topics, such as the calling of a missionary, proven methods of proselytizing, how a mission is organized, how a missionary should conduct himself, requirements for dress and grooming, suggestions for personal safety and well-being, relationships with others, letter writing, and a host of other subjects governing procedures in the mission field.

A family might want to obtain a copy of this handbook. It can be obtained through a Church Distribution Center.

INDIVIDUAL MISSIONS ALSO HAVE THEIR GUIDELINES AND RULES

In addition to the guidelines outlined in the *Missionary Handbook,* each mission may also have its own set of guidelines and procedures that are unique to its local customs, laws, and requirements. A mission in South America, for example, might have entirely different guidelines than a mission in Europe. You may obtain a copy of the guidelines either from the mission president or your missionary.

A committee of our elders and sisters developed several policies and procedures for our mission in Canada. This is an example of what an individual mission might do, but it is only one example of one mission.

- A weekly report and letter is to be written to the mission president and mailed on Monday morning each week.
- All car reports must be sent to the zone leader on the first of each month.
- You are to have only the suggested mission library with you. You are not to have any other books in your personal library while on your mission.
- For elders, hair is to be tapered and not blocked. No hair should be touching the ears.
- You are allowed to listen only to music tapes that are approved by the mission president.
- Touch football is permitted if there is no blocking and not more than six men to a team.

- Church-owned vehicles are not to be used on preparation days other than in the city in which you are laboring.
- You should end your proselytizing by 9:30 P.M. and be in your apartment by 10 P.M. to plan for the next day's activities.
- Movies are not allowed. Listening to the radio or watching television is not allowed.
- Pictures of girlfriends and families should not be displayed in the apartment. Wallet-size pictures are okay but should be kept on your person.
- Two phone calls home per year are permitted—Christmas and Mother's Day. Permission from the mission president must be obtained before making other calls outside your assigned area.
- Companions must sleep in the same room but not in the same bed.
- Correspondence to anyone within the mission outside your assigned area must be approved by your zone leader.
- No hitchhiking is permitted.
- Sisters' apartments are off limits to elders, and vice versa.
- There is a one-hour time limit for dinner appointments, including giving the family a missionary lesson.
- The only kinds of posters permitted in apartments are religious posters.
- Elders should sleep in pajamas, and sisters should sleep in pajamas or nightgowns.
- Magazines (except Church magazines) and hometown newspapers should not be read, but local newspapers in the city in which you are working may be read on preparation day.
- Tapes from home or from girlfriends are not allowed.

Remember that mission rules are established after much prayerful consideration. Those outlined above were debated pro and con by missionaries themselves, and each one had a spiritual purpose that was designed to strengthen the focus of missionaries. Each one was approved only when the decision was unanimous by the special committee.

Each mission will have its own special rules because of its geography, past experiences, social customs, and traditions. I repeat that those listed above were for one mission and at one time. Even in that mission, many of the rules might have changed in the intervening years.

Mission rules are designed so that all missionaries can live by them, even though it is recognized that stronger missionaries would not need some of them. Rules are often designed to protect the missionary from outside influences that would destroy his mission. For example, I had a good friend who was a mission president in London. One of their mission rules was that missionaries could not go to a particular neighborhood in London. One night, two elders were late returning from their labors and decided to take a shortcut through this prohibited neighborhood to save some time. What happened to them that night resulted in their excommunication and returning home in disgrace. Rules are made for the protection of the missionaries and the Church.

Many parents do not realize that distractions of almost any kind will hurt the work their son or daughter is trying to do. For example, we found that voice tapes from home—listening to younger siblings or parents or girlfriends—were so devastating to morale that it sometimes took several days for a young missionary to refocus on the work. Telephone calls on Christmas Day would rejuvenate some missionaries but would make others so homesick that they were unable to do their work. One of our missionaries could not focus on his mission because his father was sending him newspaper clippings of hometown happenings such as marriages, football games, school events, and other local news. One mother called her son every night and kept him from concentrating on his mission because he was still living daily happenings at home. She thought the mission rule about telephone calls was only for calls *from* the missionary. I couldn't figure out why the missionary was not getting into the spirit of his mission until a new companion alerted me to the problem.

One of the most important objectives of a new missionary is to get both feet in the mission field—to be totally immersed in the work. Until he does this, he will not get the spirit of his calling. He cannot be a focused missionary with one foot in the mission and the other foot at home. It is very important that the family help him become totally immersed in missionary work.

The family should always encourage the missionary to live the rules to their fullest, knowing that even small infractions lead to a loss of the Spirit. When President N. Eldon Tanner was asked to name the single most important characteristic of a missionary, he answered immediately with a single word: Obedience. Why obedience? Because all other elements of a mission depend upon obedience to the instructions of the Brethren.

My experience is that missionaries who live by the rules—all the rules—have happy and fulfilled lives, not only during their missions but also afterward. There is something about obedience that builds character, integrity, resourcefulness, and spirituality.

All of us remember the story of Samuel and Saul in the Old Testament. King Saul had been commanded to "smite Amalek, and utterly destroy all that they have, and spare them not . . . [including] ox and sheep, camel, and ass" (1 Samuel 15:3). But Saul spared the best of the sheep, the oxen, the fatlings, the lambs, and all that was good "to sacrifice unto the Lord" (1 Samuel 15:15). Samuel took away Saul's kingship—and later gave it to David—with these words: "Hath the Lord as great delight in burnt offerings and sacrifices, as in obeying the voice of the Lord? *Behold, to obey is better than sacrifice,* and to hearken than the fat of rams" (1 Samuel 15:22; emphasis added).

Samuel went on to say that "rebellion is as the sin of witchcraft, and stubbornness is as iniquity and idolatry" (Samuel 15:23). Obedience is the key to successful missionary work.

Parents, girlfriends, family members, and friends should regularly remind their missionary to follow their leaders.

MISSION ORGANIZATION

Mission presidents have two assistants to the president. A mission is divided into geographical zones presided over by zone leaders. A zone is divided into districts, presided over by district leaders. Each pair of missionaries has a senior companion and a junior companion. Elders may also be assigned to work in the mission office to assist with managing the daily affairs of the mission, but many of these assignments are now given to senior couples who have been called specifically to work in the office. They give continuing service to the myriad details involved in finances, vehicles, local laws, and medical problems of missionaries.

ASSISTANTS TO THE PRESIDENT

These are missionaries who have been in the mission long enough to have gained sufficient experience to assist the mission president in his important calling of working with the missionaries. They often participate in speaking at zone conferences, assisting with the logistics of transfers of missionaries, training district leaders and zone leaders, and managing the day-to-day routine of missionary work in the mission. Their term of service varies but is usually no more than six months. These elders usually return to the field for the final few months of their missions.

ZONE LEADERS

The geographical size of a zone will vary from mission to mission but usually consists of about twenty-four to forty missionaries, including sister missionaries and couples, depending on the distance the missionaries must travel. A zone leader (ZL) will have a junior companion. He will supervise from four to six districts. He often meets with stake leaders and other priesthood leaders in the area. Because of the differences in the size of missions and the number of missionaries assigned to a mission, the size of zones is left entirely to the discretion of the mission president. It is not unusual for a zone leader to be rotated in and out of his assignment depending on his transfers from one city to another. In other words, an elder might be a zone leader in one zone and then be transferred to another zone as a district leader or as a senior or junior companion.

DISTRICT LEADERS

A district leader (DL) will train and supervise from two to eight pairs of missionaries. He will have a junior companion. He will conduct regular district meetings in which he trains the missionaries in his district and works with other missionaries to resolve local problems and difficulties. He works closely with ward mission leaders and local priesthood leaders in correlating the mission activities in the district.

SENIOR COMPANIONS

The Church has said that every companionship must have someone in charge. Hence, a new missionary is a junior companion to a more seasoned missionary called as a senior companion. In some instances, a senior companion is transferred to another city and becomes the junior companion to someone already serving in that city.

TRANSFERRING MISSIONARIES WITHIN THE MISSION

Experience shows that missionaries are transferred from zone to zone and from district to district about every six months. Among the reasons for transfers are: (1) many missionaries need new experiences to keep them motivated; (2) experience gained in one area can be helpful in another area; (3) some missionaries become emotionally involved with local members when they stay in an area too long; (4) new missionaries must be absorbed into a mission, while others are being released to return home at the end of their missions; (5) newly called zone leaders and district leaders need to replace those being released; and (6) missionaries need a change in companions in order to keep learning new ideas and skills. There are many other reasons.

Don't be surprised if your missionary is transferred in less than six months. A mission must be flexible in accommodating changing circumstances and conditions. Transfers are one of the most serious and difficult responsibilities for a mission president and his assistants and are done only after careful and sincere prayer. Assigning a missionary to a new area and placing him with a new companion requires a keen awareness of each missionary and familiarity with all areas in the mission. In our mission, we knelt in prayer at the beginning of a transfer session. Then, after discussing and finalizing possible transfers, we again prayed to confirm each individual transfer and assignment. These transfer sessions were some of the most spiritual and insightful experiences we had in our three years in the mission field.

RELATIONSHIPS WITH LOCAL PRIESTHOOD LEADERS AND CHURCH MEMBERS

Stake presidents and bishops are responsible for missionary work in their stakes and wards. They delegate these responsibilities to ward mission leaders, who work with local Church members to assist in the total missionary program. Where there are no stakes or wards, mission presidents supervise both the missionary work and local Church members in districts and branches.

Mission presidents provide trained missionaries to assist local priesthood leaders in missionary work. They meet regularly with stake presidents, the Area Presidency, and with Area Authority Seventies to coordinate the work within their missions.

Missionaries meet regularly with stake priesthood leaders and with ward mission leaders to coordinate the work on the local level. Zone leaders, district leaders, and individual companionships are assigned to meet with priesthood leaders in the stakes and wards (or districts and branches) to plan missionary strategies and programs with local members.

Missionaries will also work with individual local members of the Church to encourage them to introduce their friends and neighbors to the Church. Working with members—whether through local priesthood leaders or by assignment to local members—is sometimes frustrating and discouraging to a devoted missionary who cannot understand why things aren't moving ahead more rapidly or why members don't do more to help them.

Members of the Church are essential to success in missionary work. The missionary who gains their confidence and who motivates them to introduce their friends and neighbors to the missionaries will have great success in his labors.

chapter four
Letters to Your Missionary

Nothing you do is more important than writing letters to your missionary. This is his link to home for the two years of his mission except for a few telephone calls on two important holidays each year. Your encouraging letters are regular and consistent reminders of your love, confidence, and interest in what he is doing.

Because letters are such a vital part of the missionary's life, they should be carefully planned and considered. I have seen missionaries who were so devastated over a letter from home that they could not return to normal work for several days. Others were uplifted and motivated from letters. The difference is the kind of letter received.

Some parents take turns writing to their missionary. Some send letters from both parents and siblings in one envelope. Sometimes one of the parents will take the primary responsibility for letters, and the other will write only occasionally. Individual circumstances in each home will determine how you handle letters to your missionary. But one thing is essential: letters from home must be regular. Few things are more discouraging to a missionary than expecting a letter and finding the mailbox empty.

THINGS TO INCLUDE IN YOUR LETTERS

Make a plan when writing to your missionary. Ask yourself what the main message of your letter will be. You might want to write down ahead of time the main purpose of your letter and a few of the points you want to cover. Stay brief and to the point, but be warm, loving, and spiritual.

Think of the impact on him that you want your letter to have—a positive, responsive, loving, supportive, spiritual, and encouraging impact—so that after he is finished reading it, he will be more determined than ever to be a committed, dedicated missionary of the Lord Jesus Christ.

After he finishes reading your letter, he should generally feel that things are well at home, that he has a spiritual family supporting him and that his letters are being read and appreciated. Also, he should feel that he has been taught a principle that will help him be a better missionary, that he has been motivated to live the mission rules and to support local leaders and the mission president, that his family and others are praying for him, and that his role is to keep studying the scriptures and take the message of the Restoration to those in his area.

You might consider one or more of the following in your letters:

- Keep your letter on a high spiritual plane (see chapter 5 for help with specific messages).
- Discuss a scripture or a recent family home evening topic.
- Discuss a family incident that has a spiritual message.
- Report on a talk in a recent sacrament meeting or a lesson in Sunday School.
- Send and discuss an article from a Church magazine or conference address by a General Authority.
- Bear your testimony.
- Express your love, appreciation, and support in what he is doing. Missionaries like to know that they're loved and missed and that their family is praying for them.
- Ask your missionary to join in praying for a goal that has been set by the family. He may also ask you to pray with him for an investigator or for a problem he is having.
- Answer his questions about home and family in a positive, uplifting way.
- Show sympathy for his concerns, but do not coddle. Be firm in your support of mission rules and procedures. Always stress obedience to leaders and to standards.

- Encourage him in the work he is doing and in solving the problems confronting him.
- Reassure him that solutions to most problems can be found in the scriptures.
- Concentrate on now. Encourage total dedication at this special time in his life when he can give his total attention and service to the Lord.

Things *Not* to include

- Newspaper clippings about sports, weddings, local crimes, and so forth.
- Negative comments about family strife and day-to-day problems.
- Frivolousness, negativism, gossip, complaints, and criticisms.
- News of the world, except as it pertains to a spiritual point you wish to make.
- Audiotapes or videotapes. And be careful with photographs—they are sometimes distracting.
- Release date and comments about "when you get home." There is a time, however, when help is needed for getting into school, finding a job, and preparing for life after the mission.

Letters from home are unquestionably the most important source of continuing family help and support during his mission. Letters tell the missionary he is loved and being prayed for. Letters help solve personal problems and disappointments. They share in emotions of joy and sorrow. Letters are absolutely essential. That's why letters should be carefully examined to ensure that they are conveying the kind of message you want to send.

Letters are like a lifeline between home and a missionary, but they are not always a one-way lifeline. Parents and family also need this contact with their missionary. My experience is that the better your letters are, the better his become. The opposite is also true—the more spiritual and uplifting his letters become, the better your letters from home become.

chapter five

Messages for Missionaries

Missionaries face many different challenges during the course of their missions. They face certain challenges in the beginning months and other challenges in the months preceding their release. Not all missionaries face the same problems. Some difficulties are unique to only a few. Others are general to almost everyone.

During our mission to Canada, we sent missionaries a general bulletin every week that focused on one possible challenge. What surprised us was that a message had a receptive audience of specific missionaries one week, while the next week's message affected others. Some messages were general and applied to mission goals and programs for all missionaries.

We encouraged the missionaries to save these messages. We found early on that a message that was not needed by a missionary that week might be needed a few weeks or months later. Senior companions often referred to a previous bulletin when helping a newer missionary make adjustments to his new mission routine. Many of these messages found their way into sacrament meeting talks after missionaries returned home. I do not take credit for all of these messages. I am grateful to many others for their assistance. Other mission presidents and their missionaries shared with me their messages. I am particularly grateful to Paul H. Dunn, Paul Felt, and Weston Killpack, three mission presidents who inspired me with their messages and encouraged me to continue writing.

Each week as I knelt in prayer to determine the contents of that week's message, I thought about the elders and sisters of our mission. Their weekly letters and reports contained hundreds of thoughts and ideas as they expressed their feelings and shared their successes and failures. Their wonderful faces and countenances entered my mind as I considered their needs and challenges. In putting together the words and phrases of the bulletin, I drew upon the testimonies and experiences of many others, including teachers, friends, fellow missionaries, church leaders, and Canadian Saints, to whom I am grateful.

Many missionaries who served with me have asked over the years if I would publish these weekly bulletins. I have resisted this because I felt that they were unique messages to a unique audience at a unique time and place.

However, as I have continued to serve in a variety of Church callings, including that of stake mission president, youth leader, regional representative, and in a temple presidency, I have come to realize that perhaps these messages might have application to today's missionaries as well as those who served with me in Canada.

I am sharing them now with some modifications for today's missionary environment. Most of what is here can be applied to many of today's missionaries. If messages might not specifically help your missionary, please ignore them unless you feel the message would be useful to his companion.

HOW TO USE THESE MESSAGES

When or if your missionary has a problem that can be related to one of the topics, you might use the material any way you wish. No attribution is necessary. Include any part of the material in your letter as your counsel and advice to your missionary.

You might wish to include an entire bulletin in your regular letters. Your missionary's mission will last 104 weeks, so you might decide in advance which of the messages you will send him, and when. Some are designed more for newer missionaries while others are for those that have been in the field a year or more. Most of them can be sent any time. Some are for specific times of the year—Christmas, for example.

The messages are printed on a single page, front and back. You may either tear out messages, photocopy messages, or print messages from the accompanying CD. Or you may want to e-mail them either in part or in their entirety. No attribution is necessary. If you use e-mail to write to your missionary, you might suggest that he copy each message or keep them in a computer file. They can be used later in district meetings, zone meetings, or sacrament meetings. My experience is that a message might not be applicable at a given time but might be of use later. You might also wish to underline or highlight important sentences or paragraphs to reinforce how you feel about the topic. It is very important for fathers to write to their missionary son or daughter. Perhaps one of these messages could be sent each week, with at least a sentence or two from the father giving his support to the message.

Combine two or three of them in a message you create yourself. Let your family members have fun deciding which paragraphs or which sentences to include in your message. Don't use quotation marks in quoting from the bulletins—just put them all together. Add your favorite scriptures or quotes from the General Authorities. You'll probably wind up with a better message than any of the ones I have written. Good luck! They are listed here in alphabetical order.

Missionary Messages

A Creed

One day in a class at Brigham Young University titled "Managing your Mind," Professor William H. Boyle gave his personal creed. It was either his own or was adapted from someone else:

> This is my creed and my philosophy. I have failed it often and shall fail it many times yet. But by these teachings of mother and father, I have lived to the best of my ability; laughed often, loved, suffered, grieved, and found consolation, and I have prospered. By friendships, I have been enriched, and the life I have lived has been a happy one. I have promised myself the following:
>
> 1. To live each day as though I may never see the morning come.
> 2. To be strict with myself, but patient and lenient with others; to give the advantage, but never to ask for it.
> 3. To be kind of all, but kindlier to the less fortunate; to be tolerant and never arrogant; to treat all men with equal courtesy.
> 4. To be true to my own in all things, and to respect all honest employment.
> 5. To remember always that my life is made easier and better by the service of others, and to be grateful.
> 6. To make as much as I can of the day's opportunities; to meet disappointment without resentment; to be friendly and helpful wherever and whenever possible, and to do so without display of temperament or of bitterness.
> 7. To keep my money free from cunning or the shame of a hard bargain, and to govern my actions so that I may fear neither reproach nor misunderstanding nor malice nor envy.
> 8. To maintain, at whatever cost, my own self-respect.
> 9. To keep faith with God, with my fellow man, and with my country.

Professor Boyle lived by this creed. He was an example for good in everything he did. His students voted him teacher of the year, year after year, because he lived by his creed. A creed is only as good as the person making it. You might sit down soon and write out your personal creed—how you will conduct your life as you associate with your fellow man. It's okay to borrow from someone else's creed if you intend to live by it.

Adjustments to Missionary Life

Adjusting to life as a missionary is more difficult for some than for others. Thoughts of home, girlfriends, college, or work are often warm, pleasant memories.

Homesickness probably causes more harm to missionary work than anything else the adversary can devise. Adjusting to food, weather, companions, rigid schedules, intense study, and all of the other elements of missionary work is not easy. The first step is to completely immerse yourself in the work. A missionary must put both feet into the mission field. One foot at home and the other in the field will never work.

If everything were solved by us or by those around us, we would never reach out to our Heavenly Father, and He knows this. A wise father wrote to his missionary daughter about homesickness:

"The only ones that can provide comfort for you now are your Heavenly Father and Jesus Christ. You become homesick so that you can learn to rely on them. They are there to help you. They will comfort you. They will strengthen you. They will lift you up when you are down or discouraged. They will take away your feelings of loneliness as you learn to rely on them."

In reporting her mission later, this sister missionary said, "I had to learn to rely on the Lord. I am a pretty independent person. I was accustomed to doing everything for myself and having things work out pretty much my way. But the Lord had other ideas. He taught me that He was in control, not me. Therefore, He gave me companions that were difficult, areas that were hard, leaders who would not lead. But every single thing that happened on my mission was to teach me something, refine a characteristic that was tough, introduce a new way for me to see things, and bring me closer to the Lord. Each time a challenge was introduced, I had a choice: I could complain about it, or I could learn from it. I'm a slow learner. Sometimes I had to learn twice. But through it all, my prayers became more real, more sincere. Little by little, I began to realize how real He really is. Transfer by transfer I began to give my will to the Lord; to see His plan rather than mine."

"Trust in the Lord with all thine heart; and lean not unto thine own understanding. In all thy ways acknowledge him, and he shall direct thy paths" (Proverbs 3:5–6).

Elder Neal A. Maxwell said that missions are a time for learning: "If we are serious about our discipleship, Jesus will eventually request each of us to do those very things which are most difficult for us to do. Sometimes the best people have the worst experiences, because they are the most ready to learn" (Carrie A. Moore, "Elder Neal A. Maxwell Dies at 78," *Deseret News*, July 22, 2004).

One missionary said that he had moments when he felt he had reached his limit. "I just could bear no more," he said. "However, the Lord knew me. He knew I was doing my best, but He also knew there was a lot more to me than I saw. He knew I was stronger than I thought I was, and there was still something to be learned."

Elder Jeffrey Holland said, "I testify that God's love and the Savior's power will calm the storms. . . . Christ knows better than all others that the trials of life can be very deep, and we are not shallow people if we struggle with them. But . . . He rebukes faithlessness and He deplores pessimism. He expects us to believe" ("An High Priest of Good Things to Come," *Ensign*, November 1999, 36).

A Partnership with God

Man has learned to do magnificent things—build pyramids, construct bridges, erect towering office buildings, lay down highways. But as man builds, nature immediately begins to undo his work, rusting away the iron and decaying the wood.

On the other hand, if man plants, nature proceeds to complete his unfinished work. Man sows a seed; up comes wheat. Man plants a sapling; up comes a tree. Such is the difference between working alone and working with God.

As you sow truth in human hearts, you work with God. A seed dropped into a heart often lies there for a long time. But with the spring of faith, the seed sprouts and pushes forward into the maturity of a lasting testimony.

The Lord has called each of you to be sowers of His message. He knows that sharing your testimony is like planting a seed or a small sapling. If not planted, it can never germinate. But once buried in good soil, it need only wait for moisture and warmth.

Your discussions are designed to provide you with an opportunity to bear your testimonies. As you teach the discussions, remember that you are setting the stage—preparing the soil and the climate for your testimonies to take root. Sharing your testimony will sow a seed. With time, this seed will develop into faith, then prayer, and finally into a lasting conviction of the restored gospel.

A story is told about John Wesley, the great religious reformer. He was leading a discussion with a group of religious notables on the subject of faith. When asked to define what faith was, no one had a good answer. Finally, someone passing by overheard the conversation and said, "Faith is taking God at his word."

Taking God at His word! Remember when the Savior told the cripple to walk, and he did; the blind man to see, and he saw? They took Him at His word. As missionaries, do you take God at His word? The Lord has promised to maintain a constant vigil over the faithful (D&C 62:9).

He can be your protector and comforter.

You show your faith by bearing your testimony. When you do this, you take God into a partnership in sowing seeds of love, trust, and joy. Each one of you has the choice of doing your missionary work alone or in partnership with God. "Draw near unto me," said the Lord, "and I will draw near unto you; seek me diligently and ye shall find me; ask, and ye shall receive; knock, and it shall be opened unto you" (D&C 88:63).

The Lord also said, "Let him that is ignorant learn wisdom by humbling himself and calling upon the Lord his God, that his eyes may be opened that he may see, and his ears opened that he may hear" (D&C 136:32).

Take God at His word. Enter into a partnership with Him to take His divine message to those whom you teach. Seek His help; testify of Him, and you will see miracles as the Spirit touches those whom you meet.

A Perfect Day

All of us have experienced days in our lives when everything was perfect, things went well, life was wonderful. Those days stand out in our memories. Have you ever wondered about a recipe for a perfect day? Here is a baker's dozen of basic ingredients that will guarantee a perfect day, every day, if they are applied.

1. Today I will adjust myself to what is and not try to adjust everything to my own desires. I will take my mission and its challenges and adjust myself accordingly.
2. Today I will strengthen my mind. I will study as I have committed myself to do. I will learn something new and useful. I will learn something about God and his ways
3. Today I will solve today's problems and will not tackle my whole life's problems at once or worry about those of yesterday.
4. Today I will be happy. Abraham Lincoln once said, "Most folks are about as happy as they make up their minds to be." I will make up my mind to be happy and will not let anything interfere with it.
5. Today I will take care of my body. I will exercise it, care for it, nourish it, and I will not abuse or neglect it. As the tabernacle of my spirit, it will be able to meet my every command.
6. Today I will exercise my soul in four ways: I will do somebody a good turn and not let him know about it; I will do at least two things I do not want to do but that I should do; I will not show anyone that my feelings are hurt; I will do everything I can do to help my companion.
7. Today I will be agreeable. I will look as nice as I can, dress as smartly as possible, talk low, act courteously, be flattering to others, criticize no one and find fault with no one.
8. Today I will have a plan and will follow it. I will set down realistic goals and priorities, and I will accomplish every one of them, including teaching.

9. Today I will spend a few moments in meditation and will commune with my Heavenly Father in prayer at least morning and night.
10. Today I will be unafraid. I will have courage as I go about my missionary activities.
11. Today I will forget myself and will do things for others. I will enjoy the spirit of sacrifice and service.
12. Today I will live the principles of the gospel and the rules of the mission. I will take pride in my ability to be obedient.
13. Today I will have a positive mental attitude. I will not be discouraged. I will look for the good in everything and everybody. My life will reflect wholesomeness and goodness rather than be a reflection of the moods of others.

Adversity

Missionaries have often asked such questions as, "Why do I have to have so many problems?" "Why is life always such a struggle?" and "Why do I have more problems than others?" Have you ever asked such questions? If so, remember that adversity makes people stronger. Consider the following examples:

THE BOLL WEEVIL MONUMENT

In Enterprise, Alabama, there is a monument erected to the boll weevil. This pest, which almost ruined the cotton industry and threatened to destroy the South, is honored not because of its destroying past but because it helped to build the South. How? Because it forced the farmers to forget about cotton and begin to experiment with other crops. Today, the South flourishes because of sweet potatoes, peanuts, and a variety of other crops. The dreaded boll weevil, the enemy, actually did the South a good turn. The bad break became a good one. The diversification of crops made the South a versatile economy that was not dependent upon the rise and fall of a single product.

LUCILLE BALL

"I Love Lucy" became an American byword. The talented actress Lucille Ball has been considered by many to be the most successful entertainers in the history of motion pictures and television. As a youngster of eighteen, she was a pretty model who found her dreams shattered by an automobile accident that confined her to a wheelchair with partially paralyzed legs. She learned to play the piano, took up music, and developed a keen sense of humor, learning to find humor in almost any subject. When she finally regained her health, her musical ability and humor combined to make her an instant star as a gifted comedienne.

ALFRED FULLER

As a young Canadian farm boy, he went to Boston to find work. He got a job selling brushes and failed miserably. He got other jobs such as delivery boy and streetcar conductor, but he kept asking himself why he failed as a brush salesman. He finally decided that the failure had not been his but that of the brushes. He bought a small wire-twisting machine and designed brushes that he thought would sell. Fuller Brushes became an international institution—the result of a young man failing and then literally twisting that failure into success.

JOHN STETSON

John Stetson, the famous hatmaker, was sent West to die. His health was failing, and he could not work. To keep busy, he amused himself by shaping a broad-rimmed hat to keep out the sun. The "Ten-Gallon Stetson" caught on and projected Stetson into an amazing business career.

While smooth sailing is wonderful and pleasant, it is in the storm that you really get to know yourself. I have mentioned many times that you never grow by just doing the things you want to do; growth only comes from doing things you don't want to do.

Misfortune and adversity should never be regarded as calamity; they may be good fortune in disguise. As necessity is the mother of invention, so is adversity the parent of genuine development. Most people follow the line of least resistance and do not really exert themselves except under great stress. When you complain about misfortune, remember that there may be a point and purpose to it that will be revealed later. "For after much tribulation come the blessings" (D&C 58:4).

Adversity

The history of the Church from ancient times to modern day is filled with stories of men and women who overcame great difficulties. Think for a moment about those who struggled to overcome physical hardship, adversities, temptations, abuse, torment, loneliness, condemnation, anguish, heartache, disasters, ridicule, and discouragement. Names such as Abraham, Moses, Job, Peter, Alma, Nephi, Joseph Smith, Brigham Young, Spencer W. Kimball, and Howard W. Hunter recall to my mind the matchless courage and valiant service that these men have inscribed in pages of time.

But what of the thousands upon thousands who fell, failed, lost, or succumbed to the temptations of Satan? Where are they in history? Do their exploits stir your mind? Do you want to follow in their footsteps? Would you teach your families of their deeds or encourage others to emulate them?

No. People tell over and over again the stories of those who persevered, who overcame troubles and adversities, who proved their obedience in times of stress, who fought the great battles of life and won.

How do you fight temptation? Discouragement? Contention between you and your companion? Ridicule at the door? Homesickness or girlsickness? Loneliness? Physical illness? The difference between a good man and a great one is the way he meets the challenges of every day, whether they be big or small.

President Hinckley has said that when he needs extra courage to face the problems of life, his thoughts turn to the Prophet Joseph Smith or to the Savior. Never were two men more scorned, abused, threatened, and tempted than were these two great examples of manhood. If they had failed or quit, what would the world be like today? Their steadfastness in the face of overwhelming odds should be an example to all of us. Olga J. Weiss wrote this poem titled "The Road is too Rough":

> "The road is too rough, dear Lord," I cried, "there are stones
> that hurt me so."

51

"My child," said He, "I understand. I walked it long ago."

"But there's a cool, green path ahead, let me walk there for a time."

"No, child," He gently answered me. "The green road does not climb."

"My burden," I cried, "is far too great. How can I bear its load?"

"Dear one," said he, "I remember its weight. I carried my cross, you know."

"But," I said, "I wish there were friends that would make their way mine own."

"Oh yes," he said, "Gethsemane was hard to bear alone."

And so I climbed the stony path, content at last to know

That where my Master had not gone, I would not need to go.

And strangely, then, I found new friends; my burden grew less sore,

As I remembered that long ago, He went that way before.

Age

One of the characteristics of the Prophet Joseph Smith was his ability to surround himself with great men, even though many of them were older than he.

Much of the work you are doing as missionaries is working with men who are older than you—ward mission leaders, bishops, branch presidents, elders quorum presidents, and other priesthood and auxiliary leaders. Even though you might at times feel reluctant to call them or visit them, remember that they are also trying to fulfill callings that have been placed upon them by the Lord.

There is no prescribed age for dynamic leadership. Although Nephi was "exceedingly young" when en route to the promised land, he was constantly showing his older brothers the right way.

Because of Mormon's faith and spiritual desires, he beheld the Lord at fifteen. At sixteen he was called to lead the Nephite army.

The Prophet Joseph Smith was only fourteen when he experienced the First Vision; when twenty-four, he organized the restored Church. Heber J. Grant was called to preside over the Tooele Stake when he was twenty-three; he was called to be an apostle while still in his twenties.

President Thomas S. Monson was called as a bishop in his early twenties; at twenty-seven he was called into a stake presidency; by his mid-thirties he was called to preside over the Eastern Canadian Mission and was called to be an apostle. No matter what your age, you are ordained as a minister of the gospel. As such, there are no certain types of leadership you must give in your area. In working with members, the following basic principles of leadership will be helpful:

1. Believe in others and teach them to believe in themselves. The Master said, "If thou canst believe, all things are possible to him that believeth (Mark 9:23)."
2. Train others well in their duties. Most members wonder how they can do missionary work and are seeking specific ways. Share with them all you know.

3. Give individual recognition for successes. Appreciation must be frequently expressed both personally and publicly. Build every member. Sincere praise is contagious.

4. Work together in unity. Love one another. Strive for teamwork and harmony in working with a member family. Help them feel the joy of being part of the missionary team.

5. Follow up. You and the family should set some dates or deadlines for various friendshipping steps. This helps them rejuggle their priorities. Then follow up.

6. Trust in the Lord. As you commit yourself with the Church family in prayer, ask the Lord to help. As David said, "Trust in the Lord with all thine heart; and lean not unto thine own understanding. In all thy ways acknowledge him, and he shall direct thy paths" (Proverbs 3:5–6).

Ammon

Success in the mission field is no different today than it was in the days of Paul, Ammon, Alma, Wilford Woodruff, or any of the other great missionaries. There is no one magic key to success—it is a process. Alma says of Ammon:

1. He was willing to sacrifice; he gave up his father's kingdom to go on a mission (Alma 17:6).
2. He had gained much knowledge and had searched the scriptures diligently. He also possessed a sound understanding of the truth (17:2).
3. He subjected himself to much fasting and prayer and thereby became available to the gifts of the Spirit (17:3).
4. He taught with power and authority of God (17:3).
5. He possessed a willingness to experience pain and had various frustrating experiences in order to grow and develop; he maintained a positive mental attitude (17:5).
6. He fasted and prayed that he would find receptive listeners and also that he would be an instrument in God's hands to proclaim His true gospel (17:9).
7. The Lord blessed him with many growing experiences and opportunities. Ammon remained patient in long-suffering and afflictions (17:11).
8. He took courage within his heart—he possessed a burning desire for greatness (17:12).
9. He was sensitive to his contact (King Lamoni) and aware of the situations he was in (17:23–24).
10. He did not lift himself up; he desired to be a servant to those whom he taught (17:25).
11. He was aware of opportunities and was willing to act upon them. He won the hearts of his contacts and became their friends (17:29).
12. He stood firm to his commitment; he protected the flocks

of King Lamoni (his investigator), even risking his own life (17:32–39).

13. He paid the price. He fulfilled all of his commitments (18:9–10).
14. He humbled himself and perceived the thoughts of King Lamoni (18:16).
15. He maintained the king's interest by asking him key questions (18:22–28).
16. He taught the gospel under the influence of the Spirit (18:34–35).
17. He persisted in teaching all who would listen, even though many did not believe (19:32–35).

Aspiring

President Ezra Taft Benson once said to a group of new mission presidents, "Aspiring to office can destroy the spirit of a mission, as well as destroy missionaries, and can, at times, be vicious."

President Harold B. Lee said that members of the Church should not strive to be a Church leader, but that they should strive to be *like* a Church leader. In that same spirit, you should strive to be like your leaders rather than to be a leader. Leadership will then follow naturally if the Lord desires that for you.

Many years ago, a young convert was visiting a high school principal in Salt Lake City about some Brigham Young University business. The principal indicated that the young convert should speak with the stake president about the matter because it involved a program that could be jointly sponsored between the high school and the stake. When the young convert asked him how to get in touch with the stake president, the principal said, "Come on; I'll take you to him."

"To my surprise," the young convert said, "he took me down the hallway to a custodian's office. He introduced me to his stake president, and I could see respect and admiration in his face as he did so." After the three of them had finished their discussion, and as the principal and the young convert were walking back to the office, the young convert remarked that it was strange that he was the high school principal and that one of the custodians was his stake president. "Not at all," he said. "We get along fine as long as he does his job as the custodian and as long as I do my job as a member of the high council." It was a lesson in Church government the young convert never forgot.

Mission policies vary. Sometimes junior companions and senior companions are switched; district leaders are sometimes released to give other missionaries the opportunity for leadership; an elder might be a zone leader one day and a junior companion the next—not because he is being disciplined but because his special talents are being utilized in the best possible way; a missionary might be a senior companion in one companionship and a junior companion in the next one.

It is the same way throughout the Church. Bishops sometimes become counselors to bishops. Stake presidents become Sunday School teachers. Area Authority Seventies become scoutmasters. High councilors become ushers. Relief Society presidents become visiting teachers. It isn't where you serve but how you serve that matters most.

> "Father, where shall I work today?" and my love flowed warm
>   and free.
> Then he pointed me out a tiny spot and said, "Tend that for me."
> I answered quickly, "Oh no, not that! Why, no one would ever see,
> No matter how well my work was done; not that little place for me."
> And the words he spoke, they were not stern, He answered me
>   tenderly,
> "Ah, little one, search that heart of thine; art thou working for
>   them or me?
> Nazareth was a little place, and so was Galilee."
>
> (Meade MacGuire, "Father, Where Shall I Work Today?" in *Best-loved Poems of the LDS People*, comp. Jack M. Lyon et al [Salt Lake City: Deseret Book, 1996])

You should not aspire for position. You should aspire to be worthy, to learn your duty, to give service, to do your best. Only in this way will the Lord bless you with the spirit of your calling.

Attitude

The basic difference in people is attitude. One of the most encouraging discoveries of this generation is that you can alter your life by altering your attitude. Here is a good illustration, shared by Stephen R. Covey:

> A young bride decided to follow her husband to an army camp on the edge of the desert in California. Living conditions were terrible. The only housing they could find was a run-down shack near an Indian village. The heat rose to 115 degrees in the shade. The wind blew constantly. Sand and dust piled up on everything. The days were long and boring. Her only neighbors were Indians, only a few of whom spoke English. Her husband was often gone for long periods of time.
>
> Finally, the loneliness and terrible living conditions got the best of her. She wrote to her mother that she was coming home. In a short time, she received a reply from her mother that contained only two lines:
>
> Two men looked out from prison bars,
> One saw mud, the other saw the stars.
>
> She read the lines over and over again and began to feel ashamed of herself. In the following days she set out to make friends with the Indians. She asked them to teach her weaving and pottery-making. At first they were distant, but when they sensed her interest was genuine, they returned her friendship. She became fascinated with their culture, history, and everything about them.
>
> She began to study the desert as well, and soon it too changed from a desolate and forbidding place to a marvelous thing of beauty. The snakes and reptiles she had feared became a lifelong obsession for study. The cacti, yuccas, and other desert plants became interesting hobbies. She collected seashells that had been left years before when the desert had been the floor of an ocean. Later, she became an expert on the area and wrote a book about it.
>
> What had changed? Not the desert, not the Indians, not the reptiles. Simply by changing her own attitude, she had transformed a miserable experience into a highly rewarding

one. (Adapted from *The Seven Habits of Highly Effective People* [New York: Simon & Schuster, 1990])

1. More than anything else, it is your attitude at the beginning of a task that will bring about its successful outcome. This is true in tracting, teaching the discussions, getting or checking out referrals, and every phase of the work.
2. Your attitudes toward others will determine their attitudes toward you. The success you achieve in life will depend partly on how well you relate to others.
3. In order to become the missionary you want to be, you must think, act, talk, and conduct yourself as would the successful missionary you want to be.
4. Attitude is not the result of success; success is the result of attitude.
5. The deepest craving of human beings is for self-esteem—to be needed, to feel important, to be appreciated. When you treat a person with esteem, you both benefit.

Attitudes

People often seek a change in their condition when what they really need is a change in their attitude. An attitude of success is a quality of mind and spirit that will give vigor and strength to everything you do.

Some people in the business world believe that success is the result of making money—that you are successful if you make a lot of money. This is not true. Making money is the result of success—you only earn a lot of money after you are successful. It's like the story of the man who sat in front of the stove and said, "Give me heat, and then I'll add the wood"; or the farmer who says, "Give me a good wheat crop, and then I'll cultivate the ground." You must put the fuel in before you can expect the heat. You must cultivate the ground before you can expect a harvest.

So it is in missionary work. Too many of you may be saying, "Lord, give me some success so I can really get to work." What you should be saying is, "Lord help me work harder so I can find success."

> If you think you are beaten, you are.
> If you think you dare not, you don't.
>
> If you'd like to win but think you can't,
> It's almost certain you won't.
>
> If you think you'll lose, you've lost.
> For out in the world we find
>
> Success begins with a fellow's mind.
> It's all in the state of mind.
>
> Life's battles don't always go
> To the strongest or fastest man,
>
> But sooner or later the man that wins
> Is the one who thinks he can.
>
> (Walter D. Wintle, "The Man Who Thinks He Can,"
> in *Poems That Live Forever*, comp. Hazel Felleman [New
> York: Doubleday, 1965], 310)

Someone once said that no one is ever defeated until defeat has been accepted as a reality and that there are no limitations to the mind except those we acknowledge. Think about those statements for a minute, and then ponder the limitations you have placed upon yourself in your missionary endeavors. Are you limiting your work with your attitude? Or, stated differently, is your attitude limiting your work?

Be positive in your attitude. Get up in the morning determined to be successful. Live the morning schedule. Love your area, your mission, your companion, your leaders, and the members. Prepare yourself through study and prayer, and then go out of your apartment with confidence and happiness—and an attitude of success. Then, somehow the Lord will help you do that which must be done. "If thou canst believe, all things are possible to him that believeth" (Mark 9:23).

Remember: Attitude is not the result of success. Success is the result of attitude.

Bad Areas

Some missionaries occasionally develop the attitude that they are in a bad area and thereby justify their poor performance.

It is interesting to observe the way various areas produce differently as different missionaries come and go. How interesting it must be to the members who live in an area year after year and see missionaries come and go—each with his own way of doing things, each with his own preconceived ideas of how the work should be done, each with his own standards of conduct and of dress.

A typical case: Elder A gets transferred to Area X. After a week, he writes his mission president, "President, I sure know why I was sent here. The last elders didn't do a thing." A couple of weeks later, he writes again, "We really have our work cut out for us here." Other weekly letters follow, and in about two months, he writes, "Things are finally coming around. Watch for things to start to happen." Another month, and he writes, "Things are just about to happen here."

Two weeks later, Elder A is transferred to Area Y and begins to write the same kinds of letters he wrote from Area X. Elder B, however, has been transferred to replace Elder A in Area X. His letters go something like this: "I sure know why I was transferred here. The area record book is in terrible shape. The ward mission leader says there hasn't been a correlation meeting in months. The members are down on missionary work because the last elders didn't work. There's a stack of referrals in the apartment that my companion says aren't worth checking out because the two or three they tried weren't interested."

Some missionaries begin walking or taking the bus to extra areas to tract. They make arrangements for bicycles or get help from the ward mission leader to go to new areas, or they find other productive activities. Others lie around their apartments and say, "This area's been tracted out."

What do you do when your area doesn't have a full organization? Or it's down because of the actions of former missionaries? Is weak in member leadership? Are you out of miles? Do you rationalize a poor attitude or poor performance, or do you take a positive attitude and turn things around?

Remember:
- You have been called by the Lord to serve in this mission.
- You have been given the necessary tools for success.
- Thousands in the Church, including your own family, pray daily for you.

The Lord has said, "I will go before your face. I will be on your right hand and on your left, and my Spirit shall be in your hearts, and mine angels round about you, to bear you up" (D&C 84:88).

May Heavenly Father bless you with a greater determination to make your own area, and hence the mission and the kingdom, the very best. Be willing to sacrifice. Reconsecrate your time, talents, and energies to serving the Lord.

Battles

What was the greatest battle ever fought? Was it the Battle of the Bulge? Was it a part of the Revolutionary War? The American Civil War? D-day at Normandy? The Battle of Waterloo? The Battle of Hastings? Taking Baghdad?

Most western historians believe it was an obscure battle near Tours, France, in the year 732 A.D. Before this battle, Muslims had conquered Syria, Palestine, North Africa, Cyprus, Sicily, Rhodes, most of the area around the Mediterranean, Arabia, Iraq, Persia, Egypt, and part of India to the borders of China. They then turned to Europe and invaded Spain in the year 711 A.D. A Muslim army crossed the Pyrenees Mountains and marched through southern France. The decisive Battle of Tours was won by Charles Martel and the Franks. The Muslims were stopped in their plans to conquer Europe. The title of Martel ("The Hammer") was given to Charles because of his frequent attacks on the Muslims as they retreated across the Pyrenees.

Had the Muslims not been stopped in France, historians feel that Islam, rather than Christianity, would have dominated all of Europe. Europe fostered such reformers as Luther, Wesley, Calvin, and Wycliffe—paving the way for religious freedom in America and the restoration of the gospel. Had it not been for the Battle of Tours, the history of the world would have been dramatically different from what it is today.

So far as each one of you is concerned, the great battles of nations really do not mean as much as your daily battles to maintain your integrity with God. And like the Battle of Tours, a win or a loss at a crucial time will change your destiny. Every battle you win takes you closer to winning the war; every battle you lose must remind you that your goal is the ultimate victory.

The greatest battles of your lives are often won or lost because of little things. Logjams in the great rivers of the West are often caused by a single log. A lumberjack seeks the log that is stemming the flow of timber. When he finds that key log and jerks it free, the drift of the current is again free to carry the mass of logs to the sawmills below.

There is also such a thing as a spiritual logjam. Sometimes you lose your momentum, enthusiasm, or dedication. In these times, you must find the key log that is stemming the flow of spiritual strength. To fight a battle without spiritual strength is like fighting a battle without weapons. Look for the key log that is stopping your progress. Is it an unforgiving spirit? Worldliness? Jealousy? Selfishness? Habit? Laziness? Pride? Jerk the obstruction out of your life, and spiritual vitality will surge forward to bring victory to you. Get the logjams out of your life.

And what do you get when you win each battle and, finally, the war? "And if thou art faithful unto the end thou shalt have a crown of immortality, and eternal life in the mansions which I have prepared in the house of my Father" (D&C 81:6).

"Wherefore, be faithful; stand in the office which I have appointed unto you; succor the weak, lift up the hands which hang down, and strengthen the feeble knees" (D&C 81:5).

Blessings

Each of you was promised certain blessings when your stake president placed his hands on your head and set you apart as an ordained minister and as a missionary for the Church of Jesus Christ. You were sent on a mission for a divine purpose, and that purpose will be fulfilled as you live up to your potential.

Your primary assignment as a missionary is to teach the gospel. To do this, you must find contacts and investigators. At times it may seem better to increase your tracting time and to find your own contacts rather than to depend upon members to get involved in friendshipping. A zone leader recently said that it would be much easier (and more productive) to spend his full time tracting rather than to depend upon members.

It may be true that temporarily your results would look better if you abandoned the member program and worked alone as missionaries in finding and teaching investigators. Life might be easier.

But are you looking for the easier way or the best way? The Church has given you a clear-cut path to follow. The Missionary Committee has said that in missions where Church members are available in numbers, missionaries must work with them in the missionary effort. It is the right way. It is the only way. It will work if you join cooperatively with priesthood leaders to make it work because it has been given to you by the Lord through our prophet. And the Lord made a covenant with everyone: "I, the Lord, am bound when ye do what I say; but when ye do not what I say, ye have no promise" (D&C 82:10).

Ponder what the Lord is saying in the above scripture. Does it apply to you? Are you sometimes frustrated about the results you get from the work you perform? The Lord also made another promise to us:

"There is a law, irrevocably decreed in heaven before the foundations of this world, upon which all blessings are predicated—and when we obtain any blessing from God, it is by obedience to that law upon which it is predicated" (D&C 130:20–21).

The way to successful missionary work is plainly laid out for you. The

Lord said that you must have "an eye single to the glory of God" in order to qualify for the work. This means serving him with "all your heart, might, mind and strength" (D&C 4:2, 5).

"For all who will have a blessing at my hands shall abide the law which was appointed for that blessing, and the conditions thereof, as were instituted from before the foundation of the world" (D&C 132:5).

Blessings come to those who earn them—and to those worthy of them. If the blessings you seek are more teaching situations, they will come if you throw off the shackles of apathy, complacency, and disobedience.

Charity

One of the greatest passages in all scripture is found in 1 Corinthians, chapter 13:

> Though I speak with the tongues of men and of angels, and have not charity, I am become as sounding brass, or a tinkling cymbal. And though I have the gift of prophecy, and understand all mysteries, and all knowledge; and though I have all faith, so that I could remove mountains, and have not charity, I am nothing. And though I bestow all my goods to feed the poor, and though I give my body to be burned, and have not charity, it profiteth me nothing. (1 Corinthians 13:1–3)

Moroni, in presenting Mormon's teachings on faith, hope, and charity, also declared that you have nothing if you have not charity.

What is charity? Mormon describes it as "the pure love of Christ" (Moroni 7:47). Many translators of the Bible call it "love." Paul says in 1 Corinthians, "Of faith, hope, and charity, the greatest is charity." Mormon says that we should "cleave unto charity, which is the greatest of all."

When asked which was the greatest commandment, Jesus said, "Thou shalt love the Lord thy God with all thy heart, and with all thy soul, and with all thy mind. This is the first and great commandment. And the second is like unto it, Thou shalt love thy neighbor as thyself. On these two commandments hang all the law and the prophets" (Matthew 22:37–40). Peter said, "Above all things have fervent love among yourselves." Paul said, "A love is the fulfilling of the law" (Romans 13:10).

Mormon said that charity "suffereth long, and is kind, and envieth not, and is not puffed up, seeketh not her own, is not easily provoked, thinketh no evil, and rejoiceth not in iniquity but rejoiceth in the truth, beareth all things, believeth all things, hopeth all things, endureth all things" (Moroni 7:45). Paul said the same in 1 Corinthians, chapter 13.

President Gordon B. Hinckley said, "How great a thing is charity, whether it be expressed through the giving of one's substance, the lending of one's strength to lift the burdens of others, or as an expression of kindness and appreciation" (Mormon Should Mean 'More Good,' *Ensign*, November 1990, 51).

Charity reigns above all other virtues—above understanding, knowledge, faith, hope, and self-sacrifice, according to Paul. All the principles and doctrines of the gospel can be summarized with love and charity.

How do you cultivate charity in your life? Read again Moroni 7:45: (1) by long-suffering, (2) by being kind, (3) by not envying, (4) by not being puffed up, (5) by being unselfish, (6) by not being easily provoked, (7) by thinking no evil, (8) by rejoicing in the truth, (9) by bearing all things, (10) by believing all things, (11) by hoping all things, and (12) by enduring all things.

Christmas Challenge

As you make your plans for Christmas this year, make this Christmas a different Christmas—a Christmas of doing something for others rather than having others do things for you. There is an obvious part of Christmas that you can feel and hear: tinsel, Christmas carols, toys and children, brightly decorated Christmas trees, Christmas lights everywhere, people busily shopping, the gaiety of the season.

Then there is the part you mostly feel: those quiet moments when each of you—alone and privately—attempts to grasp the meaning of this special day of days, this holiday of holidays. This feeling is the real side of Christmas. It might be called the quiet side of Christmas.

It is a time for remembering your friends, families, and those wonderful Christmases of the past. Most important, it is a time for remembering the Savior, Jesus Christ, and what He has done for you.

This "remembering" is the reason for Christmas gifts, for Christmas cards, for letters of gratitude—because through these little acts you show your appreciation to those who have touched your lives. You do things for those who have given their love and their kindnesses to you. This might be called reciprocal love—loving those who love you; returning the love of others.

But what of those who have not loved you? Or those who have not known you? Or those who have had no opportunity to love?

Let this Christmas be a time for lifting the lives of those who live in loneliness.

Let it be a time to light the eyes of children in need.

Let it be a time to help people remember the glorious events of the past.

Let it be a time for prayers, for renewed devotion to Him.

Let it be a time for thanksgiving, for faith in a greater future.

Let it be a time for re-examining ourselves, a rededication to eternal values.

Let Christmas be a new witness to the world of the message of Jesus Christ.

71

Let it be a time to remember that the reason for our existence is not what we are going to get out of it but what we can give to others.

To do this, and to make this Christmas a special Christmas, try spending it with people in need—in hospitals, orphanages, rest homes, convalescent homes, poorer areas within the city, and homes of widows and those in need. Start on Christmas Eve. Then on Christmas morning, have your own Christmas hour with your companion, and go out again and spend the entire day taking joy to others.

When you go, leave a spiritual thought or message. Offer to kneel and have prayer with them; leave your blessings upon them; sing Christmas carols; show that you have faith in a loving Heavenly Father and in His son; be positive about a glorious future; radiate a spirit that shows others that you have something the world needs. Your visits need not be long. You don't need to go in large groups—just you and your companion going together will be the greatest of experiences.

This is all a part of the quiet side of Christmas. Try it, won't you?

Christmas Ideas

Meetings this month probably included a session about missionary work during the Christmas season. This is a very special time of the year when people's thoughts should be turned toward others. It is a perfect time of year for you to encourage Church members to do friendshipping. Following are some ideas for you to discuss with Church families:

1. *Christmas open houses.* Every family in a ward or branch should hold an open house in their home sometime during the Christmas season. All members of the family can be involved in making invitations, delivering them, making refreshments, decorating, greeting the guests, and writing thank-you notes to those who come. This can be a great family activity. Those to be invited would be families living on the same street or in the same block. The important thing now is to get all the families in your ward or branch to set a date for a Christmas open house for their neighborhood. This is a wonderful season to get acquainted and to help celebrate the birth of Christ.

2. *The Book of Mormon as a special Christmas gift.* Many families have friends and neighbors who know they are Latter-day Saints. A Book of Mormon makes an excellent and inexpensive gift. It can be personalized by placing in the inside front cover a picture of the family and a written testimony. The Book of Mormon should also be marked according to the usual "Book of Mormon Marking Guide," which many missionaries have. The Church family should wrap the Book of Mormon in Christmas wrap and deliver it to the families they know—or have the missionaries deliver it for them.

3. *Christmas caroling.* A family might carefully select a number of neighbors and go caroling at their homes. It would be an added treat to present each family with a loaf of homemade bread, a plate of homemade cookies, a personalized copy of the Book of Mormon, or some other similar gift. Another idea would

be to get a nonmember family to join with the member family to go caroling at the homes of their friends, climaxed by hot chocolate and donuts.

4. *Christmastime family home evening.* A special Christmas family home evening could be prepared by a family, and then one or two other families in the neighborhood could be invited into their home for a family home evening. A family skit—maybe even the nativity scene—could be enacted by family members.

5. *Neighborhood Christmas tree.* A family could take the leadership in either purchasing or cutting a large neighborhood Christmas tree. Each family in the neighborhood would bring a set of lights or make some decorations for it. On a given night, everyone would gather together for a neighborhood Christmas tree night and decorate the tree. Afterward refreshments could be served in one of the homes.

6. *Christmas goodies.* Small remembrances at Christmas mean a lot to friends and neighbors. A family might bake something for their neighbors and nonmember friends such as popcorn balls, bread, cookies, fruitcake, candy, or cinnamon rolls.

Families should begin now to make plans for one or several of these ideas. You should visit every family in the ward or branch to encourage them to make their Christmas plans.

Christmas Proselyting

It is always a challenge to find ways to do effective missionary work during December. Here are ten possibilities:

1. Work with members within your ward areas to provide copies of the Book of Mormon as Christmas gifts. These books could be wrapped as Christmas gifts and delivered to specific nonmember families from a member family. Or they could be wrapped and used by you as door-openers in tracting. Tell people you have come with a special gift.

2. Tract and tell people you have a special Christmas message to share with them. This is the perfect time to discuss Christ's visit to America or the Bible story of the birth of Jesus. If they say they are too busy or that their family is visiting, use this stumbling block as a stepping stone by saying something like, "Our message is of importance to your whole family and will make the holidays seem even more meaningful and complete in your lives"; or "We have a message about the true meaning of Christmas and of the complete gospel of Jesus Christ"; or "Most people are too busy at Christmas to reflect on what Christmas really is. Our message is brief and will make your holidays more meaningful."

3. Sing Christmas carols as a good way to share the Spirit. Try to leave a spiritual thought and make an appointment to return.

4. Hold special family home evenings. Some of the best are "A Christmas Present to Honor Jesus Christ," "Come Let Us Adore Him," and "Getting Ready for Christmas."

5. Encourage members to hold get-togethers with neighbors. This is a great time of year for family home evenings together, special neighborhood Christmas programs, casual neighborhood open houses, group meetings to talk about the special meaning of Christmas, and other informal events.

6. Invite nonmembers to special ward parties or Christmas programs.

7. Contact fathers while they wait for their children to see Santa Claus.

8. Set up street and mall displays, especially on Friday nights and Saturdays.
9. Contact clubs and organizations to see if they would like a special Christmas program on the real meaning of Christmas.
10. Present a special gift to city officials, mayors, or heads of organizations. The gift could be the Book of Mormon, *Jesus the Christ, Meet the Mormons, The Real Story of Christmas,* or other similar books.

Whatever else you do, remember the Christmas spirit and keep yourselves busily engaged in missionary work. No greater happiness or joy could come to you than to see a family converted to the gospel because of your influence. The greatest gift you can give is the gospel of Jesus Christ. Your goal should be to give that gift to a family this Christmas season.

Christmas Proselyting

Using the Christmas season properly and enthusiastically will bring you more teaching opportunities than you ever dreamed possible. Here are some ideas:

1. *Help Church members in their friendshipping activities.* Get ideas into the hands of members. Offer to help them get organized, and help them with specific events they are planning. Give encouragement and support.

2. *Mall displays.* Work with zone leaders to get large mall displays into the malls of shopping centers in your area. Make up a special Christmas display, or use the posters on family home evenings, the plan of salvation, the Savior Jesus Christ, or temples. Managers of malls are reluctant to give much-needed space this time of year but will be willing to add a spiritual dimension to the season if you will approach them on this basis. Make sure the manager understands that you are not going to ask for any donations.

3. *Street displays.* Remember the scenes of Santa Clauses on the streets of large cities ringing a bell and asking for donations to the Salvation Army or other causes? The Christmas season is the best time of year to approach people. People will respect your dedication as they see you at this time of year manning a street display. During these next few weeks, more people will be downtown than at any time during the year. They will have peace in their hearts, and their families will be on their minds. People get closer to God during the Christmas season than at any time of the year. Your message is the greatest the world has ever known. Your challenge is to get it to people when they are most receptive to it.

4. *Visit members and investigators.* Leave a spiritual message at each home. Offer to kneel and have prayer with them. Sing Christmas carols, and leave your blessing with them. In all ways, show respect and love for the Savior. Make appointments for a special

Christmas family home evening, or if they are too busy during the holiday, make an appointment to return after Christmas.

5. *Use your December Sundays.* Use each one in finding investigators. Use a good share of each one in tracting and checking out referrals.

6. *Baptize.* The Christmas season is a special time of the year for joining the Church. The greatest gift you can give to others is the gospel of Jesus Christ. Encourage your investigators to prepare for baptism during the holidays. Recommit yourself to teach every day.

Commitment

The first and greatest responsibility of every missionary is to get the spirit of his mission. If he does not get the spirit of his mission, he will never really feel the comforting assurance of the Spirit, which is the motivation behind every valiant missionary.

When a missionary has the spirit of his mission, missionary work is easy and joyful, as many missionaries can testify. When a missionary does not have the spirit of his mission, missionary work is a boring and depressing drudgery.

Several ingredients are necessary to obtain the spirit of your mission. The first of these is commitment, which requires the following.

BURN YOUR BRIDGES BEHIND YOU

Jump into your mission with both feet. Keeping one foot at home and the other in the mission field will not work. So long as you maintain an interest in football scores at home, who is dating whom, which cow is having a calf, or how far the freeway construction is progressing in your hometown, you will never experience the full joy of a totally dedicated missionary. Instead, you will be constantly frustrated—being neither a missionary nor a nonmissionary but something in between.

MAKE UP YOUR MIND TO BE
A MISSIONARY THE LORD'S WAY

Too many missionaries want to do it their own way rather than submit to the will of the Lord. Put aside your personal desires and selfish motives. Total commitment means getting involved completely in the work. Learn that you are here to do His work—not to make a record so the folks back home can boast of your accomplishments.

REALIZE THAT THERE WILL BE PAIN,
PERSONAL SACRIFICE, AND DISCIPLINE

The missionary who seeks to avoid pain, personal sacrifice, and discipline has made a decision not to grow and develop himself. Tribulation and stress are temporary; they are the refining processes that provide you the opportunity to become inwardly strong. In the Lord's infinite wisdom, you are given trials at the right time and in the right amounts to insure your proper growth and future blessings. "For after much tribulation . . . cometh the blessing" (D&C 103:12).

DETERMINE A FIRM COURSE

Without commitment, a missionary is likely to draw back at every challenge, to give up at times of adversity, to become discouraged when things do not go his way. When a person commits himself, he will have less trouble making decisions because there will not be so many confusing choices and because his mind will be more clear on problems and issues. He is not so susceptible to the negative influences of others. He will receive greater help from the Lord in supporting truth and proper conduct. Elder Franklin D. Richards once noted, "Until one is committed, there is hesitancy, the chance to draw back, always ineffectiveness. The moment one definitely commits himself, then Providence moves, too'" (in Conference Report, April 1969, 21).

COMMIT YOURSELF

It is a great feeling to be a committed, dedicated missionary who lives the principles. And in this commitment you will find the joy and happiness of one who has found the spirit of his mission.

Commitments

The principle of making commitments is central to the entire plan of salvation. Taking the sacrament, being baptized, performing the ordinances of the priesthood, and taking part in temple sessions are all based on commitments and covenants.

One of the finest and highest ways you can demonstrate your faith in the Lord is to make an unqualified commitment with him to do something you know must be done, particularly those things you know cannot be done by yourself. By doing this, you demonstrate your faith that He will honor His promise to you and your faith that His power will enable you to do things far beyond your own capacities.

Stephen R. Covey says that unless you promise what you will do, the Lord will not do His part. He promises only when you promise. When you promise, you have all His promises.

To truly make a commitment, you must focus and organize the forces within you so that your mind is really made up, and then enter into your commitment with Him—a commitment to make any sacrifice to be successful. As you honor your commitment, He will honor His.

Many missionaries discover and are often amazed by this great commitment-making power. Others have not really taken it into their personal lives yet but are merely thinking about it.

Some missionaries set goals and try to reach those goals. But a commitment is much more than a goal—it is a promise, a pledge. It becomes a sacred obligation to perform.

This is the answer to bringing the fullness of the Lord's blessings to you. If you will make commitments and observe them by sacrifice, you will teach others to make commitments, and you will bring many truly converted members to baptism.

To be effective missionaries, you must enter into such commitments—to sacrifice worldly pleasures, to put aside pride and selfishness, to keep your thoughts virtuous, to detest mediocre effort, to spend less time in your rooms and more time in solid accomplishments, and to stop any criticizing or murmuring.

Study the scriptures and your patriarchal blessing. Pray earnestly for the spirit of making commitments, and then pledge yourself to complete the cause of the ministry of the Savior. Only in this way can you be successful.

Companionships

You all know from experience that you lose the Spirit if you lose a closeness to your companion. The Lord will not dwell where there is contention and strife. Members and nonmembers feel uncomfortable around missionaries who are not getting along. It is therefore one of your most important responsibilities to build unity, harmony, and love in your companionship. Here are some ideas:

1. Do not argue. If a person cannot be convinced in a good-natured conversation, let the matter drop. If you force your companion to admit you are right by a full-scale debate, your friendship will suffer more than if you had been wrong. Work as a team.

2. Do not interrupt. If a missionary is having a hard time speaking his thoughts, that is all the more reason for being a patient listener.

3. Accentuate the positive. No matter what subject comes up, try to point it in the direction of hope and happiness. Be positive, not negative; be optimistic, not pessimistic; be spiritual, not worldly.

4. Always have something interesting to talk about. Interesting subjects will come out of your readings, the scriptures, missionary experiences, meetings you attend, people you meet, and things you see. Keep them on a high plane, and make your conversations with your companion uplifting and interesting. Avoid light-mindedness.

5. Enjoy having a lack of knowledge. In other words, do not pretend to be an authority on everything. Give your companion the same pleasure in displaying his knowledge that you get in displaying your knowledge. You don't learn anything new while you are talking. You may learn something by listening—and your companion will enjoy your company more while he is expounding on his favorite subject. Ask him for suggestions.

6. Do something nice for your companion. It's the little things that count. Make a sincere gesture that tells him you are thinking of him and not yourself.

7. Let him do something nice for you. People learn to love those for whom they do the most. Watch how much your interest grows in those people you help. Don't refuse a favor from him. Leave yourself open to receive help. Don't be so self-sufficient and independent that you scare him away. Then show appreciation.

8. Keep your friendship alive by cultivating it. Many friendships get off to a fine start but stumble because of lack of follow-through. Keep it alive by nurturing it—remembering a birthday, complimenting him, letting him know you enjoy him.

9. Never say anything about your companion that would embarrass you if you said it to his face. You never help a person by criticizing him. Your role is to build up, not tear down, and to help, not destroy. Small, unkind, critical comments are often enlarged as they make their way through the missionary grapevine. Do not be guilty of damaging someone's reputation.

Your goal must always be to develop a friendship for eternity and to leave your companion a better person than when you met him. Missionary companions often become the best friends you have.

Companionships

What do I do if my companion refuses to work? Or get up? Or study? Or pray? How can I help him without contention or confrontation? At what point do I discuss the problem with my district leaders, zone leaders, or the mission president?

Life often presents challenges that require tough decisions. This is doubly true in the mission field, where rules of conduct often clash with temptations and weaknesses. How to work with lazy or less-motivated companions is a serious challenge to your efforts to serve the Lord with diligence and valor. If you happen to run into this experience, here are five basic principles that will help you serve your mission with honor:

1. You have the power to control your own actions and attitude, but you cannot control the actions or attitude of your companion.
2. You can have an impact on the actions and attitude of your companion only through example, encouragement, and actions that are consistent with missionary standards.
3. Never let your companion's actions or inactions or attitude affect your own. Keep total control of your own life by being obedient to Church standards and mission guidelines. Get up on time even if your companion sleeps in. Devote the appropriate time for study and prayer even if your companion elects not to do so. Do not let your companion lead you into any activity that would break mission rules or lead to unethical behavior.
4. Do everything you can through love and encouragement to keep your companionship on a high level of service to the Lord. One possible approach would be to say the following:
   a. "Elder, I love you too much to permit you to break mission rules."
   b. "I love the mission too much to permit you to harm its reputation."

    c. "I love my mission too much to permit you to serve the Lord with less commitment and enthusiasm than I had when I entered His service."

    d. "We need to try to work this out together. If we can't, then we need to get some help from our leaders."

5. No elder can afford to put his companion before his duty to his Heavenly Father, his mission, and his family. A disobedient elder who tries to drag you down to his level cannot be called a friend. Such a "friend" will sap your strength and ruin your mission. If you cannot work out a solution with your companion, seek the advice of your district or zone leaders on how best to help him. However, never let flagrant disobedience go unreported. If you do, you will be tainted with the misbehavior of your companion because you failed to show your first loyalty to the Lord and to the mission. In your interviews with the mission president, be open and frank and honest with him—always with an eye to helping your companion rather than condemning him.

Always stay focused on your commitment to the Lord, and continue to speak with Him when challenges and obstacles confront the potential of your companionship. After all, you are on the Lord's errand.

Compare Yourself with Joseph Smith

Most of you have a profound admiration and great love for the Prophet Joseph Smith. As you continue to study and pray about the gospel, you need to develop a standard of performance against which you measure yourself. Use the Prophet and other prophets since him as you set your own standards. Take these five qualities of the Prophet Joseph, study them, and then compare your life against them:

1. Joseph Smith had an unchanging faith and trust in God. He took God at his word. He went to God with his problems. He did not try to act alone upon his own judgment but always sought guidance and counsel from his Heavenly Father. Joseph once said, "If you wish to go where God is, you must be like God, or possess the principles which God possesses, for if we are not drawing towards God in principle, we are going from Him and drawing towards the devil. . . . Search your hearts, and see if you are like God. I have searched mine, and feel to repent of my sins" (*Teachings of the Prophet Joseph Smith*, sel. Joseph Fielding Smith [Salt Lake City: Deseret Book, 1976, 216]).

2. Joseph Smith was a humble man. He took no glory for himself but gave all credit to God and to others. Until his death, he maintained that he was but an instrument in God's hands. Humility is to know that you cannot do it alone. Joseph Smith acknowledged to everyone that all glory was God's. He said he could do nothing alone.

3. Joseph Smith loved and upheld truth. He said, "I combat the errors of the ages; I meet the violence of mobs; I cope with illegal proceedings from executive authority; I cut the Gordian knot of powers; and I solve the mathematical problems of universities, with truth—diamond truth—and God is my right hand man" (*History of The Church of Jesus Christ of Latter-day Saints*, ed. B. H. Roberts, 2d ed. rev., 7 vols. [Salt Lake City: The Church of Jesus Christ of Latter-day Saints, 1932–51],

6:78]). Truth made him courageous. Facing the violence of mobs at Nauvoo, he said: "Let every man's brow be as the face of a lion; let his breast be as unshaken as the mighty oak." His life was spent in searching for truth and sharing it with others.

4. Joseph Smith was obedient. Elder John A. Widtsoe said, "Humility always breeds obedience" (John A. Widtsoe, *Joseph Smith—Seeker after Truth*, Prophet of God [Salt Lake City: Bookcraft, 1951]). Joseph Smith's life was an example of obedience. He went from place to place, built temples, subjected himself to trials and toils, stood in the face of mobs and persecutions, never wavered in the face of adversity or criticism, and remained obedient to God in all things. The revelations he received from God made obedience a central theme of a happy life: "There is a law, irrevocably decreed in heaven before the foundations of this world, upon which all blessings are predicated—And when we obtain any blessing from God, it is by obedience to that law upon which it is predicated" (D&C 130:20–21).

5. Joseph Smith loved his fellow men. He lost himself in the work of others. When he was urged to go to Carthage, he said, "If my life is of no value to my friends, it is of none to myself" (*History of the Church*, 6:549). He cherished his friendships with those who surrounded him during his ministry. He spoke highly of them. Men loved him in return and were willing to die for the truths he espoused. Though persecutions raged around them, Joseph and his followers worked harmoniously with a love binding them together that is seldom matched in the annals of history. He spoke highly of friends and enemies.

Look at these five qualities in the life of Joseph Smith. Ask yourself every day if you have an unshaken faith and trust in God, if you rely upon God to direct you, if you will uphold truth at any personal sacrifice, if you are absolutely unwavering in your obedience to God and His anointed servants, and if you are filled with love of your fellow man.

Concentration

Concentration is simply a matter of making the right choices—to choose what you should think about rather than what you want to think about.

There are some specific techniques, however, which help in this process. They can be summarized in the following five points.

1. *Check your environment.* Get adequate lighting, and make sure that the temperature is about right. Take out a pencil and paper and make notes as you study or concentrate on a subject. Don't get too comfortable—sit at a table rather than lie down. Shut out distracting noises, and arrange with your companion for no interruptions. Make sure you get plenty of fresh air.

2. *Be aware of your physical condition.* Fight drowsiness with cold towels. Take a two-minute break occasionally for some brisk exercise; learn how long you can stay at it without a short break.

3. *Set some short-range and long-range goals.* Decide what you should do at each sitting and how far you will go in a particular day. Set a deadline for finishing a particular task; make a game of it, and check your score at regular intervals. As for a long-range goal, ask yourself, "Where am I heading if I finish this task?" In other words, what will I accomplish if I finish it—become a better missionary, a leader? Try getting a picture of what you really want. Or try the negative approach and ask yourself, "What will happen to me if I don't do this task?" Either way, make sure you know the rewards and consequences of completing the task at hand.

4. *Shut out the world around you—block out disturbances.* One of the greatest challenges facing everyone is concentrating while being barraged with distractions and competing thoughts. Some concentration-killers are: "Give up, it isn't coming"; "I'll do it tomorrow"; "I really should be doing something else"; "I wonder what's in the refrigerator"; and "A

lot of other missionaries don't know this, either." How many others can you list? Put aside thoughts of home, contacts, worries, problems, and other distractions. Concentrate! Every time you fidget, look out the window, or think about something else, you are looking for an escape. Concentration cannot stand competition. Eliminate as many escape outlets as possible.

5. *Fan your spark of interest.* Get interested in what you are doing. Make a contest out of it. ("It's me against Satan, and I'm going to win!") Get really involved in what you are doing, and become excited about the work. It is no secret that when you are interested in something, you have little difficulty concentrating on it. Indeed, the problem then becomes how to stop concentrating long enough to get other things done!

Like all things in life, no magic wand takes you from something you are not, to something you would like to be. Learning to concentrate takes hard work.

"And whatsoever ye do, do it heartily, as to the Lord, and not unto men; knowing that of the Lord ye shall receive the reward of the inheritance: for ye serve the Lord Christ" (Colossians 3:23–24).

Courage

Courage is not the absence of fear but the conquest of fear. Jean Paul Richter, a German philosopher, said about courage, "Courage consists not in blindly overlooking danger but in seeing it and conquering it."

Many people have written of courage. Confucius said, "To see what is right and not do it, is want of courage" ("Chinese Classics," *Contributor* [June 1887] 8:304). David Lloyd George said, "Don't be afraid to take a big step if one is indicated. You cannot cross a chasm in two small jumps." Sidney Smith said, "A great deal of talent is lost in the world for want of a little courage." Samuel Johnson said, "Courage is the greatest of all virtues, because if you haven't courage, you may not have an opportunity to use any of the others." An unknown author said, "Without fear there are no heroes, only fools. Never stop being afraid." Paul Whitehead put it another way: "True courage is not the brutal force of vulgar heroes but the firm resolve of virtue and reason" (in Victor L. Brown, Conference Report, October 1962, 27), and Alfieri said, "Often the test of courage is not to die but to live."

These last two quotes remind me of a talk by Mickey Mantle, the great baseball star of the New York Yankees. In part, he said, "Being brave doesn't mean being noisy. It doesn't mean acting big and brassy and knocking people down and saying 'look how tough I am.' It means doing what you have to do even when you don't want to do it; or doing what you have to do when it's hard to do it; or when you could let it slide and let somebody else do it; or when it hurts to do it.

"Suppose you and that kid you don't like on the next block have agreed to settle things with a fight after school. Maybe you know in your heart that the trouble is all your fault and the only reason you're fighting is because you happen to be big and you know you can win. You know you ought to do the right thing and apologize to the other kid, but you're afraid to, because you don't want to appear yellow. You're wondering which takes more courage, fighting or not fighting."

It takes a lot of courage to be a missionary—to not fight (debate) when you want to fight; to live rules; to stand up sometimes to a companion who wants to do wrong; to knock on doors; to speak in Church; to bear your testimony; to find a way to keep busy; to continue with members who don't seem interested in sharing the gospel; to say no to temptation; to eat your companion's cooking; to make one or two more calls after a frustrating day that should have ended an hour ago; to continue working with a bishop or ward mission leader who is so busy that you feel like you're intruding on his time; to be persistent and consistent in the face of challenges that seem almost too heavy to bear; to keep going, after being turned down time after time.

"Verily, verily, I say unto you, if they reject my words, and this part of my gospel and ministry, blessed are ye, for they can do no more unto you than unto me. . . . Fear not to do good, my sons, for whatsoever ye sow, that shall ye also reap; therefore, if ye sow good ye shall also reap good for your reward" (D&C 6:29–33).

Your calling is to teach, to testify, and to warn. It is easy to do it among friends. Courage requires that you do it in the face of adversity, discouragement, and rejection.

Courage

As you resist evil, your ability to resist becomes stronger. A few additional thoughts on this principle may increase your determination to combat the adversary.

The *Chicago Examiner* ran an editorial on courage. The point of the editorial was that you should not give up when temptations arise—that as you display courage, your courage will increase.

> In this street of life, walking in the darkness of the shadow, hungry old Satan was out hunting with his dogs, the little imps of human weakness. A man came walking through life's street. Satan said to his imps, "Go get him for me."
>
> Quickly the imp crossed the street and silently and lightly hopped to the man's shoulder. Close in his ear, he whispered: "You are discouraged."
>
> "No," said the man. "I am not discouraged."
>
> "You are discouraged," said the imp.
>
> The man replied this time, "I do not think I am."
>
> Louder and more firmly, the imp said again, "You are discouraged."
>
> The man dropped his head and replied, "Well, I suppose I am."
>
> The imp reported back to Satan, "I have him. He is discouraged."
>
> Another man passed. Again Satan said, "Go get him for me." The proud little demon of discouragement repeated his tactics. The second man walked off with shoulders stooped and a feeling of discouragement within him.
>
> A third man passed. Again the demon was told to "Go get him for me." The little imp jumped on the man's shoulder and said, "You are discouraged."
>
> "No," said the man. "I am not discouraged."
>
> "Yes you are," said the imp. "You are discouraged."
>
> "I am *not* discouraged," said the man.
>
> "You are discouraged," said the imp firmly and loudly.
>
> "I tell you I am *not* discouraged," said the man. "You lie."
>
> The man walked down the street, his head up, going

toward the light. The little imp returned to his master, crest-fallen. "I couldn't get him. Three times I told him he was discouraged. The third time he called me a liar. Now *I'm* discouraged!"

The Savior taught how to face Lucifer. "Behold, verily, verily, I say unto you, ye must watch and pray always lest ye enter into temptation; for Satan desireth to have you, that he may sift you as wheat" (3 Nephi 18:18).

As you resist a weakness or a temptation, you become a master over it. Elder LeGrand Richards said that getting rid of a weakness is like a rocket ship taking off for the moon—it takes a lot of initial thrust to get out of earth's gravity, but once you get yourself free from it, it only takes a whisper of a breath to keep you going.

Credo for a New Year

There is a time of year when you make resolutions for the new year. This is the time for serious reflection—of where you have been and where you want to go; of evaluating your strengths and weaknesses; of taking a good look at yourself, your accomplishments, and your aspirations. It is a time for setting goals for the coming year.

"All things are possible to him that believeth" (Mark 9:23). This includes the power of faith, the setting of goals, the necessity for planning, the blessings that come from following the prophet, how to work better with Church members, loving the scriptures, and keeping your sights on baptisms.

You need to work with your companion in setting goals for your area. Perhaps more important, however, is that you should use the beginning of a new year to set goals for yourself for the coming year—goals that are realistic and that are baptism-centered.

As you contemplate your goals for the year ahead, you might want to consider the following seven points of a personal creed.

1. *Build.* Build yourself by following a definite self-improvement program on a regular basis—daily scriptures, daily study, daily exercise. Build others by being positive and complimentary and by giving of yourself for others. Eliminate negativism.
2. *Exercise faith.* Learn to rely upon God rather than the arm of the flesh. Form a partnership with Jesus Christ. Know that with His help you can accomplish the righteous desires of your heart. Faith without works is dead, but so is works without faith. Have the faith that will enable you to call upon the powers of heaven.
3. *Commit yourself.* There is great strength in commitment. Take a tough mental attitude toward yourself. Do not go halfway in your commitment to the Lord. Break away from the bonds of the natural man and promise God what you will do.
4. *Keep the commandments.* Live the laws of the kingdom. Show your love for God by the way you keep His commandments.

Do not compromise your standards. Remember that faith is a gift of God given to those who are obedient. President N. Eldon Tanner once said that the greatest single characteristic of a successful missionary is obedience.

5. *Have an objective.* Know where you are going and when you plan to get there. Remember that only 5 percent of people plan their lives. Be solution oriented—be a problem solver. Write down your objectives. Remember that a goal not written down is only a wish. President Marion G. Romney once said that a desire is a "motivating conviction which moves one to action" ("Magnifying One's Calling in the Priesthood," *Ensign*, July 1973, 89). Your objectives ought to be something that moves you to action.

6. *Develop a positive mental attitude.* Know that it can be done; get busy and do it. You can change your circumstances by changing your attitude.

7. *Go the extra mile.* Don't be satisfied with mediocrity. The prophet has called for members of the Church to enlarge their vision. Do whatever must be done to reach your objective. Nothing good comes easy (D&C 136:31). Pay the price to be successful.

Danger Signs

Highway engineers have had a lot of experience with accidents. Over the years, they have developed a system of warning signs that give drivers notice of dangers that lie ahead. Such signs as "curve ahead," "dangerous intersection ahead," "slow—men working," and other similar warning signs are a way of life for everyone.

Life is a lot like the highway, except you have to look carefully to see the warning signals. Your success or failure in life is determined by how well you can see these danger signs and then take appropriate action.

In missionary work, some warning signs spell DANGER! to your work and commitment. Here are four of those signs:

1. *Doubt.* When you begin doubting your ability to get the work done, you're in trouble. The result is confusion, worry, a short temper, defensiveness, discouragement, and giving up. You must have unshakable faith in yourself. If you lack this faith, try this experiment: pick out someone you admire. Make a list of all of his characteristics. Then, make a list of all of your positive attributes (be honest—put modesty aside and list everything you feel you can do well). Compare the list of your attributes with that of the person you admire. The results are usually amazing because you will find that you have the raw materials to be the person you want to be.

2. *Procrastination.* This is one of the most insidious signals of all and sometimes the most difficult to recognize. It includes putting off important decisions, hesitating to finish a task, not following your daily plan, and hoping that problems will solve themselves or that somebody else will bail you out. The solution is to crystallize your thinking, make a plan, and set goals. Then develop the self-mastery to keep on track.

3. *Devotion to false symbols.* This is simply a surrender to egotism— to seek leadership for the glory of the office or to seek success for the wrong reasons. Some missionaries want to be well thought

of rather than to be thinkers. They worship a shadow rather than substance, and they covet the title of leadership rather than the opportunity to serve. As President Ezra Taft Benson said, a missionary should want to be like a leader rather than to be a leader. Leadership and other opportunities will then come.

4. *Complacency.* Everyone has an inner urge to take it easy. Many are satisfied with "good enough" instead of "good," or "good" instead of "excellent." Another evidence of complacency is the tendency to tear down those who strive to do better or to belittle a companion or fellow missionary who is succeeding. Remember that a complacent person will always try to get others to also be complacent. The secret to not being complacent is to set goals with deadlines.

The way to attack all of these danger signs is to develop a force of iron-willed determination. It must be strong enough to blast any obstacle from your path. As Alma said, "To him it is given according to his desires," and "[God] granteth unto men according to their desire" (Alma 29:5, 4). Desire and determination will turn your path toward success and, ultimately, to exaltation.

Desire

The indispensable force that motivates missionaries to develop talents and to share the gospel is called desire. The successful missionary develops his talents and then uses them to share the gospel with the greatest number of people. To do this, he must have desire.

Alma, in his great discourse on faith, chose desire as the basic element necessary to success in developing and growing in faith:

> But behold, if ye will awake and arouse your faculties, even to an experiment upon my words, and exercise a particle of faith, yea, even if ye can do no more than desire to believe, let this desire work in you, even until ye believe in a manner that ye can give place for a portion of my words. (Alma 32:37)

Desire is the first requisite of success in missionary work. If a young missionary brings nothing into the mission field except a deep, sincere, and earnest desire to serve the Lord and to be a good missionary and then "let this desire work" in him—prompting him to be positive and dedicated in his actions—he is assured of success. On the other hand, the most intelligent and developed missionary, without desire, is doomed to failure.

"Whosoever desireth to reap, let him thrust in his sickle with his might, and reap while the day lasts," is a phrase used by the Lord in four sections of the Doctrine and Covenants (6:3; 11:3; 12:3; and 14:3). Section 4, which each missionary has memorized, talks about "thrusting in the sickle," but the four sections quoted above talk about desiring and reaping while the day lasts. This indicates that it is not enough to desire something—you must put those desires to work through the full use of your time and energy while the day lasts.

Prayer is the beginning and end of a missionary's day. To the Lord he goes for help; to the Lord he prays for success. Prayer and desire go together. Success for missionaries will come only as fast as their desire to study, work, and pray. Desire will determine their success.

If you want a thing bad enough to go out and fight for it,
Work day and night for it,
Give up your time and your peace and your sleep for it;
If only desire of it makes you mad enough never to tire of it,
Makes you hold all things tawdry and cheap for it;
If life seems all empty and useless without it,
And all that you scheme and you dream is about it;
If gladly you'll sweat for it, fret for it, plan for it,
Lose all your terror of God or man for it;
If you'll simply go after the thing that you want,
With all your capacity, strength, and sagacity,
Faith, hope, confidence, stern pertinacity;
If neither cold, poverty, famished and gaunt,
Nor sickness, nor pain, of body or brain
Can turn you away from the thing that you want;
If dogged and grim you besiege and beset it, YOU'LL GET IT.

(Les Brown, *Live Your Dreams* [New York: William Morrow, 1992]).

Despair

In a conference address several years ago, President Ezra Taft Benson listed twelve ways to overcome despair, discouragement, despondency, and depression. The Saints are assured that "the Lord shall have power over his Saints, and shall reign in their midst" (D&C 1:36). President Benson outlined several suggestions for overcoming the adversary's designs. "If followed," he promised, they "will lift our spirits and send us on our way rejoicing" ("Do Not Despair," *Ensign,* November 1974, 65).

1. *Repentance.* "Despair cometh because of iniquity," the Book of Mormon teaches (Moroni 10:22). Transgression pulls a person down; sin creates disharmony with God and is depressing to the spirit. Those who are heavily laden should make peace with God. You must examine yourself to see if you are in harmony with God.

2. *Prayer.* "Pray always, that you may come off conqueror" (D&C 10:5). This is a key to keeping depression from destroying you. Prayer will keep you in touch with God.

3. *Service.* Losing yourself in righteous service to others will lift your sights and get your mind off personal problems or at least put them in proper focus.

4. *Work.* You should work at taking care of your spiritual, mental, social, and physical needs and of those whom you are charged to help. You must magnify your callings.

5. *Health.* The condition of the physical body will affect the spirit. Rest and physical exercise are essential. A proper diet is a necessity.

6. *Reading.* In your hour of trial, you will find peace and joy in reading the Book of Mormon, other scriptures, and the words of our prophets.

7. *Priesthood blessings.* Special blessings and anointings are helpful in time of need. Read your patriarchal blessings often; partake of the sacrament regularly.

8. *Fasting.* Periodic fasting will clear up the mind and strengthen

the body and the spirit. Prayer and meditation should accompany fasting. Fasting should not exceed twenty-four hours.

9. *Friends.* To meet often with the Saints and enjoy their companionship will buoy up the heart. The fellowship of true friends who can hear you out, share your joys, help carry your burdens, and correctly counsel you is priceless.

10. *Music.* Inspiring music will fill your soul with heavenly thoughts, move you to righteous action, or speak peace to your soul. Choose your music carefully from that approved by the mission. Do not listen to other music on your mission.

11. *Endurance.* There are times when you simply have to righteously hang on and outlast the adversary until his depressive spirit leaves you. "And then, if thou endure it well, God shall exalt thee on high" (D&C 121:8).

12. *Goals.* Every missionary needs to set short-range and long-range goals. Fill your mind with the goal of being like the Lord, and you will crowd out depressing thoughts ("Do Not Despair," *Ensign,* November 1974, 65–67).

Developing Enthusiasm

A missionary requested suggestions on how to develop enthusiasm. The following may help.

First of all, if you will look enthusiastic and act enthusiastic, you will be enthusiastic. If you will look like a missionary and act like a missionary, you will soon feel like a missionary—and then you will begin to be a missionary.

A lot of unenthusiastic men become enthusiastic when asked about their grandchildren, fishing, cars, or something else that interests them. A few missionaries who denied having enthusiasm became enthusiastic when asked about their family, motorcycles, or favorite topic.

Enthusiasm comes, then, in knowing and loving your subject. With this in mind, here are some ways to put enthusiasm into what you are doing:

1. *Know what you are talking about.* As missionaries, we should know the gospel. If we know the gospel, we will love it and will want to share it.

2. *Put enthusiasm in your voice.* Think back to businesses you have called on the telephone—can you remember the difference in the greetings? Some are bored and dull, while others are positive and enthusiastic. As missionaries, your positive cheer of greeting and bright conversation tells your member families or contacts that you love what you are doing. Leave with a cheerful, "Have a nice day!"

3. *Act enthusiastic.* Be alert when you walk. Hold yourself erect, head up. Gesture when you speak. Smile. Put a spring in your step, and walk at a fast pace. Look and act the part of a dedicated, happy, enthusiastic person.

4. *Use enthusiastic words and phrases.* Select words people like to hear. People like happy words: pleasure, joy, love, wonderful, happiness, gentle, soft. They like to hear their names used in positive terms. Use "you," "your family," "your loved ones," and other phrases that refer to them and their family. Be positive.

5. *Prepare and rehearse.* In perfecting any habit or quality, a certain amount of practice is necessary. In your companion study, practice skills such as teaching, door approaches, member approaches, and positive words and phrases. Rehearse in front of a mirror or with your tape recorder turned on. Perfection comes through practice, practice, practice. It does not come easy.

6. *Think of believability.* You have all known people who were enthusiastic but who were not sincere. State the facts and let your belief and knowledge show through. You don't need to be an extrovert to be enthusiastic. Your sincerity will demonstrate your enthusiasm.

Remember, enthusiasm maintains interest, simplicity gives power, repetition brings conviction, and testimony brings conversion.

The DIMS

Elder Marvin J. Ashton first coined the acronym the "DIMS." He said that nothing could turn out the light of your mission more quickly and completely than the DIMS.

So what are the DIMS? The letters D, I, M, and S stand for "Discouragement," "Idleness," "Murmuring," and "Sex." I'll discuss each one of these in a missionary context.

DISCOURAGEMENT

This is first on the list because it is the most common of the four and because it is one of Satan's most subtle, yet insidious tools for destroying a missionary and the work he is called to do. It creeps up on you so that sometimes you don't even know it's there. Every missionary should know and understand that almost everyone gets discouraged at times—discouraged with ourselves, with a companion, with leaders, with an area, with members. But it's what you do when you get discouraged that makes a difference. If you stay discouraged, you not only lose the Spirit, but you also you damage the spirits of others

IDLENESS

Someone said that idleness is the devil's workshop. How true this is. Idleness, laziness, slothfulness, and indolence all pal around together—you rarely see one without the other. They are some of Satan's favorite tools for destroying the work. A policeman in Los Angeles said that more young people get in trouble because they don't have anything to do than because of any other single cause. He said that crime would be cut in half in Los Angeles if people could keep busy doing constructive things. In your mission, idleness disrupts the work because it breeds contention, discontent, and, ultimately, disobedience. Learn to fill your time with scripture study, planning, and setting goals.

MURMURING

Nothing undermines morale in a mission more than elders and sisters who murmur against their leaders, members, companions, or mission life in general. Most missionaries are positive, upbeat, and a pleasure to be around. But a few seem to be unusually negative, always complaining, and griping. Murmuring against your DLs and ZLs is especially destructive. Murmuring is contagious. It needs to be stopped as soon as it begins. It's amazing what a positive word can do to stop murmuring in its tracks. If you hear someone murmuring, try saying something positive and watch the results. Don't be a negative influence in the mission. (This is not to eliminate legitimate complaints, however, which should be addressed to the mission president.)

SEX

Sex is a wonderful gift from our Father in Heaven when used for its sacred purposes. But like so many gifts, it can destroy you if used improperly. Like fire, water, and a host of other gifts from God that can also be destructive, sex has been twisted by Satan to his own use for the destroying of God's children. Sexual drives are powerful. They must be managed and controlled if you are to reach the highest degrees of the celestial kingdom.

The DIMS can turn out the lights of our missions. You must watch carefully and constantly for signs of weakness and strive for strength in overcoming them. Be prayerful. Be humble. Be constantly vigilant.

Disappointments

During the Vietnam War, a tough old sergeant was lying in his foxhole listening to an enemy radio station describe the battle he had just been in. The announcer described the battle as a rout, stating that the sergeant's infantry company had been driven back and scattered. The old sergeant looked down at his dirty, torn clothing, his bruised and battered body, and spat in the mud. "Ha, I might be driven back, but scattered—never!"

How men manage their disappointments often reveals their strengths and weaknesses. Some are merely driven back; others are scattered. What a man does when he is down determines the kind of man he is. The tests of life come when things go wrong; Satan has little influence on you when things are going right.

Despite your best efforts and intentions, all of you are bound to be disappointed at one time or another. This is especially true for missionaries because missionaries are learning new things and testing new ways of improving themselves and their methods.

As a missionary, you hope that most of your efforts will be positive. But you still have to learn to live with the bad as well as the good—with the failures as well as the successes. You cannot afford to be unduly discouraged when a door is slammed in our face, when a contact doesn't invite you back, or when one of your leaders makes a suggestion you don't agree with.

How do you react to disappointment? Do you waste time trying to find someone or something to pin the blame on? Do you take the disappointment in stride and bounce back as quickly as you can, or do you let it unnerve you? Do you turn your attention to the next problem without fretting and worrying about past failures?

Do you help other people land on their feet when they stumble, or do you make life even rougher by jumping all over them? Do you have the courage to accept occasional disappointments as the price of learning, or do discouragements prevent you from sticking your neck out again? Do you succumb easily to the defenses put up by your investigators, or do you realize that they are often testing the strength of your own convictions? As you leave a slammed door, do you approach the next one with enthusiasm and confidence, or do you let the last one bring you down?

It is only common sense to steer clear of failure. But the person has not been born who is clever enough or smart enough to succeed at everything he tries. Realistic people accept occasional disappointments as part of their callings and make the best of them.

Missionaries can be likened to three kinds of ships: barges, sailing ships, and ocean liners. Barges need to be dragged, sailing ships are great when the wind and tide are with them, but ocean liners keep fighting their way through storms. Missionaries must realize that Satan will do all in his power to slow them down, to cause disappointments, to turn them into a barge, or to make their sails go limp. At such times, your love of God and faith in the Savior will take you through disappointments to your goals.

In his final message, the prophet Moroni said we must have faith and hope and charity, and that where there is no hope there is only despair. "If ye have faith," he said, "ye can do all things" (Moroni 10:23).

Discipline

Whenever you begin to face up to life and to your personal challenges for improvement, you begin to experience an internal battle. When you make up your mind to do the things you know you must do, you also begin to realize that self-improvement takes personal discipline. To accomplish your objectives, you must be willing to experience the pain necessary to reach those objectives.

Everything has its price. Any standard of excellence must be bought with a given amount of effort. The enemies of success are laziness, discouragement, lack of confidence, impatience, selfishness, and superficiality. All of these can be overcome with one virtue: self-discipline.

To withstand pain and to experience growth, you must carry in your mind a mental picture of the success, rewards, and happiness that will be yours after paying the price. This price may include a certain amount of pain—not so much a physical pain or hurt but an emotional pain of going through excruciating changes within yourself. This is basically the principle of growth that is necessary in order for you to become aware of your potential.

Effective living includes self-discipline and self-mastery. The real adventure in life is growth through discipline and personal sacrifice. Thomas Henry Huxley said it this way:

"Perhaps the most valuable result of all education is the ability to make yourself do the thing you have to do when it ought to be done, whether you like it or not" (Oscar W. McConkie, "Ward Teacher's Message for November" 36, no. 12 [October 1933]).

Robert Louis Stevenson explained the principle of growth when he said, "You cannot run away from a weakness; you must some time fight it out or perish. And if that be so, why not now and where you stand?" (in Hugh B. Brown, Conference Report, October 1963, 85).

You realize that you have been placed upon the earth to add to your lives. You accomplish this through self-sacrifice—giving up something of less importance for something of greater importance. At times this process of giving up something can be painful even though it is for something of greater importance. This necessitates self-discipline, which leads to self-mastery.

We all experience disappointment, pain, and suffering. Life would be incomplete without them. The Apostle Paul said it best when he said of the Savior, "Though he were a Son, yet learned he obedience by the things which he suffered" (Hebrews 5:8).

Discouragement

Author Joshua L. Liebman wrote of a "tunnel of darkness" *(Peace of Mind* [New York: Simon & Schuster, 1946]). This was not the kind of tunnel carved through a mountain or seen at amusement parks but rather was a state of discouragement or depression.

Liebman pointed out that it is normal for everyone to have periods of depression. The prophet Jeremiah was so dejected that he cursed the day he was born, and Job was so depressed that he longed for death.

Harry Emerson Fosdick said that "one who expects completely to escape low moods is asking the impossible. . . . Like the weather, life is essentially variable" (Harry Emerson Fosdick, in *Reader's Digest*, Book Section, March 1959, 117–129). He also said that everyone has depressed hours, but no one needs to be a depressed person.

George Washington lost nine battles before he won the one that gave ultimate victory to his fledging nation. Abraham Lincoln lost twelve elections before he was elected president of the United States. Woolworth's first three stores were failures. Thomas Edison had nearly ten thousand failures before he finally invented the electric light. Henry Ford, when asked what he would do if he lost everything he had, said, "Give me ten years and I would build it all back again."

General W. W. Duffield spent twenty-five years working on ten-place logarithms, and his work grew to about five thousand pages of handwritten symbols. When thieves stole his bag, the tragic event nearly killed him. Wasting little time on despair, however, he began his life's work all over again. His final volume of eight hundred pages became indispensable to astronomers, actuaries, and other mathematicians of his and future generations.

Each of you as a missionary may fall under the spell of discouragement or depression. They are Satan's greatest tools for destroying both you and your work. The scriptures and the history of the Church are full of stories showing great temptations and discouragements when the prophets were on the threshold of great spiritual events. Moroni's farewell message to the Lamanites gives one answer to discouragement: "And if ye have no hope ye must needs be in despair; and despair cometh because of iniquity" (Moroni 10:22).

The Lord didn't promise that the work would be easy. He expects you to try and try again. When He told the discouraged fishermen to cast their nets again, He had them cast in the same place where they had not been catching anything. So it is with your work as missionaries—many of your contacts who turn you down are later willing to be taught. Many missionaries bear witness of this.

President Gordon B. Hinckley said to a group of missionaries, "Keep at it. Keep at it. You have to keep going. You can't stop. You just have to keep going, even in the face of discouragement" (in Gordon B. Hinckley, *Teachings of Gordon B. Hinckley* [Salt Lake City: Deseret Book, 1997], 375).

When you enter the tunnel of discouragement and despair, remember that at the end of every tunnel there is a ray of light. Follow this ray and you will be led out of darkness and into the brightness of hope and new opportunity.

Enthusiasm

Can a person be both humble and enthusiastic at the same time? Yes!

The word enthusiasm is defined as "ardent eagerness," "zeal," "fervor," "elation," "strong warmth of feeling," and "keen interest." It comes from a derivative of "God in us." It was originally coined to apply specifically to something akin to a testimony of God.

If you could act as if there were truly a god in embryo within you, think of the enthusiasm for the gospel you could show to others. If, for example, you would bear testimony with the same conviction and enthusiasm that the Apostle Paul did on Mars Hill, then your testimony would be noticed and felt by others.

Enthusiasm is not fanaticism; it is not a loud voice, fast speech, or waving arms. Nor is it necessarily found in a person who runs all the time. Enthusiasm is manifested in the missionary who, by his message and actions, stimulates others to strive to gain the same conviction or keen interest in the gospel. Enthusiasm is a smile, a diligent attitude, a firm testimony shared often, a hard handclasp, and a solid look in the eye. It is conviction, knowledge, confidence, and eagerness.

Ralph Waldo Emerson said, "Nothing great was ever achieved without enthusiasm" (*The Oxford Dictionary of Quotations*, 2d ed. [London: Oxford University Press 1950], 200). The implication is that no one ever went the extra mile without having a positive, firm conviction that what he was doing was right. Enthusiasm was an important part of Joseph Smith's life. He once said, "Excitement has almost become the essence of my life. When that dies away, I feel almost lost" (*History of the Church of Jesus Christ of Latter-day Saints*, 5:389–90). The prophet was excited about the work. He was enthusiastic about it. He could not have continued the work without that feeling of excitement and enthusiasm—that "strong warmth of feeling"—about the gospel.

Someone once said that the last four letters of "enthusiasm" (IASM) means "I am sold myself." If you will bear your testimony and teach the gospel with the firm conviction that you are sold yourself, you will influence others. Enthusiasm is contagious and will affect in a positive way those you teach.

The Apostle Paul admonished us to be "fervent in spirit; serving the Lord" (Romans 12:11). Fervor is defined as "intensity of feeling or expression" and is a synonym for enthusiasm.

Enthusiasm is not a lack of humility. Humility is "freedom from pride, haughtiness, and arrogance." Missionaries must be enthusiastically happy with members and prospective members—not proud, haughty, or arrogant but firmly convinced that the gospel will bring happiness and joy into the lives of investigators, just as it has manifested itself in their lives.

President Gordon B. Hinckley said, "Our cause is a cause to be embraced with enthusiasm" ("Stay the Course—Keep the Faith," *Ensign*, November 1995, 71).

Enthusiasm is a positive characteristic of the human personality. It is absolutely essential in our ministerial responsibilities. It is a witness that "God is in us."

Facing Adversity

The history of the Church from ancient times to modern day is filled with stories of men and women who overcame great difficulties. Think for a moment about those who struggled to overcome physical hardship, adversities, temptations, abuse, torment, loneliness, condemnation, anguish, heartache, disasters, ridicule, and discouragement. Names such as Abraham, Moses, Job, Peter, Alma, Nephi, Joseph Smith, Brigham Young, Wilford Woodruff, and Spencer W. Kimball recall to my mind the matchless courage and valiant service that these men have inscribed on the pages of time.

But what of the thousands upon thousands who fell, failed, lost, or succumbed to the temptations of Satan? Where are they in history? Do their exploits stir your mind? Do you want to follow in their footsteps? Would you teach your families of their deeds or encourage others to emulate them?

No. People tell over and over again the stories of those who persevered, who overcame troubles and adversity, who proved their obedience in times of stress, who fought the great battles of life and won.

How do you fight temptation? Discouragement? Contention between you and your companion? Ridicule at the door? Homesickness or girlsickness? Loneliness? Physical illness? The difference between a good man and a great man is the way he meets the challenges of every day, whether they be big or small.

When some people need extra courage to face the problems of life, their thoughts turn to the Prophet Joseph Smith or to the Savior. Never were two men more scorned, abused, threatened, and tempted than were these two great examples of manhood. If they had failed or quit, what would the world be like today? Their steadfastness in the face of overwhelming odds should be an example to all of us.

Olga J. Weiss wrote:

> "The road is too rough, Dear Lord," I cried, "there are stones
> that hurt me so."
> "My child," said He, "I understand. I walked it long ago."
> "But there's a cool green path ahead, let me walk there for a time."

115

"No, child," He gently answered me. "The green road does
not climb."
"My burden," I cried, "is far too great. How can I bear its load?"
"Dear one," said he, "I remember its weight. I carried my
cross, you know."
"But," I said, "I wish there were friends that would make
their way mine own."
"Oh yes," He said, "Gethsemane was hard to bear alone."
And so I climbed the stony path, content at last to know
That where my Master had gone, I would not need to go.
And strangely, then, I found new friends; My burden grew
less sore,
As I remembered that long ago, He went that way before.

President Gordon B. Hinckley has said, "Don't be gloomy. Even if
you are not happy, put a smile on your face. This is the gospel of good
news, this is a message of joy, this is the thing of which the angels sang
when they sang of the birth of the Son of God" (*Teachings of Gordon B. Hinckley*, 375).

Family Home Evenings

One of the most powerful missionary tools in the Church is the family home evening program. Every missionary should know how to conduct an exciting, spiritual, and memorable family home evening.

Missionaries must be prepared to take this inspired program to the families in their areas. Your first task is to get member families to have exciting home evenings. Some member families are not holding family home evenings regularly, and many others are holding mediocre ones.

Once you have learned how to conduct a family home evening and have taught families how to do it, your next task is to take the program to nonmember families. It would be best if member families would involve you with nonmember families, but hold family home evening without member families if necessary.

Family home evening can be used by missionaries in several ways:

1. As a tracting approach, going from door to door.
2. In street tracting, to contact fathers and families.
3. In mall and street displays, to attract the attention of families.
4. In business tracting, presenting the program to fathers.
5. With members of the Church, to teach them how to hold a family home evening with their nonmember friends.
6. With members, to become better acquainted with them.
7. With members, to have them gain more confidence in the missionaries.
8. With members, to help them select a nonmember family to friendship.
9. With members and nonmembers, to have the members introduce the missionaries to nonmembers.
10. With nonmembers to introduce them to the Church's teachings.
11. With nonmembers, to give them a discussion.
12. As a program to bring public attention to the Church's programs.

13. With nonmembers, to become better acquainted with them.
14. As a central theme for open houses in various chapels.
15. At hospitals, rest homes, and other institutions, to gain good will.
16. As demonstrations before civic groups, church groups, women's clubs, and other similar organizations.

Every missionary should have some family home evening material. It should be kept up-to-date with fun songs, spiritual thoughts, lesson materials, refreshment recipes, games, and miscellaneous items. A briefcase or small suitcase makes a perfect carrying case for all the things you need for a family home evening—manuals, elastic bands, marking pens, string, paper bags, balloons, visual aids, and other items used for games and lessons.

Missionaries should be sharing ideas at district and zone meetings and at zone conference. Help each other to become better.

Firm Foundation

A mission president told the following story:

"We moved into our first home in a new subdivision a few years after we were married. One of the things we needed most was shade around our new home. One of our first decisions was to determine what type of tree to plant.

"We decided that we couldn't wait a long time for a tree to grow, so we selected a fast-growing tree that would give us good shade within few years. We held a tree-planting ceremony and planted the tree in our front yard. Our oldest son was two years old at the time, and we looked forward to the time he could play outside under the shade of the tree.

"As expected, the tree grew rapidly. Within a few years it was the envy of the neighborhood. Its branches spread out to include much of our small front yard. Children came from all over the block to play under it. How we enjoyed it!

"One stormy evening, the wind blew and blew and blew. Our big, beautiful tree could not stand the onslaught. We watched with horror as it toppled over in the wind. We were heartsick.

"As we surveyed the tree the next morning and began the long process of cutting it up and hauling it away, we were astonished at the shallow root system of the tree. It had grown tall, but it hadn't grown very deep. The roots had grown rapidly in all directions, except down. They had not penetrated more than a foot or so into the soil to find nutrients because we had supplied everything they needed near the surface. It did not have a firm foundation.

"Sadly, we realized that in our desire to plant a fast-growing tree, we had missed important fact of life: trees, like people, need to grow slowly. Roots need to go deeply for nourishment rather than having everything given to them without work. Like people, trees have a tendency to become top-heavy if allowed to grow unchecked."

People need strong roots too—roots of ambition, integrity, loyalty, self-improvement, perseverance, spirituality, determination, love of God.

Many people do not have these roots, and when the storms of life blow and blow, they are destroyed. Everyone will face storms in life; some will stand straight and tall while others will stumble and fall.

The best anchor is the gospel of Jesus Christ. You must send your roots deeply into the soil of the Church so that you can draw from it the knowledge and experience you will need to face the storms that will surely come your way. You must feed yourselves daily with positive thinking, prayer, obedience, study, and service to others. In this way you will have the strength to endure to the end.

Only the valiant will return to the presence of God. Each one of you will therefore be tested to see if you are worthy enough and strong enough to be with Him, for how can you prove ourself unless you face adversity and challenges?

"Blessed is the man that endureth temptation: for when he is tried, he shall receive the crown of life, which the Lord hath promised to them that love him" (JST James 1:12).

This is the promise of the Lord for those who love and follow Him.

Gifts to Take Home

President Gordon B. Hinckley has suggested ten gifts to take home with you when you leave the mission field:

1. A knowledge of and love of God our Eternal Father and His Son, the Lord Jesus Christ. "And this is life eternal, that they might know thee the only true God, and Jesus Christ, whom thou hast sent" (John 17:3). Make [this] your number one gift to carry home with you.

2. A knowledge [of] and love for the scriptures. Continue to read them when you get home. Read the Book of Mormon the rest of your life. You will be inspired, and you will prepare yourselves for any opportunities that might come your way.

3. An increased love for [your] parents. You are no longer the careless young men and women you were. You have learned to appreciate and love your parents. Tell them so.

4. A love for the people among whom you labor.

5. An appreciation for hard work. Nothing happens unless we work. You will never plow a field by turning it over in your mind. . . . You won't accomplish anything by sitting in your apartment thinking of all the nice people to whom you would like to teach the gospel. Work is what makes things happen.

6. The assurance that the inspiration of the Holy [Ghost] is available to each of us when we live for it. Listen [to] the whisperings of the Spirit and follow those whisperings.

7. An understanding of teamwork. You can't do it alone. Every one of you has a companion. Don't look for his faults; he has plenty of them. Look for his virtues, and try to bring those virtues into your life.

8. The value of personal virtue. There is no room for evil thoughts in your [life]. . . . They will destroy you if you persist in them. Dismiss them. Stay away from them. Pray to the Lord for strength to rise above them.

9. The faith to act.

10. The humility to pray. Great power is available to us. The Lord

will bless us. He will guide us. He will magnify us (Gordon B. Hinckley, "Ten Gifts to Bring Home from the Mission Field," devotional, June 1983).

This was the advice President Hinckley gave to missionaries serving in several combined missions at a missionary conference. He was not talking about gifts you can buy at a store on your way home from a mission. These gifts must be developed over a long period of time. Whether you take these gifts home depends on you and your service as a minister of the Lord Jesus Christ.

Girlfriends

Helen Rowland once said, "A good woman inspires a man; a brilliant woman interests him; a beautiful woman fascinates him; and a sympathetic woman gets him."

One missionary wrote to his mission president as follows:

> "Yesterday I found out why I got my 'Dear John.' I found out that she is getting married next month. It really makes me feel [bad] as a missionary because I have spent a lot of time on my mission thinking about her and writing to her when I could have been applying myself as a missionary. My number one concern during my mission was her. So my mission has gone down the tubes along with her."

My heart aches for this elder, not so much for the loss of his sweetheart (because the Lord takes care of worthy missionaries) but for the time he lost in his ministry.

In working out a relationship with your girlfriend at home, I suggest the following considerations be agreed upon between you:

1. *Limit your correspondence.* Some missions limit letters to or from sweethearts to one letter a week. There is a purpose in this, as proven over many years of experience. Any more than this will undermine your purpose in being there and will do more to destroy your relationship with your sweetheart than anything else.

2. *Keep your letters uplifting.* Share your experiences and your testimony. Don't make your letters mushy or forlorn. Be positive in your reasons for serving and in your commitment to the work. Remember that her spirituality level must increase as yours increases—you can help hers increase by sharing your experiences with her. Use each letter to help her grow spiritually. Then when you return from your mission, she will have gone through your experiences with you, and you will be that much closer because of it.

3. *Don't visit or telephone.* Nothing destroys a missionary's spirit

as much as a visit or phone call from a sweetheart. It has taken some elders several days or weeks to recover from such a personal contact. There is nothing that can be said by telephone that cannot be said in a letter. Telephone calls do more harm than good—on both ends of the line.

4. *Work hard and trust in the Lord.* Be prayerful about your relationship; concentrate your efforts on being the best missionary you can be.

Glory

When all my work seemed in vain
And all my hopes had been slain;
When I had tried and failed in every way
To find a soul to teach some day;
And after a long week I had toiled
To find my work had all been foiled
At last, I finally knelt in prayer
And said, O' Lord it isn't fair
That I should work so hard for you,
And yet my people all fall through.
I've come out here for two long years
And endured hardships and overcome fears.
I have preached the gospel with all my might
From early morning till late at night.
All of these rules I have applied
Yet everything has failed that I have tried.
O' Lord, I have prepared myself to teach,
And yet no souls are within my reach.
O' Lord, you know I'm working hard;
Isn't it about time I got my reward?
Please tell me what I should do
That I might be able to satisfy you.
Then the answer came to me
And set my mind and conscience free.
He said, my son, it's the same old story.
Your eye's not single to my glory.
The reason you have tried in vain
Is because you're trying to build your fame.
The reason I have let you fail
Is because you let your pride prevail.
I've let you wander in the dark and fumble

Because I'm trying to make you humble.
And the reason your people all fell through
Is because your work is not true.
My son, I'm afraid you're just a fake;
You're not baptizing people for my sake;
You think of numbers ten by ten
To raise your stature in the eyes of men.
You're thinking only of your own success,
And that type of person I will not bless.
Here is one thing you must realize—
Your actions and thoughts are before my eyes.
I'll never give my blessing to you
Until your heart is pure and true.

(author unknown)

Goals

The following information came from a meeting for new mission presidents:

> Some years ago there appeared an error in the method of proselytizing, and many people were baptized who were not converted. This caused concern among the Brethren. We want people to have a testimony. But when we expressed some concern about many of these baptisms, the pendulum swung all the way across the other direction, and many mission presidents came to feel, mistakenly, that they should never discuss baptism with investigators at all. That is the trouble with pendulums—they nearly always swing all the way in one direction or the other. That problem has been corrected. . . . From now on, brethren, we expect that every year there will be a great increase in conversions and baptisms. We hope that stake and full-time mission presidents will understand this. We do believe in setting goals. We live by goals. In athletics, we always have a goal. When we go to school, we have the goal of graduation and degrees. Our total existence is goal-oriented. Our most important goal is to bring the gospel to all people. We must convert more people. We must find ways and means.
>
> Our goal is to achieve eternal life. That is the greatest goal in the world. The Brethren are not opposed to goals. We do not want stake and full-time mission presidents to establish quotas for the missionaries. Rather, we expect them to inspire missionaries to set their own goals, and make them high enough to challenge their very best efforts, and work to achieve them. (Regional Representatives' Seminar, April 1975; as cited in Ezra Taft Benson, "President Kimball's Vision of Missionary Work," Mission Presidents' Conference, April 1985)

We must have goals to make progress, encouraged by keeping records. It is proper for a missionary to set his own goals, as the swimmer or the jumper does. We believe in goals, but the individual must set his own. Mission presidents should stimulate and encourage missionaries to make and reach goals for themselves. Goals should always make us reach and strain. Success should not necessarily be gauged by always reaching the goal set but by progress and attainment.

A good golfer never plays against his opponent; he plays against par. A good runner runs against time; a good bowler works for 300. When they play against par, time, or a perfect 300, top performance is obtained. A mediocre game may be good enough to beat a poor opponent. The world is full of men who aimed only to be a little better than the other man of mediocrity. The history of the world is made by men who shoot for par and make it or better it.

Each companionship must prayerfully consider how they can set and achieve high goals. Use your weekly planning sessions, your daily planner, and your daily planning session as outlined in *Preach My Gospel* to set your goals and to reach them.

Goals

There are ten basic steps in the setting and achieving missionary goals:

1. *Be prayerful.* Always set goals in an atmosphere of spirituality and harmony. In a regular planning session, missionaries should pray together for guidance in setting goals.
2. *Evaluate the past.* "Those who fail to look at the past are condemned to make the same mistakes in the future." Learn from the past. Evaluate past goals and achievements. Notice where you failed or succeeded previously. Notice where others have succeeded and how.
3. *Set realistic goals.* Based upon your evaluation of the past and your evaluation of your own abilities and the area in which you labor, work with your companion in setting realistic goals for the coming week or month.
   a. Compare your goals with the results of other companionships in your mission.
   b. Stretch yourself. Reach for the stars. Never be satisfied with past accomplishments; always try to improve.
   c. Work on your weaknesses. Analyze your companionship to see where you are falling down or where improvement is needed.
4. *Write down your goals.* A goal not written is only a wish. Be specific. Then place your goal sheet where you can see it.
5. *Make a plan to reach your goals.* The achievement of a goal usually requires many intermediate steps. Your plan may involve as many as four or five steps, or it may be a daily plan to reach weekly or monthly goals.
6. *Commit yourself.* Get on your knees in prayer and commit yourself to your Heavenly Father and to one another that you will reach the goals you have set. Do not take this covenant lightly.
7. *Visualize.* Picture yourself in the act of performing your plans or completing your goals. This is the power of positive thinking.

This increases your desire to finish and is a reminder of your goals.

8. *Evaluate your progress.* Check up on yourself. Analyze your plan to see if you are on course or if you are falling behind. This is a vital and important step. If not done, you will often find yourself falling far short of your goals.

9. *Adjust your plan.* This does not mean to change your goals. During your evaluation, you may find yourself falling behind or doing the wrong things to reach your goals. You may need to change your plans. Astronauts call this a midcourse correction. The goal is still there—you merely change your plan to achieve it.

10. *Achieve your goals.* Don't give up until you reach them. Work, work, and work until you experience the glorious feeling of accomplishing what you set out to do.

Goals for a New Year

The beginning of a new year is traditionally a time for analysis—reviewing the past year, evaluating strengths and weaknesses, promising to accomplish certain things during the coming year, and taking a good overall look at ourselves and our future.

Elder Paul H. Dunn listed ten things for you to remember as you set your goals. If you will use them, your goals will blossom into eternal accomplishments:

1. Remember that man is that he might have joy.
2. Remember that joy comes by developing and using your talents, not only for yourself but also for humanity.
3. Remember to approach your daily problems with love in your heart for those involved. Work and do your best. Trust in God for your reward.
4. Remember not to worry too much about the yesterdays or fear too much about the tomorrows, for the yesterdays are gone forever, and the tomorrows may never come. But greet each dawn as the beginning of a new adventure, where the interplay of faith, love, and work either makes life richer or more miserable, depending on your efforts and attitudes.
5. Remember to rise above adversity and trouble, for these exist to increase your patience and sympathies for mankind. Men, like rivers, become crooked by following the line of least resistance.
6. Remember to be optimistic at all times—everything has its bright side.
7. Remember to do something good for someone each day and thus increase the number and intensity of your friendships. Friendships constitute great wealth. Never hesitate to win friends by losing yourself in their service.
8. Remember that a true Latter-day Saint always has an encouraging word and kind deed for others.
9. Remember to pray always; don't leave your knees until you

know the Lord will answer your prayers.

10. Remember to do things that increase your faith in God. With such faith you will resolve all the conflicts of your mind and soul, and it will carry you through discouragement and despair. You will be untroubled and without bitterness, and you will have sweet peace of mind.

May the Lord bless you in your labors as you live by the commitments of your stewardship.

Goals—Follow Through

"Clearly understood goals bring our lives into focus just as a magnifying glass focuses a beam of light into one burning point" (Ezra Taft Benson, *The Teachings of Ezra Taft Benson* [Salt Lake City: Bookcraft, 1988], 384).

President Benson made this statement at a mission presidents' seminar. What a beautiful statement it is! He also said: "When we set goals, we are in command. If we know where we are going, we can judge more accurately where we are now and make effective plans to reach our destination. . . . If we can state our goals clearly, we will gain a purpose and meaning in all our actions. . . . Without goals, our efforts may be scattered and unproductive. Without knowing it, we may be torn by conflicting impulses or desires."

President Thomas S. Monson said, "When we deal in generalities, we shall never have success; but as we deal in specifics, we will rarely have a failure" ("The Aaronic Priesthood Pathway," *Ensign*, November 1984, 41). "When performance is measured, performance improves; when performance is measured and reported, the rate of improvement accelerates" (Thomas S. Monson, *Favorite Quotations from the Collection of Thomas S. Monson* [Salt Lake City: Deseret Book, 1985], 61).

Ralph Waldo Emerson said that the world makes way for a man who knows where he is going. The tragedy is that so few people in the world know where they are going. Social scientists say that less than 5 percent of the population have taken the time to define specific goals for themselves. Many people think they have goals, but in reality most of them are nothing more daydreams.

What is the difference between goals and daydreams? The answer lies in four fundamentals: (1) a goal must be written down; (2) it must be specific; (3) a plan must be developed for accomplishing it; and (4) it must be followed through.

A goal must be visualized or seen in the mind. Wilbur Wright saw himself flying. Edison saw a world of light. Michelangelo saw a statue in every block of marble he faced. An architect sees a building in his mind and begins to shape it in his imagination before he puts it on paper.

But simply dreaming about a building will not create the structure. Every detail must be planned on paper. A set of blueprints is drawn. A step-by-step procedure must be made with a detailed plan of action. Then someone must take these plans and follow them in every detail if the building is to be built as it was designed by the architect. Wilbur Wright, Thomas Edison, and Michelangelo followed the same procedures as they worked toward their goals.

After clearly defining your missionary goals, you must develop a specific plan of achievement—a step-by-step blueprint that will lead you to accomplishment. It must be written down. This plan must include numerous short-range goals that lead to the long-range objective, a time schedule for each step, and a check-up system to keep yourself on the right track.

But all of this is wasted effort without one final ingredient: follow-through. You must discipline yourself to follow the plans you have outlined. You must organize your time, energy, talents, knowledge, and efforts toward a careful follow-through of the plans you have made. As you kneel in prayer each day to review and plan, confirm with your Heavenly Father those things you intend to do—and then do them. Action makes the difference between success and failure.

God

Sometimes you find people who do not have a belief in God. Many in society have forgotten the source of all knowledge. As Gen. Omar Bradley, army hero during World War II, once said, "We have conquered the mysteries of the universe but have rejected the Sermon on the Mount." The following quotations from a few great men in history might help you with investigators who do not believe in God.

Voltaire: "If a clock proves the existence of a clock maker, and the world does not prove the existence of a Supreme Architect, then I consent to be called a fool."

Bruce Barton: "When a load of bricks, dumped on a corner lot, can arrange themselves into a house; when a handful of springs and screws and wheels, emptied onto a desk, can gather themselves into a watch, then and not until then will it seem sensible . . . to believe that all these thousands or millions of worlds could have been created, balanced and set to revolving in their separate orbits, all without any directing intelligence at all" (in Hugh B. Brown, *Continuing the Quest* [Salt Lake City: Deseret Book, 1961], 522).

Edwin Conklin: "The probability of life originating from accident is comparable to the probability of the Unabridged Dictionary resulting from an explosion in a print shop" (Bruce Barton, "If a Man Die, Shall He Live Again?" *Improvement Era* 46, no. 4 [April 1943]).

Thomas A. Edison: "I know this world is ruled by Infinite Intelligence. It required Infinite Intelligence to create it and it requires Infinite Intelligence to keep it on its course. . . . It is mathematical in its precision" (in Henry D. Taylor, Conference Report, October 1970, 18).

Werner Von Braun, space scientist: "In our modern world many people seem to feel that science has somehow made such 'religious ideas' untimely or old-fashioned. But I think science has a real surprise for the skeptics. Science, for instance, tells us that nothing in nature—not even the tiniest particle—can disappear without a trace. Think about that for a moment. Once you do, your thoughts about life will never be the same. . . . Nature does not know extinction. All it knows is transformation!" (in Richard L. Evans, Conference Report, October 1970, 87).

Albert Einstein: "The man who regards his own life and that of his fellow creatures as meaningless is not merely unfortunate but almost disqualified for life" (in Thomas S. Monson, *Favorite Quotations from the Collection of Thomas S. Monson* [Salt Lake City: Deseret Book, 1985], 100).

Henry Eyring: "The more I try to unravel the mysteries of the world we live in, the more I come to the conception of a single overruling power—God."

LaBruyere: "The very impossibility in which I find myself to prove that God is not, discloses to me His existence" (in N. Eldon Tanner, "Ye Shall Known the Truth," *Ensign*, May 1978, 14).

Great Teaching

Many missionaries have wondered how they can become great teachers. Someone who took classes from Dr. Richard Gunn, a BYU professor who received an award from BYU for being a great teacher, said that his great qualities are (1) love for the people he is teaching, (2) love of the subject he is teaching, (3) a knowledge of the subject he is teaching, (4) enthusiasm, and (5) the ability to convey all of this to his classes.

Missionaries must posses the first four of these qualities. Only in the fifth quality is there a slight difference between Brother Gunn's needs and yours. That difference is not so much in the size of his classes (four hundred) compared with yours (from one to six) but in the purpose of your teaching.

All religious teaching should be directed to bringing the investigator to commit to do the thing we are teaching. As missionaries you must therefore be aware that there is a difference between entertaining people, instructing people, and teaching them for commitment. Although you need ability to convey this message to your contacts, it is more important that you have the spirit of your teaching.

1. A great missionary must be in harmony with the principles he is teaching. You only teach what you really are, and what you really are, you radiate. (If you really are a half-hearted missionary, that is what you radiate. If you really are a dedicated, sincere missionary, that is what you radiate.)
2. A great missionary must look within for the greatest source of strength and learn to tap the source of divine power. He must be worthy of and live close to the Spirit.
3. A great missionary must be prepared to teach investigators how they can have a spiritual experience, an awakening, a rebirth of the Spirit.
4. A great missionary must assure his contacts that he is willing to make sacrifices with them. When you ask your contacts to commit themselves to do something—to stop smoking,

for example—you must also make a commitment to do something—to visit them every day, for example.

5. A great missionary must know how to use his missionary tools: the principles in *Preach My Gospel*, the scriptures (memorizing working scriptures), testimony.

6. A great missionary bears a strong testimony with sincerity and conviction. Testimonies are used to strengthen investigators and members and are used to seal all commitments.

If you will (1) love your people, (2) love your subject (the gospel), (3) gain a knowledge of it, and (4) be enthusiastic about it (bearing testimony), the Spirit will then work through you to convey that testimony to others. "And the Spirit shall be given unto you by the prayer of faith; and if ye receive not the Spirit, ye shall not teach" (D&C 42:14).

Group Meetings #1

One of the best ways to help a ward member fulfill his challenge to be a missionary is to either hold a group meeting or to participate in one. By holding one in his own home or by bringing his nonmember friends to one being held in another home, a member is helping someone hear the message of the gospel.

What is a group meeting? Basically, it is a meeting held in the home of a Church member to which are invited several other Church members and several nonmembers. The ideal group consists of about two to six members, three to eight nonmember friends, and one or two pair of missionaries. (If you only have one or two nonmembers, reduce the number of members.) Here's how to hold one:

1. *Choose the topic of discussion for your group meeting.* Among topics which may be selected are: the Book of Mormon, family home evenings, the Church's program with families, eternal marriage, Joseph Smith, living prophets, the plan of salvation, or the Church. Experience has shown that the Book of Mormon is one of the best. You may want to take advantage of specialists in the ward or stake to speak on their specialties or for well-known personalities to speak. In every case, however, remember that the meeting is designed to teach doctrinal principles to those who attend. It is not a time for only chatting and socializing.

2. *Carefully plan the arrangements.* Work through the ward mission leader to arrange for speakers (missionaries, special guest speakers, bishopric, high council members, or stake presidency). Two speakers are usually needed—one to give an introductory message and the other to give the principal discourse of the evening.

3. *Determine those who should be invited.* In some cases, you and the ward mission leader will select particular members to attend and will also select nonmembers who are being taught. At other

times, the ward mission leader will ask a few families to get together and invite nonmembers to attend. Sometimes you will work with one of your friendshipping families to host a group meeting and plan who should be there. There will be times when a few families will get together and plan a group meeting, and each family will invite a nonmember family. No matter how a group meeting gets started, the planning should be carefully and prayerfully done at least two to three weeks before the scheduled date.

4. *Invite the selected nonmembers.* Those invited should be asked sincerely, directly, and well in advance. They might be approached by you or a Church member as follows: "Some of our best friends will be over on Friday to discuss the Book of Mormon and its relevance today. We would be honored if you and your wife could join us." There are several approaches, but the important principle is that you be honest and forthright. They should know before attending that you will be discussing a particular subject.

Many members are looking for ways to friendship nonmember families but are afraid to do it alone. Group meetings can be great spiritual experiences, and the "strength in numbers" feeling can give many members the courage to go ahead.

Group Meetings #2

Plan in advance what you will do at the group meeting. Your two speakers should have been selected. You and other members should get together a day or two in advance and make assignments. Decide who will conduct the meeting (usually the man in whose home the meeting is held). Choose individuals to give the prayers, conduct songs (this is optional, but choose familiar Christian hymns and not a distinctively Mormon hymn), bear brief testimonies, and ask specific questions during the discussion period (if there are specific points you want brought out that the nonmember guests do not ask).

Light refreshments should be served at the beginning. Serving them before the meeting will add to the intimacy and informality. The non-member guests will feel more relaxed as they get acquainted. Those arriving late will be on time for the program, and guests will leave on a high spiritual plane at the end of the meeting.

The atmosphere should always be easy, intimate, personal, and informal. Help your guests relax. Make sure that members and nonmembers sit with each other.

The format will be: (1) welcome, (2) opening prayer and blessing on the refreshments, (3) song (optional), (4) refreshments, (5) introduction of speakers, (6) speakers, (7) testimonies, (8) discussion (if appropriate), (9) closing remarks by host, with testimony, (10) closing prayer.

Talks should set the spiritual tone. Assuming that your group meeting will center on the Book of Mormon, the following would be in order. The host would introduce the subject in his welcome by briefly relating the Joseph Smith story. The first speaker would set the tone of the meeting by speaking approximately ten minutes to relate the origin of the Book of Mormon, to mention something about the period of history covered therein, and in other ways to prepare the guests to receive the spirit. The second speaker would take about thirty minutes to discuss the Book of Mormon.

   a. Stress the Book of Mormon's simplicity, clarity, relevance, and spirit. Cite appropriate biblical references, and show how the Book of Mormon eliminates confusion and questions. Read several passages on various subjects.

b. Guests should never leave with the feeling that the Book of Mormon is just "nice" or simply "interesting." Show how the earnest seeker can put the Book of Mormon to the test and determine for himself that it is of God.

c. Have enough copies of the Book of Mormon and the Joseph Smith pamphlet for each person so that passages can be easily followed as they are read.

d. Testify of the urgency of finding out whether or not the Book of Mormon is revelation from God. Then give passages to show its greatness.

Close the meeting on a high spiritual note. Leave time for testimonies and a short discussion, but do not get involved in argument or debate.

Group Meetings #3

Follow-up on group meetings is vital. As with all other facets of missionary work, the group meeting is just one link in a chain of events that will cause a person to accept the gospel. But it is an important link. Its success will depend upon how well you follow up.

Work with your friendshipping families. Keep a record of the members who attended and which nonmembers they invited. Member families should be utilized in following up on the nonmembers. If family "A" invited family "B," then encourage family "A" to continue to work with family "B."

Meet with your friendshipping family to discuss the next step. This should be done the next day, if possible. Don't let the enthusiasm of the group meeting diminish because of a time lag. Discuss with the husband and wife what should be done next. The friendshipping family could:

1. Contact the nonmembers immediately and extend sincere and deep appreciation for their attendance.
2. Visit the nonmember family, and take them a homemade loaf of bread or some other personal gift to let them know they care.
3. Invite the nonmember family to attend a Church meeting or event.
4. With a few member families, invite the nonmembers over to a dinner or party. The members invited could be the same ones who attended the group meeting, or it could be a different group.
5. Spend a few minutes discussing the group meeting with them either to answer their questions or to offer to sit down and read scriptures or pamphlets with them.
6. Invite them over for a family home evening. Offer to go to their home to show them how to have a family home evening, or offer to have you (the missionaries) go to their home to put on a family home evening.

The follow-up is up to you. Don't expect the member family to do it. Members will usually depend on you to provide the ideas and follow-through. Be enthusiastic. Be positive. Be encouraging. Be supportive. Be creative. Be prayerful.

Start giving discussions as soon as possible, but don't get overanxious. Some families who attend a group meeting will want to get started on the discussions immediately, but these will be the exceptions. Most families will need a family home evening (or two or three) and additional friendshipping before they will accept the missionaries. Be patient. Get the friendshipping family to arrange for you to teach the discussions, if possible.

Get your member families to try a group meeting. They become a spiritual memory.

Guidelines for Goals

Listed below are ten things to remember in setting goals. If you will use these in setting your goals, they will blossom into eternal accomplishments.

1. Remember that man is that he might have joy (2 Nephi 2:25).
2. Remember that joy comes by developing and using your talents, not only for yourself but also for humanity.
3. Remember to approach your daily problems with love in your heart for those involved. Work and do your best. Trust in God for your reward.
4. Remember not to worry too much about the yesterdays or fear too much about the tomorrows, for the yesterdays are gone forever, and the tomorrows may never come. But greet each dawn as the beginning of a new adventure where the interplay of faith, love, and work either makes life richer or more miserable, depending on your efforts and attitudes.
5. Remember to rise above adversity and trouble, for these exist to increase our patience and sympathies for mankind. Men, like rivers, become crooked by following the line of least resistance.
6. Remember to be optimistic at all times; everything has its bright side.
7. Remember to do something good for someone each day, and thus increase the number and intensity of your friendships. Friendships constitute great wealth. Never hesitate to win friends by losing yourself in their service.
8. Remember that a true Latter-day Saint always has an encouraging word and kind deed for others.
9. Remember to pray always. Don't leave your knees until you know the Lord will answer your prayers.
10. Remember to do things that increase your faith in God. With such faith you will resolve all the conflicts of your mind and soul, and it will carry you through discouragement and despair. You will be untroubled and without bitterness and will have sweet peace of mind.

Guidelines for Working with Members

There are three broad categories for finding prospective members: (1) that which you do on your own as missionaries (such as tracting, telephone tracting, street meetings, business contacting, open houses, speaking at civic groups, visitors' centers, and contacting people at shopping centers or in downtown locations), (2) referrals that come to you from distant places (such as from visitors' centers, friends, relatives, and so forth), and (3) that which is done by members of the Church among their neighbors, friends, and associates (known as friendshipping).

Each of these has its place in the overall missionary program, but working with members is many times more effective and long-lasting in the conversion process. If you can work properly with members within the framework of priesthood correlation, this will be your greatest opportunity for teaching the gospel.

The following are some guidelines to be used in working with members:

1. You must work through your ward or branch mission leaders.
2. Missionaries must always retain their identity as ministers. Childish behavior will suggest to the members that you are not yet sufficiently mature to be trusted with their friends or neighbors. Keep your ministerial dignity.
3. The effective relationship with members is finely balanced. Missionaries must be businesslike. You must not become overly familiar with family members.
4. If you are businesslike, busy, successful missionaries, you will get member help because the members will want to participate in successful work.
5. Approach members in a spirit of helping them share the gospel with their friends. Do not talk about their "duties," "obligations," or "responsibilities."
6. Remember that most member families want to friendship. The reasons they don't are: (a) they don't know how, (b) they are

       afraid, (c) they are too shy, (d) they don't have time, or (e) they don't trust the missionaries to do a good job.

7. Find out the real reason that they do not friendship, and then go to work on that reason. Remember that the missionaries' role in this phase of the work is to teach members how. By teaching them how, they will gain confidence in themselves (and in the missionaries), and they will be so excited about the work that they will find the time.

These are general guidelines. You might also review chapter 9 in *Preach My Gospel*. Remember that the first responsibility of the missionary is to prepare himself—by being humble, prayerful, and prepared to teach.

Happiness

"Happiness is the object and design of our existence; and will be the end thereof, if we pursue the path that leads to it; and this path is virtue, uprightness, faithfulness, holiness, and keeping all the commandments of God" (Joseph Smith, *History of the Church of Jesus Christ of Latter-day Saints,* 5:134–35).

In this beautiful statement, the Prophet says not only that happiness is the objective in life, but he also explains how to go after it. Lehi, in writing to Jacob, said, "Men are, that they might have joy" (2 Nephi 2:25). Later in the same chapter, Lehi said, "The devil . . . seeketh that all men might be miserable like unto himself" (2 Nephi 2:27). The purpose of man, therefore, is happiness. God wants you to be happy; conversely, Satan wants you to be unhappy.

President David O. McKay said, "There are three means of achieving the happy, abundant life: first, making God the center of one's life; second, using the free agency given to man; and third, rendering service to others." Each of these three means is related to the path outlined by Joseph Smith:

1. *Make God the center of your life.* Joseph Smith said that you must keep the commandments of God, that you must be holy, and that you must be faithful. Richard Wagner said, "Joy is not in things, it is in us." The Savior said, "The kingdom of God is within you" (Luke 17:21). He also said, "For whosoever will save his life shall lose it: and whosoever will lose his life for my sake shall find it" (Matthew 16:25).

2. *Use the moral agency given to you.* Happiness consists in mastering evil tendencies. There cannot be happiness without the freedom to choose. If the spirit of man is in bondage or enslaved, there cannot be true progress. You must find a way for your spiritual self to control your physical self. Sir James Barrie said, "The secret of happiness is not in doing what one *likes* to do but in liking what one *has* to do." Joseph Smith said that

you must have virtue and uprightness. Horace Mann said, "In vain do they talk of happiness who never subdued an impulse in obedience to principle. He who never sacrificed a present to a future good, or a personal to a general one, can speak of happiness only as the blind do of colors" (in *Horace Mann: His Ideas and Ideals*, comp. Joy Elmer Morgan [Washington, D.C.: National Home Library Foundation, 1936], 149; as cited in Marvin J. Ashton, "Be of Good Cheer," *Ensign*, May 1986, 66).

3. *Render service to others.* Happiness only comes to those who try to make others happy. Robert Ingersoll said, "Happiness is the only good. The place to be happy is here. The time to be happy is now. The way to be happy is to help make others so." Gretta Palmer said, "Happiness is a by-product of an effort to make someone else happy."

The great German philosopher of the eighteenth century, Immanuel Kant, said that the great aims in life must be the perfecting of yourself and the happiness of others. "Service is the rent we pay for the space we occupy in the hearts of our fellow men" (in Eldred G. Smith, Conference Report, April 1967, 77). President David O. McKay said, "He who seeks for happiness alone seldom finds it, but he who lives to give happiness to others finds that a double portion has come to himself" (David O. McKay, *Pathways to Happiness*, comp. Llewelyn R. McKay [Salt Lake City: Bookcraft, 1957], 188).

Happiness is not an external condition. It is a state of the spirit and an attitude of the mind.

Happiness Is . . .

Have you ever wondered why some missionaries are happy and dedicated in their work, while others are unhappy? Or why some missionaries have so many problems while others don't? Or why some missionaries are busy and successful while others keep saying that things will get better?

Most mission offices have pictures of their missionaries. There is seldom a day when your mission president does not look at your individual picture and offer a silent prayer in your behalf, or thank Heavenly Father that he has sent you to the mission, or hope that your investigator will accept your baptismal challenge, or hope that you will throw off the shackles that bind you so that you can become the missionary you were sent here to be, or worry with you about the recent surgery of a parent, or think about dozens of different things.

As your mission president analyzes each individual missionary (those who are here now as well as those who have come and gone), he cannot help but reflect upon the differences—how some have so many problems while others have so few, how some are so happy while others are sad, why some find success while others do not, how some take their callings seriously while others do not.

There is a difference between happy missionaries and unhappy missionaries. This difference can be summed up in one word—obedience. Those who are doing the Lord's work the way it should be done are happy; those who are slothful are unhappy. Consider the following:

1. Those who are living the rules support the rules and are blessed. Those who do not live the rules complain about them and are unhappy. The way to get a testimony of tithing is to pay our tithing. The way to get a testimony of mission rules is to live them. The Prophet Joseph Smith said, "I made this my rule: when the Lord commands, do it" (*History of the Church*, 2:170). The General Authorities have not only had many years of experience in missionary work, but they also receive direction from the Lord in the administration of

missionary work. You should have trust in them and follow
their leadership.

2. Those who are studying are expanding their knowledge of
the gospel. They find happiness and joy as their testimonies
increase. Those who are not studying are unhappy as they
wonder why they are not finding the spirit of their mission.
Using two hours every day in studying the gospel is crucial,
and yet many missionaries use this time for writing in journals,
making out reports, or finding a way to get out of studying.
These are two precious hours every day. Use them wisely and
consistently, and you will return from your mission anchored to
the scriptures. If you refuse to study, the storms of life will blow
you away because you do not have that anchor.

3. Those who are sacrificing and going the extra mile are those
who are happy. Those who procrastinate and go through the
motions are unhappy. Happiness comes from knowing that
you are doing well in your calling. When you are slothful, you
cannot be happy.

The formula for missionary happiness is so simple that it is amazing
that more missionaries cannot see it. Obedience is happiness. Disobedience
brings turmoil, conflict, frustrations, discouragement, failure, loss of
respect, lack of spirituality, a weakened testimony, and unhappiness.

Each missionary should regularly kneel in prayer and promise God
that he will do those things he has come on his mission to do.

Happiness

President Gordon B. Hinckley has said, "It is very important to be happy in this work . . . this is the gospel of happiness. It is something to be happy about, to get excited about" (*Teachings of Gordon B. Hinckley* [Salt Lake City: Deseret Book, 1997], 256).

To be happy, President Hinckley admonished, you must "reach out and bless others in all that you do, that, because of your efforts, someone may live a little closer to the Lord and have a little greater happiness in his or her life" (*Teachings of Gordon B. Hinckley*, 255).

Then he added: "That is the end of our existence, when all is said and done: to build happiness in the lives of people, because the thing we teach is the Lord's plan of happiness" (255).

One can expect problems. There will be disappointments in your work with your ward mission leader or in your encouragement of members. An investigator may ask you not to come back again. Your companion may not want to work as hard as you do. Ridicule might be heaped upon you by people on the street.

Jenkins Lloyd Jones, a newspaper columnist, once wrote: "Anyone who imagines that bliss is normal is going to waste a lot of time running around shouting that he's been robbed. Most putts don't drop. Most beef is tough. Most children grow up to be just people. Most successful marriages require a high degree of mutual toleration. Most jobs are more often dull than otherwise. . . . Life is like an old-time rail journey—delays, sidetracks, smoke, dust, cinders, and jolts interspersed only occasionally by beautiful vistas and thrilling bursts of speed. The trick is to thank the Lord for letting you have the ride" ("Big Rock Candy Mountains," *Deseret News*, June 12, 1973, A4).

President Hinckley also said, "If we will live the gospel, if we will put our trust in God, our Eternal Father, if we will do what we are asked to do . . . we will be the happiest and most blessed people on the face of the earth" (*Teachings of Gordon B. Hinckley*, 255).

Referring to Alma 12:10–11, Elder Neal A. Maxwell said, "Only by aligning our wills with God's is full happiness to be found. Anything less results in a lesser portion" (Neal A. Maxwell, *If Thou Endue It Well* [Salt Lake City: Bookcraft, 1996], 51).

And Richard L. Evans, writing more than fifty years ago, said, "Our Father in Heaven is not an umpire who is trying to count us out. He is not a competitor who is trying to outsmart us. He is not a prosecutor who is trying to convict us. He is a loving Heavenly Father who wants our happiness . . . and who will help us all he can if we will but give him . . . [our] obedience and humility and faith and patience" (Richard L. Evans, in Conference Report, October 1956, 101).

President Hinckley said, "Keep the faith. Your happiness lies in following the gospel of Jesus Christ. That's the case with all of us . . . happiness lies in walking in righteousness. Happiness lies in faithfulness and in righteousness" (*Teachings of Gordon B. Hinckley*, 256).

God wants his children to be happy. He especially wants His missionaries to be happy. He and the prophets have told you how to be happy. Your job is to do as they say.

How To Concentrate

One of the questions most often asked by missionaries is, "How do you concentrate?"

Concentration is an acquired skill, not a mysterious force or a born talent. It is a victory, not a gift; a reward, not an inheritance. Like most good things in life, you have to work for it.

You concentrate on those things that interest you. You have a greater interest in some things than others. Getting interested in two or three things at a time is like trying to catch two or three rabbits at the same time—you end up with none of them. "The secret of success is constancy of purpose," said Benjamin Disraeli, and concentration requires that you determine your goal and then get on with it. If you don't know where you are going, any road will get you there" (in Richard J. Marshall, *Home Teachings with Purpose and Power* [Salt Lake City: Deseret Book, 1990], 117).

Try a little experiment: look up from this page for just a moment. See how easily you can focus your attention on anything in your immediate field of vision. You can fix it on the window, a picture on the wall, or the doorway. You can focus your vision on anything you want to. You make the decision.

You and you alone decide what object or subject you want to concentrate on. It is simply a series of choices you care enough to make. To concentrate is to choose. This is simple. Yet it is seldom understood and holds the key to any successful attempt at concentration.

These two points, then, comprise the secret of concentration: (1) the interest you have in the subject, and (2) your ability and desire to discipline yourself to make the right choices when temptation takes you away from that subject.

Analyze yourself to see how much interest you have in learning about the gospel. Everything has its price. Pay the price by learning to focus on the subject before you. Avoid distractions. Discipline is the secret of concentration.

Humility

"Be thou humble; and the Lord thy God shall lead thee by the hand, and give thee answer to thy prayers" (D&C 112:10).

"Be clothed with humility: for God resisteth the proud, and giveth grace to the humble" (1 Peter 5:5).

"And no one can assist in this work except he shall be humble and full of love" (D&C 12:8).

You can hear from many sources that humility is a great virtue. But what is it? How can you gain it? How can you know if you have it? How can you find it in others?

Humility is what you have when you think you don't have it or what you don't have when you think you do. Webster calls it "not proud or haughty; not pretentious; unassuming; meek; modest." President David O. McKay said that humility is being submissive and obedient.

The Prophet Joseph Smith emphasized the value of humility when he said, "Let not any man publish his own righteousness, for others can see that for him; sooner let him confess his sins, and then he will be forgiven, and he will bring forth more fruit" (*History of the Church*, 4:278–79).

Og Mandino said in *The Greatest Salesman in the World*:

> If I become overconfident, I will recall my failures.
> If I feel complacency, I will remember my competition.
> If I enjoy moments of greatness, I will remember moments of shame.
> If I feel all-powerful, I will try to stop the wind.
> If I become overly proud, I will remember a moment of weakness.
> If I feel my skill is unmatched, I will look at the stars.

I know of an elder who could have been a great missionary. He had been a stake missionary before he arrived in the mission field and had held several important positions in his small branch. People had told him that he was going to be a great missionary, and he believed them.

Unfortunatley, it took nearly his entire mission for him to realize that without the Spirit he was nothing—that bringing people into the

Church depended upon the Spirit, not on him. Humility requires that its possessor seek the Spirit and that he have a willingness to learn, a genuine desire to serve others, a due regard for the opinions of others, dedication, and appreciation for what he has and for what he receives.

May you all strive to follow the Master when he said, "But he that is greatest among you shall be your servant. And whosoever shall exalt himself shall be abased; and he that shall humble himself shall be exalted" (Matthew 23:11–12).

Improving Ourselves

Most of you have heard stories about President Heber J. Grant and his determination to improve—how he was such a poor penman that he practiced penmanship until he became a teacher in penmanship at the University of Utah; how he was picked last so many times in baseball that he practiced throwing a baseball for hours until he played on a championship baseball team; how he sang so poorly that he practiced singing until he became reasonably good at it.

What gave President Grant the will to succeed? The self-discipline? The determination to improve himself? In an article in the *Improvement Era* in 1899, he paid tribute to a lesson in the National Fifth Reader. He said that made a profound impression on him that he never forgot.

> There is no trait of human character so potential for weal or woe as firmness. To the businessman it is all important. Before its irresistible energy, the most formidable obstacles become as cobweb barriers in its path. Difficulties, the terror of which causes the pampered sons of luxury to shrink back with dismay, provoke from the man of lofty determination only a smile. The whole story of our race—all nature, indeed—teems with examples to show what wonders may be accomplished by resolute perseverance and patient toil.
>
> It is related of Tamerlane, the celebrated warrior, the terror of whose arms spread through all the eastern nations, and whom victory attended at almost every step, that he once learned from an insect a lesson of perseverance, which had a striking effect upon his future character and success.
>
> When closely pursued by his enemies—as a contemporary tells the anecdote—[Tamerlane] took refuge in some old ruins, where, left to his solitary musings, he espied an ant tugging and striving to carry a single grain of corn. His unavailing efforts were repeated sixty-nine times, and at each time, [as] soon as he reached a certain point of projection, he fell back with his burden. . . . But [on] the seventieth time he bore away his spoil in triumph, and left the wondering hero reanimated and exulting in the hope of future victory.

How [great] the lesson this incident [portrays]! How many thousand instances there are in which inglorious defeat ends the career of the timid and desponding, when the same tenacity of purpose would crown it with triumphant success! . . .

Be, then, bold in spirit. Indulge no doubts—they are traitors. In the practical pursuit of our high aim, let us never lose sight of it in the slightest instance: for it is more by a disregard of small things than by open and flagrant offenses that men come short of excellence. There is always a right and a wrong; and if you ever doubt, be sure you take not the wrong. Observe this rule, and every experience will be to you a means of advancement. ("The Nobility of Labor," *Improvement Era*, December 1899, vol. 3, no. 2)

This was the creed that gave Heber J. Grant his great desire to improve himself—to make strengths out of his weaknesses. He said, "If we fall into the habit of making resolves in relation to ourselves, and of constantly breaking them, such a course will tend to make us careless in the fulfillment of promises to others."

As Shakespeare said, "To thine own self be true, And it must follow, as the night the day, Thou canst not then be false to any man" (Hamlet, act I, scene iii, lines 78–80; as quoted in Gordon B. Hinckley, *Be Thou an Example* [Salt Lake City: Deseret Book, 1981], 55).

Inside Ourselves

As you continue to dedicate your life to the Lord's ministry, you should become more and more conscious of the fact that each of you is really two persons. One is your outside self, who is seen and watched by others, who lives and speaks and acts in public—the person you reveal to others with varying degrees of frankness.

The other is your inner self, which is partly hidden even from your closest friends and sometimes which you yourself only dimly comprehend. It is this inner self, your better self, which the Master sees and values. He sees the real person. It was because of this insight that He could distinguish between the woman and her accusers, between the fishermen and the scribes and Pharisees.

Man, when alone with God, knows there can be no pretense, no make-believe, no outer self. It is a time when your soul is naked and perhaps ashamed, when you can really concentrate on prayer and a closeness with God because you are no longer distracted by fear of discovery. All that you are, or hope to be, is known to our Heavenly Father.

Missionaries are expected to put forth to the world a good example of the outer self. You must look, act, speak, and be like ministers of the gospel. To some missionaries, this is only a front. Their inner selves succumb to the temptation of the flesh. Their self-esteem dwindles and their resistance disintegrates. The inner selves of other missionaries are at peace because they know they are doing their best.

You must respect yourself in order to have the confidence to convince others of the truthfulness of the gospel. As you live the rules and commandments, you gain self-respect and confidence. You can teach with confidence and conviction. You can bear testimony with sincerity and sureness.

Henry David Thoreau said, "What a man thinks of himself, that it is which determines, or rather indicates, his fate." Abraham Lincoln said, "If at the end, when I come to lay down the reins of power, I have lost every other friend on earth, I shall at least have one friend left, and that friend shall be down inside of me" (in Ernest L. Wilkinson, *Lifting One's Sight, BYU Speeches of the Year* [October 1, 1963], 14). It is vital that you think well of yourself if you are to find happiness and success.

You are here to serve the Master—not to serve the mission president or your district leader or zone leaders. Your outer self can fool your companions and your leaders; it can even sometimes mislead yourself. But as you kneel in prayer each night to discuss with God your stewardship, both He and you know how well you have labored in the area entrusted to your care.

Each one of you should strive to live your life so that you might be able to say, as the Prophet Joseph Smith said as he was on his way to Carthage, "I have a conscience void of offense toward God and towards all men" (*History of the Church*, 6:630). Each of you should emulate President Spencer W. Kimball, who said that he never willfully did anything wrong.

The challenge is to bring your inner self into harmony with God and then to have your outer selves reflect accurately the standards of your inner selves.

It Can Be Done

President Ezra Taft Benson once said that we need missionaries to match our message. You know that you have the greatest message the world has ever known, but the effectiveness of that message depends upon the messengers who take it to the people. You must be equal to that great calling.

Your time in the mission field is short but eternally important. Some missionaries succeed in varying degrees of achievement while others seem to stumble along—trying to stay enthusiastic but somehow not obtaining the results they desire.

What makes the difference? As one looks over a mission, it is not the people, not the time of year, or the area. Nor is it the number of hours spent in proselyting. It is the attitude of the missionaries and their awareness of what can be done. A good attitude produces good results, a fair attitude produces fair results, a poor attitude produces poor results.

Good missionaries will do things that other missionaries refuse to do. Good missionaries make things happen, while poor missionaries stand by and wonder why things aren't happening. Many of you feel that all you have to do is to give a talk, knock on doors, stand by a street display, visit a few members, or spend seventy hours proselyting, and the Lord will do the rest. But it's how smart you work that counts—not the number of hours you spend but how you spend the number of hours.

Rewards in the mission field will always match our service. A missionary who knows how to be a missionary and who is totally dedicated to being the best is rewarded for his service. An area will go up or down depending upon the missionaries who labor there. Your goal must be to be the kind of missionary who will make things happen in any area under any set of circumstances and who can be relied upon to set things right. You must change your circumstances rather than letting circumstances change you.

President Hinckley has asked the Saints to increase baptisms. Members will expect missionaries to be prepared to teach those whom they friendship and to assist them in their friendshipping activities. Your thoughts, actions, desires, plans, and energies must be directed toward conversions. It can be done because the prophet has directed it. Your only limitation is yourself.

There is a new missionary spirit permeating the world. Special fasts and a rededication of areas are taking place; members are beginning to feel a new commitment to spreading the message of the restoration; the prophet's call for raising the bar is happening before your eyes; friendship-ping is being done with a sense of urgency; plans are being made; families are being prayerfully selected; the missionary guide, *Preach My Gospel*, is moving the work along faster than ever before.

President James Faust has said that missionaries must provide the zeal to accompany the maturity of the members. Therefore you must get excited about the work. You must prepare yourself to teach every day and to baptize regularly.

Judging Others

Despite the warning, "Judge not, that ye be not judged" (Matthew 7:1), you may have a tendency to look critically at others, particularly your companions and your district and zone Leaders.

Each time you meet a new companion, leader, or another elder, you may make an entry in our mental notebook: "he is conceited, selfish, opinionated, lazy"; or, "he is nice, but his new authority has gone to his head"; or "he ought to be more enthusiastic (or humble, sincere, devoted)."

People form snap judgments about others. Perhaps it is this propensity to form hasty opinions that prompted Thomas Carlisle to say, "Before we censure a man for seeming what he is not, we should be sure that we know what he is."

The companion who seems conceited, selfish, lazy, and opinionated may just be trying to cover up an inferiority complex. The companion or friend who is inconsiderate may be hiding other personal inadequacies. The new district leader may be trying his best to lead with love and kindness, but his inexperience gets in the way. A new companion may have annoying habits, but remember that his experience has been different from yours. The elder who seems aloof and indifferent may be having serious problems at home or is going through a down time.

One of the great hymns in the LDS hymnbook is hymn 235, "Should You Feel Inclined to Censure":

> Should you feel inclined to censure, Faults you may in
> others view,
> Ask your own heart, ere you venture, If you have not
> failings, too.
> Let not friendly vows be broken; Rather strive a friend to
> gain.
> Many words in anger spoken, Find their passage home
> again.
> Do not, then, in idle pleasure, Trifle with a brother's fame;
> Guard it as a valued treasure, Sacred as your own good
> name.

> Do not form opinions blindly; Hastiness to trouble tends;
> Those of whom we thought unkindly, Oft become our
>   warmest friends.

In getting along with your companion or leader, remember that agreement is not nearly as important as understanding. Try to put yourself in his place, or try to decide what is behind his actions. Think how you would act and feel under similar circumstances. If nothing else, learn from him what you would *not* do.

If judge you must, do it in a spirit of love and concern for your fellow missionaries. As the Savior said, "For if ye love [only] them which love you, what reward have ye?" (Matthew 5:46).

Keep the Covenants

A few years ago, the president of a mission had a remarkable experience. When he first arrived in the mission, the baptisms, the proselyting hours, and the productivity of the mission were running high. It continued for several months and then began to decline. He began implementing various programs and ideas to stimulate the work, and still the productivity of the mission declined.

He prayed about the problem, fasted about it, talked it over with his assistants and others. Finally, early one morning as he was driving to a meeting, an answer was given. Unexpectedly, he heard a voice say to him "Tell the missionaries to keep the covenants they have made with me so I can bless the people."

It came as a surprise to him, and that very day he began talking about the covenants each missionary had made in the temple and began bearing down on living the standards. Many were struck with guilt—one even indicated that he had ceased wearing his temple garments. Others confessed that they had been slothful, had become complacent, and had broken many mission rules. There was an air of serious reflection, sorrow, and repentance.

He went from meeting to meeting, carrying the same message: "Keep the covenants . . . so I can bless the people." It wasn't long until the whole picture changed in the mission. Missionaries began serving the Lord with a renewed purpose. They began to live the rules. They began to act and look like missionaries. They were happy. The Lord blessed their labors. They became successful missionaries. The Lord blessed the people with testimonies.

As you reflect on your own experience of going to the temple for your own endowments, you will recall some of the specific covenants and sacred obligations you took upon yourself. How well are you doing at keeping the covenants you have made with the Lord? Are you standing in the way of His blessing the people?

Those who keep covenants are happy; those who break covenants are unhappy. President James E. Faust said that one of the main reasons for you coming to earth is to show Heavenly Father that you can keep covenants. The Lord has said, "Verily I say unto you, all among them who know their hearts are honest, and are broken, and their spirits contrite, and are willing to observe their covenants by sacrifice—yea, every sacrifice which I, the Lord, shall command—they are accepted of me" (D&C 97:8).

He also said, "All victory and glory is brought to pass unto you through your diligence, faithfulness, and prayers of faith" (D&C 103:36).

May each of you do the things you have covenanted with the Lord that you would do, that He might then be able to "bless the people."

Laws of Motion

Sir Isaac Newton advanced three great principles of motion. You can relate them to your own progress ("motion") as a missionary.

Keep in mind that Newton's laws involved three entities: (1) an object, which in this case will be the missionary; (2) a force, which in this case will be the motivations which move you; and (3) motion or movement, which in this case will be the progress you make. His three great laws follow, with a paragraph about how that law can be applied to missionary work.

1. "An object at rest tends to remain at rest until acted upon by an external force." Translated into missionary work, this means that a lazy missionary tends to remain lazy (not moving ahead, not progressing) until he is motivated (moved upon by an external force). This force could be a desire to make a good showing to the mission president, the fear of what others might think, a competitive spirit to excel, or a powerful talk or sermon given by one of his leaders. But these kinds of motivations need constant renewals, and the missionary will find himself starting and stopping, starting and stopping, starting and stopping— with accompanying ups and downs in his spirit during his ministry. Remember: the basic, underlying force that motivates a great missionary is an unequivocal love of God, Jesus Christ, and all mankind. Other forces and motivations enter in, but they are insignificant when compared with the greatest force in the universe, that of love. It is the pure love of Christ that moves a great missionary to go the extra mile, to make the one additional contact, to become so hungry for someone to teach that he will sacrifice whatever is necessary to find that someone.

2. "An object in motion tends to remain in motion until acted upon by an external force." Translated, this means that a good missionary will stay good until someone or something gets him off the right path. New missionaries come out fired with

zeal until a first companion teaches him how *not* to work. One missionary said about a former companion, "Yes, he has a good companion now who lives the rules, but he will wear him down, and they will soon be corrupt." Do you make your companion a better person, or do you wear him down? Other forces that slow down the motion or progress of a missionary are homesickness, fear, discouragement, laziness, bad attitude, worldliness, sin, contention, self-pity, and a host of other tools used by Satan to slow down your work. How do you work against these forces? You can do it only by working hard, living the rules, and sacrificing worldly and personal pleasures because of your pure love of Christ.

3. "For every action, there is an equal and opposite reaction." Translated into our work, this means that your actions will have a good or bad effect on members and contacts. If you act like missionaries, people will treat you like missionaries. If you lose your ministerial dignity while trying to be overly friendly with a family, they will lose respect for your callings as missionaries. You cannot hope to be missionaries and act like high school students. Your actions will work against you.

"Be of good cheer, for I will lead you along. The kingdom is yours and the blessings thereof are yours, and the riches of eternity are yours" (D&C 78:18). Your progress during your mission will continue with you for eternity, and it is vital that you stay in motion in the right direction. How? By loving Him. Why? *Because* we love Him.

Leadership

Position or leadership will come to those who the Lord feels can do the work or to those who need a particular calling. Each calling you receive prepares you for additional service and for a future calling. Every calling prepares you for the next one—you just don't know what it will be.

As missionaries, each one of you is a leader. Even though you must work under the direction of the bishops and ward mission leader, even though you are cautioned not to get too pushy with members, even though you are reminded that you are here to assist the members in their missionary work—nevertheless, you must gently persuade, remind, guide, and move the work along. Surprisingly, the members expect this of you. The bishops expect this of you, and the ward mission leaders expect this of you. If you sit back and do nothing, they soon lose confidence in you. If things are not going well in a ward, you cannot sit back and blame the bishop or ward mission leader. As missionaries (leaders), you must find a way. If the work is going well, you must give credit to others. You must follow the Lord's counsel:

"Only by persuasion, by long-suffering, by gentleness and meekness, and love unfeigned; by kindness, and pure knowledge, which shall greatly enlarge the soul without hypocrisy, and without guile" (D&C 121:41–42).

1. *Persuasion.* It's not so much what you say that counts; it's the total impression you convey. Enthusiasm, persistence, awareness, empathy, and patience are all virtues of persuasion. Aggressiveness, impatience, and pressure do not persuade.

2. *Long-suffering.* Work with the members and leaders. Recognize that they do not yet have the commitment to missionary work that you have—that their time and interests are divided among their family, employment, Church callings, and other responsibilities. One of your challenges is to teach them how to include missionary work in their list of top priorities.

3. *Gentleness.* "There is nothing so strong as gentleness, and there is nothing so gentle as real strength," said St. Francis de Sales

(in *Favorite Quotations from the Collection of Thomas S. Monson*, 210). Gentleness is consideration, tenderness of feeling, and love. Take time to be gentle.

4. *Meekness.* Meekness is the quality of being teachable and open-minded. "Teach them to humble themselves and to be meek and lowly in heart; . . . Teach them to never be weary of good works, but to be meek and lowly in heart" (Alma 37: 33–34).

5. *Love unfeigned.* Everyone can sense when a person is not being genuine. As a leader, you must learn to love your fellow Saints and to work closely with them. Unfeigned love is love with genuine concern. You must really care.

6. *Kindness and pure knowledge.* Learn how to build people up, to make them better, to make them happier, to bring them closer to God. An act of kindness is an act of love. When you do something for others, you are generally the one who gains the most. The more you know about God (pure knowledge), the more you become like Him.

Listening

"Nature has given us two ears, two eyes, and but one tongue, to the end that we should hear and see more than we speak." This statement was made by Socrates, the Greek philosopher who lived four hundred years before the birth of Christ.

Earl Nightingale recently said that about 85 percent of all human problems could be solved if, instead of talking, people would learn to listen. "Silence," he said, "just plain ordinary, run-of-the-mill silence, can work wonders when it comes to getting along with other people."

Conversation is a lot like table tennis: *ping!* You say something witty, constructive, and provocative; but don't forget to *pong!* Listen. Some people are so busy trying to ping that they don't realize that conversation is a two-way street. Even when another person is talking, they aren't listening because they're too busy thinking about what they are going to say. George Atwell has said, "The art of conversation consists as much in listening politely as in talking agreeably." The scriptures say, "He that answereth a matter before he heareth it, it is folly and shame unto him" (Proverbs 18:13). Here's a little verse learned long ago:

> Her words were small, and seldom bright,
> And never made to glisten;
> But she was joy to all she knew—
> You should have heard her listen!

If you keep talking, you only say what you already know. If you listen, you might learn something you don't know. Plutarch said, "Know how to listen, and you will profit even from those who talk badly" (in "Aaronic Priesthood Under 21," *Improvement Era* 57, no. 2 [February 1954]). Wilson Mizner said that "a good listener is not only popular everywhere, but after a while he knows something." And Bernard Barach said, "Most of the successful people I have known are the ones who do more listening than talking."

Listening is more than just hearing. Most people feel they are good listeners because they have the self-restraint to be quiet while another is talking. To truly listen is to hear with understanding—to view the issue and to feel as the speaker does about it; to stand in the other man's shoes and see it as he does. It isn't necessary to always agree, but you must understand how the other person feels.

As to how you should listen, King Benjamin said it most effectively:

> My brethren, all ye that have assembled yourselves together . . . I have not commanded you to come up hither to trifle with the words which I shall speak, but that you should hearken unto me, and open your ears that ye may hear, and your hearts that ye may understand, and your minds that the mysteries of God may be unfolded to your view. (Mosiah 2:9)

James Stevens wrote, "I have learned . . . that the head does not hear anything until the heart has listened, and what the heart knows today the head will understand tomorrow" (in Marvin J. Ashton, "Family Communications," *Ensign*, May 1976, 52).

The capacity to listen is important. A great amount of time is spent in teaching to read, write, and speak. You need to learn much more about listening. For as Jacob said in the Book of Mormon, "And wo unto the deaf that will not hear; for they shall perish" (2 Nephi 9:31). Listen to God, to your missionary leaders, to members, to investigators, to priesthood leaders.

Love

Jesus said, "If a man love me he will keep my words: and my Father will love him, and we will come unto him, and make our abode with him" (John 14:23). This is a wonderful promise.

The gospel of Jesus Christ is a gospel of love.

There is a story about three men who stood at the threshold of a cottage. Their knock at the door was answered by one of the children, who asked their names and the purpose of their visit.

One of the three spoke, saying, "My name is Love. My companions' names are Luck and Riches. We are seeking places for rest and refreshment. One of us would be pleased to receive the hospitality of this home tonight. We and the choice of whom it is to be, we leave to you."

The child was bewildered. She ran and called the other members of the family. They gathered quickly to decide which of the three distinguished callers they would receive. They repeated over and over again the names of their would-be guests, studied their characteristics, and listened again to the request that was made.

Finally, the choice was made. In unison, they exclaimed, "We will entertain Love!" But they were perplexed to find that Luck and Riches accompanied Love into the home. Observing their astonishment, Love turned to his hosts and said with a divine smile, "Be not alarmed. Whenever I am made a welcome guest, there my companions also will make their abode" ("A Love Story," *Improvement Era* 28, no. 10 [August 1975]).

The Savior taught that a person's real influence is measured by the people he serves and the quality and unselfishness of that service. Joseph Smith taught that if a man really wants to get ahead, then he must strive to push others ahead. When you begin to understand that the greatest thing in the world is the human soul and that your greatest joy comes through helping someone gain exaltation, everything will fall into place for our missionary work.

Someone said that you begin to live only when you begin to love, and that you begin to love only when selfishness dies and you live to bless others. Muscle or force can split a shield and even destroy life, but only the unseen power of love can open the hearts of men. Og Mandino said:

> I will greet this day with love in my heart. Henceforth will I love all mankind. From this moment, all hate is let from my veins for I have not time to hate, only time to love. From this moment I take the first step required to become a man among men. . . . If I have no other qualities, I can succeed with love alone. Without it, I will fail, though I possess all the knowledge and skills of the world. I will greet this day with love, and I will succeed. (*The Greatest Salesman in the World* [New York: Bantam, 1968])

The Doctrine and Covenants states, "And faith, hope, charity, and love, with an eye single to the glory of God, qualify him for the work (D&C 4:5). It also tells us, "And no one can assist in this work except he shall be humble and full of love, having faith, hope, and charity" (D&C 12:8).

Start each day with love in your heart—love for one another, love for your leaders, love for members with whom you work, love for your investigators, and love for yourselves. If you will do this, then you will have love for God and He will have love for you.

Managing Our Minds

The mind is the greatest invention of all time. It is an instrument of tremendous capabilities. It is probably the least understood of all the tools in the universe. A British neurophysicist has said that it would cost billions of dollars to construct a computer that would remotely approach the capabilities of the human brain.

Because of the significant role the brain plays in our lives, it is important that you learn to properly harness and develop this great source of power and strength. The key to this is sometimes called Mind Management, or managing the mind.

In a way, you create your own mind. Every thought contributes to your future habits and circumstances. The key to happiness is what you put in your mind. The key to success is within your own thoughts.

William James said, "Our mind is made up by what it feeds on." The Bible says, "For as he thinketh in his heart, so is he" (Proverbs 23:7). President Gordon B. Hinckley has said, "Each of us, with discipline and effort, has the capacity to control our thoughts and actions" ("Reverence and Morality," *Ensign*, May 1987, 47). Ralph Waldo Emerson said, "Thoughts rule the world" (in Hugh B. Brown, *Continuing the Quest* [Salt Lake City: Deseret Book, 1961], 331). The modern computer techie says, "Garbage in, garbage out," implying that with computers you only get out what you put in.

Your mind is like a field of soil. Whatever you plant—weeds or flowers—will grow. The same is true of your mind. If you plant negative thoughts, discouragement, lack of commitment, and so forth, they will rapidly grow until they overwhelm you. On the other hand, if you plant positive thoughts and nourish them, they will grow into a bountiful harvest. In other words, the key to success is in your mind and what you put into it.

One mission president said that your mind could be called your individual Control Room because it governs nearly everything you do. As you manage your mind, your faith can be increased, your lives can be given direction, success can be yours. Whatever you do begins in your Control Room.

Studies have shown that most people use only 10 percent of their time in constructive thinking. The other 90 percent is lost in negative thinking, daydreaming, or wandering. You must therefore learn to increase the amount of time you spend in constructive thinking.

Managing your mind includes (1) goal setting, (2) prayer, (3) a course of action to meet the goals, (4) constant focus on your goals, and (5) action. The secret, then, is to be constantly "engaged in a good cause" (D&C 68:27). Someone once said that "whatever a missionary thinks about or talks about when he doesn't have to think or talk is indicative of his dedication."

You do create your own mind. As Elder Neal A. Maxwell said, "We must be careful of what we allow in our mind, for it will be there for a long time, reasserting itself at those very times when we may be most vulnerable" (*We Will Prove Them Herewith* [Salt Lake City: Deseret Book], 44).

Just as an idle mind is the devil's workshop, so it is that "all things are possible to him that believeth" (Mark 9:23). You can manage your mind. Believe it.

Member Goals

In the guide to missionary service, *Preach My Gospel,* the First Presidency has presented a comprehensive look at missionary work today. Among other things, their message to missionaries and priesthood leaders includes:

1. Missionary activities must be centered in the family; families must take the initiative in preparing neighbors and friends to hear the gospel.
2. Priesthood leaders must take the lead in training and motivating Church members to do friendshipping.
3. The First Presidency has outlined the way missionary work should be done. If you will do it the way they have directed, they have promised you success. If you try to do it your own way or the way it used to be done, you have no promise.
4. The role of the full-time missionaries is to be better prepared, to be more spiritually mature (so that they can teach by the Spirit), and to become more persuasive teachers.
5. Any encouragement of members (sometimes called *pressure*) should come from their priesthood leaders and not from missionaries.
6. Local Church leaders and members are the best allies of missionaries. Respect them and strive to build good relationships with them. Your attitude should be, "How can I help?" Seek to be a blessing, not a burden, to the members and leaders in your area.
7. Home teachers, the ward mission leader, and the full-time missionaries all help the quorum leader train and motivate quorum members to do friendshipping.
8. The primary function of the full-time missionaries is to teach the gospel to investigators. Missionaries might also ask members to help them teach a particular topic or lesson.

President Ezra Taft Benson has said that "clearly understood goals bring our lives into focus just as a magnifying glass focuses a beam of light into one burning point" (*Teachings of Ezra Taft Benson*, 384). As missionaries, you must give full support to ward mission goals and do everything you can to assist the members. Your assignments are (1) training as needed and as requested by priesthood leaders; (2) providing ideas and know-how; (3) giving help and aid where necessary; (4) inspiring members to want to do more; and (5) teaching those who have been prepared to hear the gospel.

Most members are afraid to do missionary work. Others are too busy or don't know where to begin. Your task as missionaries is to encourage and love the members and to build confidence in them and yourself.

Member Work

Three keys make productive missionary work: (1) family-to-family friendshipping (when a member family shares the gospel with a nonmember family), (2) cooperation between members and the missionaries to reach and teach investigators, and (3) fellowshipping new converts after baptism.

Missionaries are called and ordained to preach the everlasting gospel. "Say nothing but repentance unto this generation," said the Lord (D&C 6:9; 11:9). "Wherefore, you are called to cry repentance unto this people" (D&C 18:14). It is impractical to expect that missionaries alone can warn the millions in the world. Members must be finders. The valuable time of teaching missionaries is too often spent in finding.

Members should shoulder this responsibility. All members know of nonmembers they can refer to the missionaries. Every father, mother, and youth in the Church should share the gospel by giving a Book of Mormon, telling the account of the Prophet Joseph Smith, or inviting their acquaintances to a special meeting. If members are in tune, the Spirit of the Lord will speak to them and guide them to those with whom they should share the gospel. The Lord will help them if they will listen.

On occasion, missionaries might ask members to assist in the teaching of investigators. This is especially true when recent converts can teach and bear testimony on specific topics.

It is the responsibility of the members to provide missionaries with the names of individuals and families to teach. Sometimes members forget that it is better to risk a little ruffling in the relationship of a friend than it is to deprive him of eternal life by keeping silent. Families are bringing families into the Church in great numbers. This is the way it should be.

You have another revealed program that has in it the power of heaven. Several decades ago when President David O. McKay presided over the Church, he gave impetus to the missionary work in the stakes of Zion. He coined the term "every member a missionary," and it was obvious that it would be a giant step toward the accomplishment of missionary goals

(David O. McKay, in Conference Report, April 1959, 121–22).

President Gordon B. Hinckley has said that every convert needs three things:

1. A friend in the Church to whom he can constantly turn.
2. An assignment. Every convert deserves a responsibility.
3. Membership in a quorum or auxiliary. ("Focus of Area Training: Family Converts," *LDS Church News,* December 13, 1997)

The ward council will take the lead in providing these things. Missionaries will help as requested. Fellowship must take place, with your assistance.

The First Presidency is serious about the importance of missionary work. You must also get serious about it and convey that seriousness to the wonderful members of the Church.

Missed Opportunities

Most people do not appreciate the opportunities they have at the time they are available. During high school and college, for example, few students really appreciate the value and purpose of their education until long after they leave school. Life is much the same way. If you could constantly be aware of the importance of your daily actions as they relate to your total lives—and to eternal life—you would take better advantage of every precious hour.

Church leaders have watched missionaries come and go for many decades. The most common thing they hear is, "If only I could live my mission over again."

Some mission presidents have said that the most discouraging interview with missionaries is that final, last interview just before they go home. Not all of them are discouraging, but all too many of them are—as the missionaries look back and see how much more effective they could have been.

Most of these "I wish I could live my mission over again" returned missionaries fall into five general categories:

1. "I guess I was afraid." They had the greatest of intentions when they got into the mission field. In their letters and testimony meetings, they promised to rededicate themselves. But they never did. They never made the effort to do any more than to follow. When their companions did things against the rules, they went along because they were afraid to stand on principle. They were afraid to tract, afraid to sacrifice, afraid to tell the mission president what was in their hearts, afraid to set up street displays, afraid to bear their witness. They kept thinking that the great virtues of a missionary would come to them, but they found out too late that these virtues only come through hard work and selfless sacrifice.

2. "I didn't have good leadership." They felt during their missions that they didn't get the right training, the right supervision, the right example. They complained that those who were called to

183

be DLs, ZLs, or APs really hadn't earned their positions but had received their callings because they had sought favor with the mission president. To cover up their own inadequacies, they broke rules and made fun of leaders so that other elders wouldn't accuse them of trying to make points with the mission president. When they weren't called to be leaders, they criticized the selection of others.

3. "My girl was more important then my mission." They spent so much time writing to, thinking of, worrying about, and talking about the sweetheart back home that not much energy was left for missionary work. Most of these missionaries ultimately marry someone else.

4. "I never really got the missionary spirit." They spent their time worrying about things at home, spent too much time with members of the Church, went through the motions without sacrificing, and never really committed themselves to the work. They felt that mission rules were meant for others. They put in their two years but never experienced the joy of hard work and dedicated effort—of going the extra mile, of making every minute count.

5. "I never really learned the gospel." They avoided study and spent their time daydreaming or doing busy work to justify their lack of study. Sometimes they would pad their reports so that wasted time would not show up on mission records.

Missionary Attributes

Many people ask the question, "How do you learn to be a missionary?" Seven basic things must be learned:

1. To become a missionary, you must learn to think. You must seek truth, study, weigh all the evidence, ponder, gain knowledge, learn your duty, be informed about the gospel, be aware of the techniques of the work, keep your thoughts pure, keep your eye single to the glory of God, and realize that "as he thinketh in his heart, so is he." Confidence, conviction and persuasion come from knowledge.

2. To become a missionary, you must learn to have faith. You must have faith in God, be obedient to Him, pray to Him, rely on Him. You must have faith in yourself, in your leaders, in your calling, in the people you teach. You must have faith that the work will move ahead—that it can and must be done.

3. To become a missionary, you must learn to give. You must learn to give of your love, understanding, kindness, sympathy, forgiveness, energy, ideas, work, time, encouragement, devotion. You must get outside yourself and into the lives of others. You must give. As Emerson put it, "The only true gift is a portion of thyself" (in *Favorite Quotations from the Collection of Thomas S. Monson*, 188).

4. To become a missionary, you must learn to be humble. You must know that you cannot do it without God's help; that behind a successful missionary program are the thoughts, ideas, and help of many others; that you must seek counsel from those who are wiser and more experienced than yourself; that only by putting forth your total effort can you hope to be worthy of help from God. You must learn that gratitude to others is necessary if you are going to succeed.

5. To become a missionary you must learn to set goals. You must seek new levels of performance, new and greater objectives, regular

self-improvement. You must discipline your life to achieve these goals and to follow the programs given to us by the General Authorities. You must keep your expectations high and learn to dream, to be unafraid of new problems and new directions. Above all, you must never let dreams die or allow goals to be abandoned.

6. To become a missionary you must learn to be a friend. You must learn to go more than halfway, to be positive in your words and deeds, to show genuine concern for others. You must let others feel of your spirit and gladness. You must have the pure love of Christ—to love even those who use you or persecute you. You must learn the magic words that build, help, inspire, and encourage. You must share what you have with others and learn that people "don't care how much you know until they know how much you care" (in Richard J. Marshall, *Home Teachings with Purpose and Power* [Salt Lake City: Deseret Book, 1990], 119).

7. To become a missionary you must learn to meet failure. You must resolve that if you fail, you will fail while trying to succeed. You must realize that you cannot always control what happens to you, but that you can control your response to failure. Remember that the mark of a great man is what he does when he becomes discouraged. Know that the only person who can permanently defeat you is yourself. Every missionary has his down days, but he must not wallow in self-pity. He must get up and get busy and know that a person never fails until he gives up.

Missionary Work

The prophets have made great pronouncements concerning your responsibility to do missionary work. These responsibilities are equally shared by all members of the Church, including full-time missionaries. "For of him unto whom much is given much is required" (D&C 82:3). The prophets have spoken:

> The Lord commands every soul to whom this message comes that it is his responsibility, not only to receive it, but also to carry it to his neighbor. (*Take Heed to Yourselves* [Salt Lake City: Deseret Book, 1966], 28)
>
> —Joseph Fielding Smith

> God will hold us responsible for the people we might have saved, had we done our duty. ("It Becometh Every Man," *Ensign*, October 1977, 5)
>
> —Spencer W. Kimball

> I know this message ["every member a missionary"] is not new, and we have talked about it before, but I believe the time has come when we must shoulder arms. I think we must change our sights and raise our goals. (*The Teachings of Spencer W. Kimball*, ed. Edward L. Kimball [Salt Lake City: Bookcraft, 1982], 585)
>
> —Spencer W. Kimball

> After all that has been said, the greatest and most important duty is to preach the gospel. (*History of the Church*, 2:478)
>
> —Joseph Smith

> Preach that the responsibility of declaring this plan of life, this way of life, this plan of salvation, rests upon the entire membership of the Church. (In Conference Report, October 1966, 7)
>
> —David O. McKay

> Surely taking the gospel to every kindred, tongue, and people is the single greatest responsibility we have in mortality.

(*The Teachings of Howard W. Hunter,* ed. Clyde J. Williams [Salt Lake City: Deseret Book, 2007], 246)

—Howard W. Hunter

God help us to fulfill our responsibility . . . of bringing the glad tidings of the gospel to our friends and neighbors. (In Eugene England, *Converted to Christ through the Book of Mormon* [Salt Lake City: Deseret Book, 1989], 9)

—David O. McKay

These are only a few of the thousands of statements made by Church leaders concerning our opportunities and obligations for sharing the gospel. Many others are in chapter 1 of *Preach My Gospel.* As missionaries, you must shoulder even greater responsibility in this work because of your unique callings.

Music

This subject will be of intense interest to some of you, of moderate interest to a few, and of no interest to others. But it is a subject that affects all of you because music permeates all of your lives in one way or another.

The First Presidency said to all priesthood leaders:

> Through music, man's ability to express himself extends beyond the limits of the spoken language in both subtlety and power. Music can be used to exalt and inspire, or to carry messages of degradation and destruction. It is therefore important that as Latter-day Saints we at all times apply the principles of the gospel and seek the guidance of the Spirit in selecting the music with which we surround ourselves. (In Boyd K. Packer, "Inspiring Music: Worthy Thoughts," *Ensign,* January 1974, 25)

President Ezra Taft Benson said, "Music creates atmosphere. Atmosphere creates environment. Environment influences behavior" ("Satan's Thrust—Youth," *Ensign,* December 1971, 53). President Boyd K. Packer has said, "In our day, music itself has been corrupted. Music can, by its tempo, by its beat, by its intensity, dull the spiritual sensitivity of men" ("Inspiring Music—Worthy Thoughts," *Ensign,* January 1974, 25).

President Packer also said, "There is so much wonderful, uplifting music available that we can experience to our advantage. Our people ought to be surrounded by good music of all kinds."

In attempting to define a music policy for missionaries, Church leaders have had two thoughts uppermost in their minds: (1) the guidelines recommended by President Packer for music throughout the Church, refined by the level of spirituality and the needs of ministers of the gospel; and (2) the need to avoid popular music that would be full of memories for those who hear it. As for the latter point, one mission president said, "Even today I am taken back to a junior prom, a certain date, or a special occasion when I hear certain songs that were popular in my youth."

After careful and prayerful consideration, a mission president will develop a policy concerning music tapes and recordings. Many suggest that only music by the Tabernacle Choir is appropriate. If you have other tapes other than those approved by your mission, you should send them. Those who persist in violating mission rules concerning music will not be able to fulfill the purposes for which they were called on their missions.

These two years of your lives should be different from other years. Dedicate yourselves to the gospel. Raise your standards of conduct above those of the world. Sacrifice worldly pleasures for spiritual virtues. Put aside thoughts and feelings that detract from total commitment to God. As ministers, you should contemplate Paul's message to the Corinthians: "When I was a child, I spake as a child, I understood as a child, I thought as a child: but when I became a man, I put away childish things" (1 Corinthians 13:11).

Your prayerful consideration of these procedures will bring you a realization that wholesome, uplifting music during your mission will bring you blessings of the Lord.

Obedience

Elder L. Tom Perry said, "Daily obedience and clean living and wholesome lives build an armor around you of protection and safety from the temptations that beset you as you proceed through mortality" (L. Tom Perry, "Called to Serve," *Ensign*, May 1991, 39). Never is this more true than during missionary service.

Many years ago, President N. Eldon Tanner had just returned as president of the European Mission (which included all the missions of western Europe). He was asked what was the single most important attribute of a successful missionary. Without hesitation, he said, "Obedience."

In the Old Testament, Samuel chastised Saul for his failure to follow God's commandments. Saul had been ordered to destroy the Amalekites and all they owned. But Saul destroyed only those things he thought were "vile and refuse," and spared the best of the animals to sacrifice to the Lord. Samuel said to Saul, "Behold, to obey is better than sacrifice" (1 Samuel 15:22). Because of his disobedience, Saul's kingship was taken from him.

A mission president told this story: "I remember when I was a small boy, my father worked out of town during the week and was home only on weekends. One week as he left he gave me a job to do during the week. It was a job I didn't want to do, but our chicken coop really needed a new coat of paint. Instead, I worked hard all week to get the chicken coop and the fenced-in area around it looking spotless. When my father returned at the end of the week, the chicken coop had never looked better—it was a marvel to behold. I was proud of it. Even the chickens seemed proud of it. But it didn't save me from getting a spanking! I had performed a good service, but it was not that which my father had told me to do."

President David O. McKay said, "We are here to enjoy life in its fullest and most complete sense; but the message of the gospel of Jesus Christ is this: that to live, one must live in obedience to law, physical law, intellectual law, spiritual law. Transgressions of law always brings unhappiness; it always brings death when carried to the ultimate end" (David O. McKay, in Conference Report, October 1920, 42).

Obedience is not the mark of a slave but is one of the prime qualities of leadership. Look around at your leaders in the Church—your bishop, your stake president, your elders quorum president. Were they called to their positions of responsibility because they resisted authority? They learned that obedience is an absolute essential in the organization of the Lord's Church.

If you do not obey, the power to obey disappears. Your capacity to recognize good is weakened. "And that wicked one cometh and taketh away light and truth, through disobedience" (D&C 93:39).

Elder James E. Talmage wrote, "Man can achieve naught of excellence in matters material or spiritual except through the exercise, the utilization, of that supreme form of energy, obedience." Aristotle said, "Wicked men obey because of fear, and good men obey because of love" (*Useful Quotations*, ed. Tyron Edwards [New York: Grosset and Dunlap, 1933], 428; in Ted E. Brewerton, "Obedience—Full Obedience," *Ensign*, May 1981, 68). Henry Ward Beecher said that laws are servants, and he rules them who obeys them.

Obedience is the key to spirituality. If you find yourself lacking in contacts, having companion problems, getting discouraged, questioning your abilities, or feeling alone, perhaps you should look carefully at your degree of obedience.

One Thing at a Time

"Life by the yard is hard, but life by the inch is a cinch" (in *Favorite Quotations from the Collection of Thomas S. Monson*, 261).

Most people try to take life in big gulps rather than just a sip at a time, but those who take time to savor each individual experience or blessing will taste of the joys of living.

Elder Sterling W. Sill said that the best way to eat an elephant is to cut it up into little pieces (*The Five Fingers of Leadership Success*, Brigham Young University Speeches of the Year [February 9, 1965], 5). This is the way it is with most everything you do. For example, many of you look at the five lessons in *Preach My Gospel* and think how hard it will be to learn all of them; others cut them into small pieces and learn a concept at a time. New missionaries often look at the two years that lie ahead of them and think how long they will be, but the wise missionary is one who sets his goals and then strides ahead one step at a time.

Most people are guilty of looking at a task and then turning away from it because it looks too big. Your weekly planning session is one step in cutting the year into small pieces. Another aid for you is your daily planner, and if you will use it each evening to plan your next day, you will find that life really is a cinch by the inch.

No task is too large, no challenge too great, no mountain too high, no sorrow too heavy, and no goal too far if you will keep this simple truth in mind. Remember that the race is won not by the swift but through the steady, faithful persistence of those who persevere. The final step upward is the result of many, many steps in that same direction.

Life is a one-way street—you cannot go back and change what you did yesterday. But you can profit from yesterday's experiences, make plans for the future, and then go ahead with the confidence and conviction that you are doing what's right. Every success in life has a price tag on it. Success in missionary work has several such price tags, including diligence, dedication, and devotion.

If at times life seems almost overwhelming with problems and disappointments, try analyzing the ways they can be cut into smaller pieces—one thing at a time.

Opportunity

Alexander Graham Bell once said, "When one door closes, another opens; but we often look so long and so regretfully upon the closed door that we do not see the one which has opened for us" (in Brent A. Barlow, *Understanding Death* [Salt Lake City: Deseret Book, 1979], 83).

Dean Johnson, author of a book titled *Business and Man,* formulated a "Law of Opportunity" as follows: "Opportunity offers itself to men in proportion to their ability, their will for action, their power of vision, their experience, and their knowledge of their business. Inversely, opportunity is concealed from men in proportion to their slothfulness, their reliance upon others, their passion for imitation, and their ignorance of their business."

Translated into missionary work, this means that your opportunities for success depend upon your ability, your dedication, your vision, your experiences, and your knowledge of the gospel and its programs. When a spiritual opportunity comes along, you will not only grab it—you will be prepared for it. Your goal, then, must be to achieve the qualities of success.

Determination and concentration require energy to give them body. Mere resolutions are worthless unless they are promptly followed by act and deed. Resolutions (or goals) are of no worth unless you do something about them. They are like music—silent unless performed; like a seed—sterile unless planted and cultivated; like faith—dead without works; like standards of conduct—worthless unless put into practice.

Those who value present comfort more highly than the attainment of a purpose usually shy away from goals and other ambitious thoughts. Those who appreciate a challenge know that they will likely get some splinters in their hands while they are climbing the ladder of success. They are willing to pay the price.

A purpose is vital to the spirit of achievement. Force of purpose will generate the will to labor earnestly and perseveringly and thereby enable you to be as successful a missionary as you want to become. It is

195

important for you to have a feeling of necessity about what you are doing. This gives you the power to overcome difficulties.

Success is seeing difficulties in a task without shrinking away from them. Every person looking for opportunity must expect to encounter reverses. Difficulties show men what they are made of. The first rule in coping with frustrations is to expect your full share of them. They are part of our daily living. They are like the sand traps on a golf course, put there to prove the skill of the golfer.

Faintheartedness holds out small hope of accomplishment. The timid and hesitating missionary is likely to find everything impossible, chiefly because it seems so to him. President Spencer W. Kimball said, "Life gives to all a choice. You can satisfy yourself with mediocrity if you wish. You can be common, ordinary, dull, colorless; or you can be clean, vibrant, progressive, useful, colorful, rich" (*The Miracle of Forgiveness* [Salt Lake City: Bookcraft, 1969], 235).

Ask yourselves what you will wish tomorrow that you had done today. This can give purpose to your decisions. It helps you to see opportunity. The secret of success is to be ready for opportunity when it comes. Don't regret tomorrow what you should have done today.

Opportunity

In the days before modern harbors, ships had to anchor outside a port until a flood tide came to carry them in. The ships thus at anchor were described in Latin as being *op portu,* "in front of port." As the time for the turning of the tide approached, skipper and crew were alerted as the tide reached its crest. All sprang into action at the critical moment. They knew that if they missed the tide, they would have to wait for another one.

Shakespeare likened this experience to the affairs of men and caught the exact meaning of *opportunity* when he said, "There is a tide in the affairs of men, which, taken at the flood, leads on to fortune; omitted, all the voyage of their life is bound in shallows and in miseries" (in Spencer W. Kimball, in Conference Report, October 1970, 71).

Opportunity is not a tangible thing—something that can be lost and then found again. Once lost, it is lost forever. Another opportunity may present itself, but the previous one is gone forever. And if you have another opportunity, will you have learned enough from the first one to take advantage of it? There is a proverb that says, "The dawn does not come twice to awaken a man." Life is a one-way street—you cannot go back and change the things you did, or didn't do, yesterday.

The Apostle Paul, in writing to the Galatians, said, "And let us not be weary in well doing: for in due season we shall reap, if we faint not. As we have therefore opportunity, let us do good unto all men, especially unto them who are of the household of faith" (Galatians 6: 9–10).

A former missionary has written that while he was on his mission, he spent most of his time thinking about home. Now that he is home, he spends most of his time thinking about his mission. Lost opportunities? They are all around us!

The men who were able to ride the tide into port were prepared—by their knowledge and experience, their skills, and their readiness—to take advantage of the full flood of the tide. Here are some ideas to help you be ready for your tides of opportunity:

1. *Believe in yourself.* Expect breaks to come your way. Expect

your Heavenly Father to bless you because you know you are doing all that is required of you. Have a positive attitude toward yourself and your success. Know it will happen.

2. *Make your experience work for you.* Review what you have accomplished. Look at your experience (both good and bad), and see how much you have learned from them.

3. *Evaluate your strengths and weaknesses.* Take an honest look at yourself. Recognize the important things. Take an inventory of your skills and talents. Don't hide behind excuses or rationalize away your limitations. Emphasize your strengths.

4. *Expose yourself to opportunities.* Be on the hunt at all times. Be aware of what is going on around you. Be imaginative. Work out a plan (most good things don't just happen). Learn your duty and then do it.

5. *Follow through.* Be prepared for difficulties. Turn your hurdles and obstacles into challenges. Let your mistakes be your teachers. Watch out for those who will try to turn you away from your goal. Be persistent. Be faithful. Stick it out.

Opposing Forces

"For it must needs be, that there is an opposition in all things" (2 Nephi 2:11). The reason for opposition is so that the children of God, through the principles of moral agency, may develop the power of choice in their lives—to choose the promptings that build and uplift rather than those that tear down and destroy.

The influences of Satan can be subtle and deceiving. Many who have a testimony of the Lord Jesus Christ do not believe in the adversary. Satan is real. He exists, he is here among us, and his mission is to destroy each one of us. He is the opposition.

How do you overcome the power of Satan? There are many ways, but here are four:

1. *Learn to recognize Satan.* "Whatsoever thing persuadeth men to do evil, and believe not in Christ, and deny him, and serve not God, then ye may know with a perfect knowledge it is of the devil" (Moroni 7:17). In analyzing your promptings from within, you can be sure it is of Satan if it leads to selfishness, pride, lust, personal desires, rejection of righteous counsel, disobedience, rebelliousness, or contention, or if it is incompatible with our stewardship. "And that which doth not edify is not of God, and is darkness" (D&C 50:23).

2. *Learn the limitations of Satan.* One of the most comforting verses in all scripture is D&C 6:16: "Yea, I tell thee, that thou mayest know that there is none else save God that knowest thy thoughts and the intents of thy heart." This means that Satan does not know what you are thinking—that he must rely on your actions to discover your weaknesses. He must therefore seek to control your thoughts from the outside. This brings you into a partnership with God and gives you the power to overcome and to persevere. "Keep all the covenants and commandments by which ye are bound; and I will cause the heavens to shake for your good, and Satan shall tremble"

(D&C 35:24). Satan also becomes discouraged. That is why it is so important to be strong and unwavering in our obedience to God's laws.

3. *Learn how God can help you.* Work and pray for the influence and power of the Holy Ghost, which brings understanding, light, and edification. "Every thing which inviteth to do good, and to persuade to believe in Christ, is sent forth by the power and gift of Christ" (Moroni 7:16). You must constantly evaluate the promptings from within, realizing that the Spirit of Christ and the Holy Ghost will prompt you to righteous works. Several indications can assure you that the inner prompting is from God: if it is compatible and in harmony with your stewardship; if it is compatible and in harmony with the scriptures, prophets, and leaders; if the results are good, positive, and righteous; if it serves others; and if it edifies and leads to light and understanding.

4. *Learn your own strengths and weaknesses, and act to improve.* God would never tempt you to do an unrighteous act. If such a temptation comes, you automatically know from whence it comes. Evaluate your past actions. Know where you have fallen down and where you have stood straight and tall. As you resist evil, your ability to resist becomes stronger. This is the way to perfection. There are no shortcuts, no easy way, no coasting downstream. The Apostle Paul showed us the way: "Put on the whole armour of God, that ye may be able to stand against the wiles of the devil. . . . Above all, taking the shield of faith" (Ephesians 6:11, 16).

Opposition

Any cyclist will tell you that both the front and back wheels of a bicycle are of equal importance. The back wheel delivers the power necessary to propel the bicycle forward, while the front wheel determines the course the bicycle will follow.

Many men have learned to use their back wheels only. They can set themselves in motion. What they lack is a steering wheel. Oliver Wendell Holmes used to say, "I find the great thing in this world is not so much where we stand, as in what direction we are moving" (in *Favorite Quotations from the Collection of Thomas S. Monson*, 158).

How does a man determine the course he will take or what direction he will follow? An enlightening story is told by Lady Asquith, whose husband was prime minister of England during the early years of World War I. She was riding on her estate when she saw a tramp. Taking up conversation with him, she asked him an interesting question: "How do you decide which way to go?" The tramp replied, "I always go with the wind at my back."

Here is the philosophy of the hobo, the derelict, the drifter, the bum—the man who will never face anything.

Coasting downhill, drifting downstream, or sailing with the wind at your back are the easy paths to follow. Remember the kite you used to fly? When it drifted with the wind, it would falter. But get it to fight the wind, and it would soon rise and soar with the grace of a seagull.

When you set your course as a missionary, do not shy away from adversity, hardship, or opposition. Remember that growth and progress come from surmounting those little stumbling blocks.

Indeed, you should be grateful for them, for they provide the challenges that give life its opportunities and zest. They are the winds that will lift you to the heights of achievement and success.

Optimism

The word *optimism* comes from the Latin word *optimus,* which means "best." Hence, optimism is a disposition to look on the best or bright side of things or to believe that everything is for the best.

Missionaries sometimes talk about positive mental attitude, confidence, seeing the good side of things, trust in the future, encouragement, and hoping for the best. Optimism is all of these things—and then some.

A young boy was riding his bicycle to school one day when his front wheel skidded on some loose gravel, and he lost control. He skidded into a tree and was thrown from his bike. He skinned his arm, lost a tooth, and ruined his slacks. Picking himself up and dusting himself off, he proceeded to push his bike to school. About a block down the street, a car careened around the corner and ran into the boy and his bicycle. Seriously injured, he was taken to the hospital in an ambulance. After the doctors had set his broken bones and bandaged his wounds, his father noticed that he was grasping something in his right hand. He asked his son what it was that he was holding so tightly in his clenched fist. The boy opened his fist and showed his father a quarter. "I found this quarter when I fell off my bike," he said. "This must be my lucky day."

Optimism is the ability to see the good things of life, to see good in others, to work hard for the cause in which you believe, to build up things rather than to tear them down. Here is something called "The Optimist's Creed":

> [Promise yourself] to be so strong that nothing can disturb
> your peace of mind.
> [Promise yourself] to talk health, happiness, and prosperity
> to every person you meet.
> [Promise yourself] to make all your friends feel that there is
> something good in them.
> [Promise yourself] to look at the sunny side of everything.
> [Promise yourself] to think only the best, to work for only
> the best, and to expect only the best.
> [Promise yourself] to be just as enthusiastic about the success of others as you are about your own.

[Promise yourself] to forget the mistakes of the past and to press on to greater achievements in the future.

[Promise yourself] to wear a cheerful countenance at all times and to give a smile to every living creature you meet.

[Promise yourself] to give so much time to the improvement of yourself that you have no time to criticize others.

[Promise yourself] that you will be too large for worry, too noble for anger, too strong for fear, and too happy for the presence of trouble. (Christian D. Larson, *Science of Mind*, 71 [June 1998], 50)

Believe in working, not waiting; in laughing, not weeping; in boosting, not knocking. Believe in today and the work you are doing—in courtesy, generosity, kindness, and gratitude. Most of all, believe in a wise, loving Heavenly Father who is watching over you and who is interested in the lives you touch.

Pain and Sacrifice

Robert Louis Stevenson explained the principle of growth when he said, "You cannot run away from a weakness; you must some day fight it out or perish; and if that be so, why not now and where you stand?" (in Hugh B. Brown, Conference Report, October 1963, 85).

The way to grow as a person is to do the things you do not want to do. You have been placed upon the earth to gain a mortal body—to add to your life, learn self-mastery, gain experiences, prove your love to our Heavenly Father, and share the gospel with others.

You accomplish these things through sacrifice—by giving up something of less importance for something of greater importance. At times, this giving up of something is painful—even though it is for something of greater importance.

Thomas Henry Huxley stated it this way: "Perhaps the most valuable result of all education is the ability to make yourself do the thing you have to do when it ought to be done, whether you like it or not" (in Henry Eyring, *Reflections of a Scientist* [Salt Lake City: Deseret Book, 1983], 21–22).

The real adventure in life is growth through discipline and personal sacrifice. To withstand pain and to experience growth, you must carry in your mind a mental picture of the success, rewards, and happiness that will be yours through paying the price. Paying the price may include pain and self-denial. But isn't that what life is all about?

President Joseph Fielding Smith said, "No mortal life would be complete if there had been no disappointments, no pain or physical discomfort, nor suffering" (Joseph Fielding Smith, *Answers to Gospel Questions*, 5 vols. [Salt Lake City: Deseret Book, 1957–1966], 5:91).

The missionaries in one mission recently met together and decided to make a commitment to the Lord. After fasting, they promised the Lord that they would make certain sacrifices. In return, they asked that they receive certain blessings. They made the sacrifices, and the Lord blessed them.

How many of you ask for the blessings but are unwilling to make the sacrifices? You set goals and make commitments to reach those goals but then fail to pay the price to be worthy of receiving His help.

When you begin to face up to life—to recognize your weaknesses and to make plans for improvement—you experience an internal battle. When you look at your life and decide to do those things you know you must do, you must also realize that self-improvement requires sacrifice and pain and self-denial. The Apostle Paul explained it best when he spoke of the Savior's example: "Though he were a Son, yet he learned obedience by the things which he suffered" (Hebrews 5:8).

Part-Member Families #1

A mission president once asked his missionaries how they would approach a nonmember husband whose wife was a member of the Church. Their answers: "Get better acquainted with him." "Let him know that I am a friend." "Help him in his work."

Basically, these responses are correct. You need to get to know a person before you can begin the process of conversion. But look at the odds you are fighting: two missionaries and a wife vs. the husband's drinking friends, smoking friends, dirty-story-telling friends, and all the other forces pulling him away from the gospel. In many ways, the battle seems lopsided in Satan's favor.

Remember too that the wife and others have probably tried every conceivable approach with him. He knows all the programs designed to bring him into the Church. The home teachers have had a try at him; maybe six or eight pairs of missionaries have tried and failed; the bishop and other priesthood leaders have had him to parties, sports events, and other occasions; he may know the past discussions better than the missionaries. In other words, he may appear to be immune to all attempts to convert him.

How, then, can you hope to reach him when so many people have failed? There are no pat answers—no tried-and-proven methods—but the following ideas may help:

1. *Correlate with your priesthood leaders.* Priesthood leaders have the responsibility for working with part-member families. With their help, prayerfully select a part-member family (if you do not have one in mind). They may have a program under way or a plan made. Meet with the home teachers, quorum leader, bishop, and others who will know the background and problems of the person who is selected.

2. *Ask the Lord for help.* In addition to prayers offered with your priesthood leaders, covenant with the Lord that you will give the family your very best efforts, and then live so that you will be worthy of His help.

3. *Find out why he is not a member.* It could be lack of interest, Word of Wisdom problems, bad opinion of other members, bad feelings toward someone, transgressions, fear of involvement, pride, fear of losing friends, misunderstanding of Church doctrines, a hang-up with specific Church principles, or other reasons. If you can find the real reasons for his reluctance, you can then look for ways to overcome his objections.

4. *Make a plan.* With your priesthood leaders, devise ways to bring all of the Church's resources to your aid. Organize a committee, bringing several other members to help. Plan, improvise, use all of the creative tools at your command to figure out ways to get people to help friendship the person. If he golfs, get golfers to help. If he collects stamps, get stamp collectors to help. If he likes fishing and hunting, get fishermen and hunters to help. Surround him with new friends that have similar interests. These friends must be genuine. They must be interested in him and his friendship—whether he ever joins the Church.

There are four more possible steps. The above four are merely the preliminaries.

Part-Member Families #2

Part-member families #1 discussed four preliminary steps in beginning labors with part-member families. The basic principle was to involve other people. Once you begin to recognize and take advantage of the power of the Church in accomplishing any given task, there will be no stopping the work. Learn to use the organization of the Church. Continuing from #1, here are four additional steps.

5. *Encourage Church members in the family to live the gospel.* President Boyd K. Packer says that if it is difficult to get a man to Church, then the wife should do everything she can to make him feel at Church while he's home. Begin where he is, in the home, by having him take his rightful place at the head of the family. Getting him to Church may be an important step in his conversion, but it isn't necessarily the first step. Too often people judge a man's activity or testimony by his attendance at Church. The home and family are units of the Church. President Packer says that when men feel comfortable with the Church at home, then they begin to go to Church with their families. Encourage the family to live the gospel in all they do. Be sure to teach the discussions to the family. Teach when he will be there too.

6. *Use the family home evening program.* Get the family together for a family home evening. Approach the father and offer to put on the first one, or offer to give a part of it. Teach the family some games, give the lesson, or be in charge of refreshments. When you are in the home, defer to him as the head of the family. Let him know he is in charge. Try to get him to kneel and lead the family in prayer. If you cannot have a family home evening in his home (or feel that you shouldn't), get one of the member families on your committee to invite the family to one of their homes for one. If used properly, family home evening can be one of your most important tools in the conversion process.

7. *Be friendly.* Visit the family. Go out of your way to do something special for all of them, especially the nonmember. Help him in his work if you can. Let him know you are genuinely interested. See him sometimes outside the home.

8. *Follow up.* Keep various members of your committee working on different activities. They expect you to coordinate things. Keep feeding ideas to them: baking cakes, sending birthday cards, having lunch together, meeting the man downtown, holding neighborhood parties or dinners, including the couple in social activities, taking them to Church-sponsored events, introducing them to other Church members, and a host of other possibilities. Think of ways to reach the man. Pray about it regularly. Be a coordinator, and work on it regularly—nearly every day.

Remember that the conversion process works on the principle of love—love from family, love from missionaries, love from priesthood leaders, love from the ward family. Once he knows that everyone really cares, it will have an effect on him. You can overdo such a special project, but it would be far better to err by doing too much rather than by doing too little. Also remember that in working with part-member families, patience and understanding are absolutely essential to success. He may never join the Church, but he and his family will be happier and more fulfilled. And his newfound friends in the Church will surround him with love and good will.

Pay the Price

There was once a man who wanted to be a U.S. Senator. His friends immediately swung into action to get him elected. They arranged for all kinds of meetings in front of different clubs, associations, and other groups. They wanted to get him as much public exposure as possible.

But he started to pick and choose. He wanted to take the meetings that were convenient and to avoid those that were hard. He wanted a comfortable campaign.

He soon had no campaign at all. In fact, it finally ended when one of his closest friends was delegated to go tell him: "You'll never be a U.S. Senator; you don't want it badly enough."

Elder Paul H. Dunn told a story about a young man who visited a friend of his. The young man's clothes were threadbare, his shoes were cracked, and poverty was written all over him. "I'm going to be a doctor," he said, "and I wondered if you could direct me to a job to help pay my medical school expenses." Elder Dunn's friend thought to himself that the young man might as well try to buy Dodger Stadium. He explained how long it would take to get through medical school and how much it would cost. With all the tact that he could summon, he pointed out that the whole idea was beyond the young man's reach, and he suggested other alternatives.

The young man listened patiently and courteously, but he wanted to be a doctor. He believed he could be a doctor. A doctor he was going to be. And that was that. He became a doctor and is now practicing in Los Angeles.

Jack Dempsey was boxing in New Jersey many years ago while he was the heavyweight boxing champion of the world. A boxer who had made a reputation as a good fighter was in one of the preliminary fights that night, but the sportswriters had written him off because he had brittle hands. His name was Gene Tunney. That night he lost his fight because of his weak hands, but he decided that he was going to become the heavyweight boxing champion of the world.

He knew his weakness was his hands. He knew what he would

have to do to reach his goal. He bought two hard rubber balls, and day after day put one in each of his hands and squeezed them every time he got the chance. At the same time, he worked regularly at punching the heavy bag—lightly at first, then more and more aggressively as his hands became stronger. Finally, his weakness became his strength—two of the strongest hands in the history of boxing. He defeated Jack Dempsey and became the heavyweight boxing champion of the world. In a return bout, he defeated him again and then later retired undefeated as champion. Gene Tunney knew what he wanted; he paid the price to get it.

Your role as a missionary is to teach. That is the reason you were sent to your mission. The Lord expects it of you. Teaching should be your primary goal. It should permeate your every thought. It should be uppermost in every planning session. You should be obsessed with a desire to teach and bear testimony as were Alma, Abinadi, Ammon, Paul, and other great missionaries.

Look at your mission; take a look at what you say you want. How much do you really want to teach? What are you doing to find teaching situations? Are you really paying the price? If you want to teach the gospel badly enough, you will do it.

Persistence

Persistence is the key to success. A large research firm made a study and found the following:

48 percent of salesmen make one call and quit.

25 percent of salesmen make two calls and then quit.

12 percent of salesmen make three calls and quit.

5 percent of salesmen make four calls and quit.

10 percent of salesmen make five or more calls and make 80 percent of the sales.

In other words, 80 percent of all sales were made by 10 percent of the salesmen—and were made after five or more callbacks. Most salesmen don't fail; they just give up.

Benjamin Disrali said that "genius is the power to make a continuous effort" (in Sterling W. Sill, *The Wealth of Wisdom* [Salt Lake City: Deseret Book, 1977], 113). Calvin Coolidge said, "Nothing in the world can take the place of persistence. Talent will not—nothing is more common than unsuccessful men with talent; genius will not— unrewarded genius is almost a proverb; education will not—the world is full of educated derelicts. Persistence and determination alone are omnipotent" (in *Favorite Quotations from the Collection of Thomas S. Monson*, 164).

Persistence is the power to go on resolutely in the face of difficulty. It is the missionary who never gives up, the man of faith who perseveres, the ability to try and try again, the person who gives until it hurts and then who gives some more until it feels good. It is the person who keeps getting up one more time than he gets knocked down, the person who will not accept defeat, and the quality that makes good men great and great men greater.

Look at the men and women you admire most in life. The chances are that they are successful because they were willing to pay the price of success. That price usually included persistence. Few men ever achieved success the first time they tried. The extra effort of men such as George

Washington, Abraham Lincoln, Thomas Edison, and Henry Ford led to their success. It reminds me of a little ditty:

> It matters not if you try and fail,
> And fail and try again;
> But it matters much if you try and fail,
> And fail to try again.
> (In Paul H. Dunn, Conference Report, April 1979, 7)

Persistence is the key to success. Persist in your labors in the face of whatever obstacles Satan throws at you. The persistent missionary is the successful missionary.

Persistence

Heber J. Grant's father died nine days after he was born. When Heber was a boy, his bishop, seeing the condition of the Grant home, offered to take money from fast offerings to build a new roof. "Oh no you won't," said Sister Grant, "I have sewing here . . . and this house will take care of me until my son becomes a man and builds a new one for me."

The bishop felt that she would never get her new home because Heber was "the laziest boy in the thirteenth ward." The bishop thought Heber was lazy because he spent so much time throwing a ball against the bishop's adobe barn.

But Heber had a reason for throwing the ball against the barn. He was tall and lean but very frail. He loved baseball but was always the last one chosen on the last team. Heber J. Grant did not like defeat. He began pushing his way to the top in baseball. He would practice by himself for hours. Some times his arm would ache so badly he couldn't sleep at night, but he eventually played on the territorial championship team. When he was twenty-one, he built a new home for his mother (see Heber J. Grant, "One Man's Memory of an Honored Mother," *Improvement Era* 39 [May 1936]).

You have all heard of President Grant's desires to be a good penman. As a boy, he was poor at writing. He began pushing again, this time pushing a pen. He became one of the best penmen in Utah and later taught penmanship at the University of Deseret. In the same way, he learned to sing. His favorite saying was, "That which we persist in doing becomes easier for us to do, not that the nature of the thing is changed, but that our power to do is increased" (Ralph Waldo Emerson, in Heber J. Grant, "Overflow Meeting," Conference Report, April 1901, 63).

Robert Bruce was a gallant Scottish patriot who worked most of his life to free Scotland from British rule. He lost many battles and was forced to hide from his enemies in a hut deep in the forest. "It is of no use to fight any more," he said. "Our enemies are too strong for us." As he sat contemplating his plight, he saw a spider hanging from a thin thread, trying to swing itself from one beam to another. Six times it failed. Bruce remembered that he had at that time lost all six of his major battles. "If that spider persists until it succeeds, then I shall also continue," he told himself. When the spider persisted and won, Bruce rallied his soldiers, won independence for Scotland, and became its first King in 1328 (see Sir Walter Scott, *Tales of a Grandfather* [n.p., n.d.], 109–10).

Helen Keller, the great woman who overcame blindness to become a symbol of service to others, said, "We can do anything we want to do if we stick to it long enough" (in Roderick L. Cameron, *Grant Oratorical Contest,* Brigham Young University Speeches of the Year [December 1, 1964], 3). John J. Pershing, the famous General of World War I, said: "If you have a fall . . . pick yourself up and start over immediately. If you do, in the long run life won't beat you." Theodore Roosevelt said, "The world wants men who do not shrink from temporary defeats in life, but come again and wrestle triumph from defeat" (in Anthony Wons, *Tony's Scap Book* [Chicago: Reilly and Lee, 1930], 87). Most important to us, Jesus said, "He that endureth to the end shall be saved" (Matthew 10:22).

The Lord is pleased with those who promise much and give more, who start the race strong and finish strong, who accept responsibility gladly and give their best, who are counted ready to stand because of their stalwartness and unwavering faith.

> Tis the sticker who wins in the battle of life,
> While the quitter is laid on the shelf;
> You are never defeated, remember this,
> Until you lose faith in yourself.
> (In Sterling W. Sill, *Principles, Promises, and Powers* [Salt
> Lake City: Deseret Book, 1973], 226)

Personal Relationships

A few months after moving to a small town, a woman complained to a neighbor about the poor service at the local drug store. She hoped the neighbor would repeat her complaint to the owner of the drug store.

Next time she went to the drug store, the druggist greeted her with a big smile, and told her how happy he was to see her again. He told her that he hoped she liked their town, and he invited her to let him know if there was anything he could do to help her and her husband get settled. He then filled her order promptly and efficiently.

Later, she reported the miraculous change to her neighbor. "I suppose you told the druggist how poor I thought the service was?" she asked. "Well no," the neighbor said. "I hope you don't mind, but I told him you were amazed at the way he had built up this small-town drug store, and that you thought it was one of the best run stores you had ever seen."

Can you apply this principle to your missionary work? Try it on your district leader or zone leader or on a future companion. Teach the principle to Church members at a family home evening or in a visit to their home. Talk about it in Church when you are called upon to speak. Bear it in a testimony meeting. Teach it to your contacts and investigators.

The basic principle is that compliments are better than complaints. You should treat people like the person you want them to become. Almost miraculously, they become that person.

One time a person complained that no one liked him. He had few friends, his family life was a disaster, he had lost a succession of jobs; even relatives had given up visiting his home. There is a list of what might be called Ten Negative Personality Traits. Out of the ten, this man had seven or eight. It's no wonder he was isolated from others.

If you need friends, or if people seem to disappear when you come around, or if members are not friendshipping the way you want, or if you feel that no one likes you, evaluate yourself against these ten negatives:

1. A compulsion to show off knowledge, experience, virtues, or ability.

2. Exaggerates to the point that it is almost lying.
3. Moodiness. Friendly one day, unfriendly the next.
4. Bossiness. Must run everything; never gives others a chance to lead.
5. Not reliable. Word is no good, promises never kept, commitments broken.
6. Chronic complainer. A real crepe-hanger; murmurs, gripes, mutters.
7. Nosy. Asks personal questions that are none of his business.
8. Gossipy. Knows everything about everybody, including you, and tells all.
9. Says things in anger and then tries to smooth things over with favors.
10. Always fishing for compliments but never gives any.

Sit down and compare your personality traits against these ten. If you score more than one or two, you may know why you are lonely even if you have many fine traits.

Persuasion

To persuade is to lead someone to a belief or to a course of action. Your work as missionaries—both in teaching nonmembers and in helping Church members understand their great opportunities in friendshipping—revolves around your ability to persuade them to believe or to act.

What good is it for missionaries to have the authority to make converts if they do not have the ability to make converts? Jacob said that he labored diligently among his people, that he might "persuade them to come unto Christ" (Jacob 1:7). Moroni, in quoting Mormon's teachings, said that that which "inviteth to do good, and to persuade to believe in Christ, is sent forth by the power and gift of Christ" (Moroni 7:16). Mormon said, "I would that I could persuade all ye ends of the earth to repent and prepare to stand before the judgment-seat of Christ" (Mormon 3:22).

Why are some people so much better at the art of persuasion than others? Are there any guidelines to follow, any commonsense rules that will help when you are trying to get another person to do it your way? Can you use these principles to help you as missionaries? Dr. Norman Vincent Peale has listed six hints on dealing with others in what he calls "The Very Gentle Art of Persuading People." See how you rate on them:

1. *Always look at your proposal from the other person's viewpoint.* This may seem elementary, but it's astonishing how often would-be persuaders fail to do it. They're so intent on their own objectives that as they talk, the other person begins to feel he's being exploited or used. This sets up inner resistance. If, on the other hand, your approach takes into consideration the welfare of the person you're trying to persuade, something in him is going to sense it and respond to it.

2. *Avoid the hard sell; it's counterproductive.* No one likes to be cornered. No one likes to be pressured. There's a point at which persuasion becomes demand. Even if you force apparent agreement, the other person will resent you for it.

3. *Stay constantly aware of the effect you're creating.* If it's favorable, move ahead. If not, draw back. The person who fails to do this isn't a persuader; he's a bore.

4. *If you find the front door locked, go around to the side.* Good persuaders don't try to pry open a closed mind. They think of possible alternatives. If an investigator cannot at this time accept a basic principle, find one he will accept, and then build on that common ground.

5. *Whenever possible, create a climate of acceptance in advance.* Happy, relaxed people are responsive, cooperative people. Fretful, moody people are not. This is where members can do so much good—by cultivating a nonmember family to the point where our message will be acceptable. The Savior was a master at persuading: when he had people in a responsive mood, he persuaded them in the direction He wanted them to go.

6. *Finally, let your enthusiasm show through.* This is perhaps the most important rule of all because no worthwhile persuasion can be accomplished without it. It's easy to resist a halfhearted persuader. After all, he hasn't been able to persuade himself. But an enthusiastic missionary is one who cares, and real caring is the most contagious thing in the world. Bear your testimony, and bear it with conviction.

Planning #1

Your lives are made up of planning. Some do it well, and others either do it poorly or too late. Still others make a plan but do not have the self-discipline to live by it. Those who take time to carefully make a plan and then master the art of living by it become successful, happy, peaceful people.

There are five basic periods (or time zones) for which missionaries should be setting plans. These are:

1. Planning for the immediate. Today, tomorrow, tonight, this afternoon, or anytime in the next few days.
2. Planning for the week. Planning things to be done a week at a time.
3. Planning for the next month. The length of time you will be in an area or have a specific companion, or a calendar month for accomplishing activities, group meetings, firesides, and so on.
4. Planning for the long range. This would be the length of your future mission, the next five years, the next ten years, or the plans for your life.
5. Planning for the eternities. This would be your plan for after earth life is over.

It is easy to see that each one of these time zones will phase into the others. If you plan each day carefully, the week will be a success; if you plan each of your missionary areas carefully, your mission will be a success; if your mission is a success, your life will be a success; and if your life is a success, your eternal joys will be great. Each one of these time zones is dependent upon the others.

The planning of long range and eternal goals (numbers four and five above)—and the necessary intermediate steps for achieving them—is something each missionary should be doing constantly.

Planning for the immediate (daily planning), planning for the week, and planning for the month are done regularly in your daily and weekly planning sessions.

Carefully review the suggestions about missionary service in *Preach My Gospel.*

Planning #2

Planning #1 discussed the five time zones in planning. All of you should be planning for the immediate, the week, the month, the future, and for eternity.

You have heard the old adage, "If you fail to plan, plan to fail" (in Victor L. Ludlow, *Principles and Practices of the Restored Gospel* [Salt Lake City: Deseret Book, 1992], 333). There is another admonition, equally important, which says, "Plan your work, and work your plan."

The basic "plan your work" tool of the missionary is the missionary daily planner outlined in *Preach My Gospel*. This basic planner is used in your weekly planning session to plan your week and then is used each evening to plan the next day. Daily planning and weekly planning (in fact, all planning) require four basic steps.

1. *Review.* Look at the past and analyze. Pinpoint weaknesses, failures, and successes. Determine the causes of failures and successes. Ask yourself, "Where have I fallen down?" "What good did I accomplish today?" and "How could I have done better?"

2. *Set goals.* You should know where you are going before you get started. Remember—goals must be written down and kept in front of you. A goal not written down is only a wish.

3. *Determine priorities.* Once goals have been set, priorities must be established. Which goal do I reach first? What are the intermediate steps for reaching that goal? What goal is next on my list? What are the intermediate steps?

4. *Schedule.* Once you know (1) where you are going, (2) what is to be your first objective, and (3) the intermediate steps for getting there, then you must decide when you want to arrive. This means that each intermediate step must be scheduled for a particular time and place. In this type of scheduling, everything you schedule (or plan) is written down to accomplish a predetermined goal or intermediate step. Thus,

your life becomes organized because you always know where you are going and how and when you are going to get there.

Many missionaries plan their next day by listing their appointments first. Then they fill in with other things. But if they will go through the four steps of planning every night—carefully setting their goals for the next day and setting priorities—they will soon begin having a purpose for every action they take.

When you make an appointment, accept a dinner engagement, or visit a member, you should have a definite objective in mind. This objective should fit into the goals you have set for that particular day or week. As you become goal-oriented—and judge each move as it relates to your goals—you begin organizing ourselves so that you can "plan your work and then work your plan" (in "Gleaner Girls," *Improvement Era* 38 [March 1935], 38).

Once you learn to plan properly, these skills will become so important that you will carry them into your lifetime of accomplishments. It is estimated that only 5 percent of the population sets goals and makes plans, so you will have a wonderful advantage in your professional career.

Preparation Day

Preparation days are relatively new in missionary work. Until a few years ago, missionaries were expected to work seven days a week and take a little of each day to do their laundry, cleaning, letter writing, and so on.

Then someone suggested a "Diversion day"—a day that could be used for many personal activities and which would allow the missionaries to concentrate on missionary work the other six days of the week. Diversion day became too much of a diversion, and the General Authorities decided to authorize the current preparation day.

The basic premise, however, remains the same: this is the day to use for all of your personal activities—laundry, cleaning, writing letters, learning more about the culture of the people in your area, attending the temple when one is available, and so on. The intent is for you to prepare yourself for the coming week's missionary labors.

Unfortunately, some missionaries continue to use other days of the week to do their laundry, clean apartments, get haircuts, and buy clothing in order to leave preparation day free for sports and similar activities. This is not in keeping with the spirit of the decision to provide a preparation day for those kinds of activities.

You should still dress as missionaries if you are in public places such as museums, art galleries, special exhibits, and cultural centers. Do not travel outside your district without your zone leader's approval. If you want to travel outside your zone, get permission from the mission president. Stay with your companion during all activities. Read the *Missionary Handbook* for a full discussion of activities for this day.

If used properly, this day can become the special day for which it is intended—taking care of your nonmissionary duties and preparing yourself physically and emotionally for the coming week's activities.

Always be found in proper places with proper thoughts and engaging in proper activities, and the Spirit of the Lord will strengthen you and make your preparation day what it should be.

Pretty Good

Charles Osgood of CBS Radio knows the difference between "good" and "pretty good." He wrote the following poem to remind us that "pretty good" might not be good enough.

> There once was a pretty good student, who sat in a pretty
> good class,
> And was taught by a pretty good teacher, who always let
> pretty good pass.
> He wasn't terrific at reading, he wasn't a whiz-bang at math,
> But for him, education was leading straight down a pretty good path.
> He didn't find school too exciting, but he wanted to do pretty well,
> And he did have some trouble with writing, and nobody had taught
> him to spell.
> When doing arithmetic problems, pretty good was regarded as fine.
> Five plus five needn't always add up to ten, a pretty good answer was nine.
> The pretty good class that he sat in was part of a pretty good school,
> And the student was not an exception; on the contrary, he was the rule.
> The pretty good school that he went to was there in a pretty good
> town,
> And nobody there seemed to notice
> He could not tell a verb from a noun.
> The pretty good student, in fact, was part of a pretty good mob,
> And the first time he knew what he lacked was when he looked for a
> pretty good job.
> It was then, when he sought a position, he discovered that life could
> be tough,
> And he soon had a sneaking suspicion, pretty good might not be good
> enough.
> The pretty good town in our story was part of a pretty good state,
> Which had pretty good aspiration, and prayed for a pretty good fate.
> There was once a pretty good nation was pretty proud of the greatness
> it had,
> Which learned much too late
> If you want to be great
> Pretty good is, in fact, pretty bad.

(Charles S. Osgood, "The Osgood File," copyright 1986, CBS)

"Pretty good" is not good enough for great missionaries. Work together to raise your standards to a higher level.

Priorities

Your weekly letters and reports to the mission president are important and are much appreciated. One mission president said, "What a spirit they contain! Never have we felt the Spirit of the Lord so abundantly as when reading of the experiences you are having. Your weekly letters are very important to us. Keep them coming."

As your mission president reads your letters and visits personally with you and discusses your goals, one thought keeps coming to his mind: A missionary really isn't a missionary until he can teach the lessons. Without knowing what and how to teach, how can he be teacher?

Much is being done to find improved ways of utilizing the teaching abilities of the missionaries (and less of your time in the finding process), but all of these ideas hinge on your ability to teach the gospel as revealed by the leaders of the Church in *Preach My Gospel.*

Your first priority, then, is to become an excellent teacher of the gospel. To become a successful teacher, four steps will help if you will do them consistently:

1. *Study and restudy the five basic lessons in chapter 3 of* Preach My Gospel *until the concepts become firmly implanted in your mind.* Once this is done, teaching by the Spirit will come naturally to you. Be sure to memorize the scriptures accompanying the lessons. These lessons contain the essential doctrines, principles, and commandments of the restored gospel.
2. *Work with your companion.* Spend time each morning in individual preparation, and then spend time giving the concept out loud to your companion.
3. *Pray for help.* As a servant of the Lord, you are entitled to His help. But don't expect it until you're putting forth your best effort.
4. *Teach every chance you get.* Practice at district meetings, zone meetings, in the homes of members, at firesides, and wherever and whenever you can. If you are asked to speak in a sacrament meeting, a family home evening, fireside, or other meeting,

use the concepts of the lessons, and speak forcefully and confidently.

May the Lord bless you in your great work and in your sincere efforts to prepare yourself to meet the challenges of becoming a great teacher. As the Brethren have said: By knowing the basic concepts of the lessons in *Preach My Gospel*—and loving them and living them—you can then teach with confidence and conviction.

Repentance

A missionary once indicated that he and his fellow missionaries had been reflecting upon James 5:19–20 in their zone meeting: "Brethren, if any of you do err from the truth, and one convert him; let him know, that he which converteth the sinner from the error of his way shall save a soul from death, and shall hide a multitude of sins."

They had interpreted this scripture to mean that a person who converts and baptizes someone will be forgiven of his sins without going through the normal channels of repentance. This is not true. There is no way to circumvent the process of repentance.

Repentance includes (1) abandonment of the transgression, (2) confession to one in authority, and (3) restitution, where possible. Once these steps have been fulfilled, the transgressor must then go to his Heavenly Father in sincere prayer and ask for forgiveness. Forgiveness is a separate process requiring both repentance and living the commandments: "Nevertheless, he that repents and does the commandments of the Lord shall be forgiven" (D&C 1:32).

"How long must I wait to be forgiven?" is a question often asked. "How often and for how long a period must I ask my Heavenly Father to forgive me?" is another frequent question. The answer is that there is no set time. In some cases the warm, sweet spirit of forgiveness comes over a person after several days of daily prayer (following repentance), while in others it may be weeks or months or years.

The important thing to remember is that the transgressor must seek forgiveness—it does not come automatically simply because he has fulfilled the steps of repentance. Living the commandments is also required—and this is a lifelong process.

One of the commandments is to share the gospel with others; that is what James meant when he talked of hiding a multitude of sins when we convert a sinner. It is also what the Lord meant when he said, "For I will forgive you of your sins with this commandment—that you remain steadfast in your minds in solemnity and the spirit of prayer, in bearing testimony to all the world of those things which are communicated to you" (D&C 84:61).

Most people could use some of the promises in James 5:19–20. In *The Miracle of Forgiveness*, President Spencer W. Kimball said, "A sound way to neutralize the effects of sin in one's life is to bring the light of the gospel to others who do not now enjoy it" (204). He further said, in commenting about James 5:19–20, "We could expand it somewhat and remind the transgressor that every testimony he bears, every prayer he offers, every sermon he preaches, every scripture he reads, every help he gives to stimulate and raise others—all these strengthen him and raise him to higher levels" (205). These comments by President Kimball presume that you have already repented of your transgressions and are now seeking forgiveness, and that you are in the process of showing your Heavenly Father that you have earned forgiveness.

Resourcefulness

Many years ago, each mission president was given the opportunity to submit a confidential report about his missionaries. This is no longer done, but the questions were interesting.

The report asked questions about expenses, education, medical problems during the missionary's mission, knowledge of the gospel, conduct, trustworthiness, willingness to do missionary work, conformity to mission rules, and other questions.

One of the most interesting questions was the one about the missionary's resourcefulness. This is an important attribute for a missionary to possess, and it is something that can be acquired if you work hard enough at it.

What is resourcefulness? The dictionary defines it as "the ability to meet and handle situations." It is the ability to solve problems—working around, through, under, or over an obstacle.

It means never giving up until you find a way to solve the problem confronting you; it is perseverance—"if at first you don't succeed, try, try again"; it is being creative—trying solution after solution until you find one that works; it is common sense—using your brain instead of your brawn; it is faith—praying for guidance and then working until it comes true; it is obedience—being worthy to receive the inspiration necessary to get the job done.

Too many missionaries go through the motions of their missions without ever stepping back and taking a good, hard, long look at what they are doing. Resourcefulness is finding new and better ways to get the work done, to find new solutions to old problems, to find answers to new problems, to overcome, to invent, to create, to discover.

How do you become resourceful? How do you develop resourcefulness? The answer might be found in Alexander Hamilton, who said, "Men give me some credit for genius. All the genius I have lies in this: when I have a subject at hand, I study it profoundly. Day and night it is before me. I explore it in all its bearings. My mind becomes pervaded with it. Then the effort which I make, the people . . . call the fruit of genius. It is the fruit of labor and thought" (in Hugh B. Brown, *Contributing to the Quest* [Salt Lake City: Deseret Book, 1961], 529–30).

Herein lies the road to resourcefulness. It is the ability to concentrate on a given problem. You must be willing to put forth great mental effort to find the answer. You must think through the problem until you find a way to solve it. For example, what do you do if your ward mission leader will not hold a regular correlation meeting? What do you do when tracting day after day brings no results? How do you get referrals from members when they keep telling you they don't have any? How do you get a member to hold a group meeting? How do you get more teaching situations? How do you better control your thoughts? How do you improve companion relations? How do you get members to select a family to friendship? There are answers to all of these questions, but they vary from area to area. It is up to you and your companion to find the right answer for your area.

Resourcefulness will determine your success or failure in finding your answers. The secret is to (1) use good, common sense; (2) be persistent by never giving up until you find the solution to your problems; and (3) be faithful and prayerful and trust in the Lord.

Retakes

Most people have been involved in picture days in school, when a photographer comes to town and takes pictures of everyone for the yearbook or for class pictures. One of the standard rules is "no retakes." This means that the photographer will not be able to take your picture again if you do not like the way your picture turns out. It simply costs too much money to come back a second time.

One senior in high school recalls being caught in a "no retake" squeeze. When the pictures finally came back for his yearbook, he was severely disappointed in his photograph, which would be printed for all history to see. As editor of the yearbook and an amateur pilot, he foolishly decided to fly 150 miles away and get a new picture taken. The deadline for printing the yearbook was past, but his vain mind could see no alternative other than to hurry to the city and get back as soon as possible. Ignoring bad weather warnings, he went to the airport, arranged for an airplane, and took off into a strong headwind.

The trip nearly ended in disaster. Shortly after taking off, he was fighting a blinding dust storm with winds of fifty miles per hour. His little Porterfield airplane could only do sixty-five miles per hour, so he was actually making only fifteen miles per hour toward his destination. After battling for nearly two hours on a three-hour tank of gas, he was still within sight of where he had started! He finally landed back where he started from—poorer, frustrated, wiser. He decided that maybe some things in life were more important than a picture in a yearbook.

As he looked back on that experience, he was reminded that life is much like the "no retake" policy of those photography firms. For example, you will not be able to retake your mission; you will not be able to live it over again. Once completed, the day-to-day happenings of your mission are gone—recorded permanently as they happened, with no opportunity to do them over again.

Compare film in a camera with our life on earth. Film is made in semidarkness and stored in a dark container. It is wound into a camera in darkness. The camera lens is opened for a fraction of a second, allowing light to be focused on the film. An image is made on the film which becomes a permanent part of it. The film then continues in the dark, is removed from the camera without exposure to light, and then goes into a darkroom for developing and printing.

In the context of eternity, your short life here on earth can be likened to that film. Earth life is only 1/100th of a second in the timelessness of eternity, yet the image made on your soul in that brief exposure to mortality will be with you forever. What you do with your life—how you use the precious gift of mortality, no matter how brief it may be—determines whether you return to God's presence.

There are no retakes in life. You can live each day but once. You can fill your mission but once. Even though the great principle of repentance allows you to erase from your life the mistakes you have made, you will not be able to go back and replace the time lost. You could wish for nothing better than to look back on the picture of your mission and be happy with the image you see.

Sayings #1

Many people like to save little thoughts and sayings. Listed below is a random sample of some thoughts pertaining to missionary work that might be interesting to you:

1. Definition of a missionary: A missionary is like a duck—calm and unruffled on the outside, but paddling like crazy underneath.
2. Discouragement is like a baby. The more you nourish it, the bigger it gets.
3. Keep your face always toward the sunshine, and the shadows will fall behind you.
4. When success turns your head, you're facing trouble.
5. Life is a long lesson in humility. We need tough days to drive us to our knees.
6. Positive thinking is the only way to produce positive results.
7. The man who does his best today (on his mission) will be a hard man to beat tomorrow (after his mission).
8. The distance a missionary goes is not as important as the direction he is going.
9. The smallest good deed is better than the greatest intention.
10. Difficulties strengthen the soul as labor strengthens the body.
11. The nearer we come to God, the greater His light can shine upon us.
12. You cannot hope to enjoy a harvest without first laboring in the field.
13. A good leader is someone who can step on your toes without messing up your shine.
14. There are few, if any, jobs in which ability alone is sufficient. Also needed are loyalty, sincerity, enthusiasm, cooperation, and dedication.
15. The person who gets ahead is the one who does more than is necessary—and keeps on doing it.

16. Nothing is easier than murmuring; no talent, no self-denial, no intelligence, no character is required.
17. The goal of criticism is to leave the person with the feeling that he's been helped.
18. A person rarely succeeds at anything unless he enjoys doing it.
19. Those who lose their temper usually lose.

Sayings #2

1. There is nothing so fatal to character as half-finished tasks.
2. Make promises sparingly, and then keep them faithfully no matter what the cost.
3. Never let an opportunity pass to say a kind and encouraging thing to or about someone.
4. You have to stay awake to make your dreams come true.
5. He who postpones the hour of living right is like the person who waits for the river to run dry before he crosses.
6. A smile is the window of the soul indicating that the heart is at home.
7. Perhaps the best thing about the future is that it only comes one day at a time.
8. Think of your own faults when you are awake and of the faults of others when you are asleep.
9. What do we live for if it is not to make life less difficult for others?
10. You cannot do a kindness too soon because you never know how soon it will be too late.
11. Never does the human soul appear so strong as when it foregoes revenge and dares to forgive injury.
12. Every noble work is at first impossible.
13. Always remember that the soundest way to progress in any organization is to help the man ahead of you get promoted.
14. What I spent, I lost; what I possessed is left to others; what I gave away remains with me.
15. Character is much like window glass—when it is cracked it is cracked inside and out.
16. No one would have crossed the ocean if he could have gotten off the ship in a storm.
17. Before criticizing someone, ask yourself three questions: (1) Is it true? (2) Is it kind? (3) Is it necessary?
18. All I have seen teaches me to trust God for all I have not seen.

19. There are two weaknesses against which most of us must guard ourselves. The first is the habit of trying to reap before we have sown; the other is to create alibis for the mistakes we make.

20. Does the going seem a little easier lately? Better check. You just might be going downhill.

21. When you're through learning, you're through.

22. You never get a second chance to make a good first impression.

Sayings #3

1. Remember that in an argument the one who is doing most of the talking is usually the one who is wrong.
2. If you have a choice between making either yourself or your companion look good, choose your companion.
3. If you cannot give in during an argument, do it anyway as an exercise in self-discipline.
4. When the going gets tough, the tough get going.
5. When you get to the end of your rope, tie a knot and hang on.
6. Don't be content to be second-rate—aim high even if you miss.
7. Many people who think they have arrived are surprised to find that they have been traveling in reverse gear.
8. The surest way to knock the chip off a man's shoulder is to pat him on the back.
9. If you can't win, make the one in front of you break the record.
10. Most of us know how to say nothing; few of us know when.
11. If your troubles are deep-seated and of long standing, try kneeling.
12. Some minds are like concrete—all mixed up and permanently set.
13. One of the best ways to avoid trouble and ensure safety is to breathe through your nose. It keeps your mouth shut.
14. You can tell that some people aren't afraid of work by the way they fight it.
15. The man who looks down on his neighbors is always surprised that they don't look up at him.
16. The poorest of all men is not the one without a cent but the one without a dream.
17. The only exercise some people get is jumping to conclusions, running down people, sidestepping responsibility, and pushing their luck.
18. To do for the world more than the world does for you—that is success.

19. If you want to leave your footprints in the sands of time, wear your work shoes.
20. No matter how stony the path, some forge to the front; no matter how easy the going, some fall behind.

Famous Sayings

Several years ago, a well-known research firm in the United States—Daniel Starch Associates—conducted a survey to find out which statements, philosophies, spiritual thoughts, or quotations had meant the most to people. They researched thousands of famous sayings by philosophers, poets, statesmen, writers, and spiritual leaders; they read hundreds of books, including the Bible, the Koran, and many others.

Then they interviewed thousands of people in all walks of life—businessmen, dentists, housewives, oil drillers, steelmakers, carpenters, secretaries, morticians, ministers, lawyers, chemists, teachers, electricians, and many others—to see which of these famous statements had meant the most to them in their lives.

From all of these interviews, they selected the "Top Ten Sayings of All Time" and published them in a booklet called *Words to Live By*. Here they are:

1. Do unto others as you would that they should do unto you (a paraphrase taken from both Matthew 7:12 and 3 Nephi 14:12).
2. Know thyself (attributed originally to Socrates by Plato).
3. Anything that is worth doing at all is worth doing well (Earl of Chesterfield).
4. If at first you don't succeed, try, try again (William E. Hickson).
5. The three great essentials of happiness are (1) something to do, (2) someone to love, and (3) something to hope for (unknown).
6. The only way to have a friend is to be one (Ralph Waldo Emerson).
7. As a man thinketh in his heart, so is he (Proverbs 23:7).
8. Knowledge is power (Thomas Hobbes).
9. Actions speak louder than words (an ancient proverb).
10. An ounce of prevention is worth a pound of cure (an old English proverb).

As you look over these ten statements and consider their worth in the lives of missionaries, you can see that every one of them has a special meaning to you. These ten statements can have an impact as you work with members, labor with investigators, serve with your companion, correlate with leaders, set goals, hold your inventory sessions, pray, analyze strengths and weaknesses, lead others, and seek to become better missionaries.

You will have your own special sayings or favorite scriptures. Many people have written them down and carry them in their wallets or planners. You should find those special words that have great meaning in your life and memorize them or keep them readily available for constant review. Daniel Starch Associates did not have the Book of Mormon, the Doctrine and Covenants, or the Pearl of Great Price when they made up their list. Your list should include statements from these priceless scriptures, such as, "Therefore, O ye that embark in the service of God, see that ye serve him with all your heart, might, mind and strength, that ye may stand blameless before God at the last day" (D&C 4:2).

Self-Control

The question of self-control is a compelling question and includes:

- Control of thoughts
- Control of appetites
- Control of actions
- Control of attitudes
- Control of emotions
- Control of what we do with time
- Control of the direction in which we point our lives toward eternity

When God gave you moral agency, you were in a sense trusted to yourself, and you became accountable.

But whenever someone does something he shouldn't, he is inclined to justify himself, to seek to shift responsibility, to say that pressures or outside influences moved him to do what he did, and that he is not responsible for his actions.

Some become enslaved with compulsive habits or yield to appetites or to improper actions and plead that they are helpless before their habits—that they are compelled or persuaded that temptation was stronger than their will to resist.

But you can choose what you think by the sheer determination to do so. Blessedly, you can repent. You can turn from a wrong road. But you are responsible. You are accountable for your thoughts, words, and actions.

You must have the character and the conviction to keep self-control. Thomas Carlyle said, "Conviction is worthless unless it is converted into conduct."

"He that hath no rule over his own spirit is like a city that is broken down, and without walls" (Proverbs 25:28).

"He that is slow to anger is better than the mighty; and he that ruleth his spirit [is better] than he that taketh a city" (Proverbs 16:32).

Look about you. You will see bishops, stake presidents, General Authorities, and other leaders who have been entrusted with great responsibilities because they have proven themselves valiant. To be valiant requires an undeviating course toward eternal life. Always strive for greater self-mastery, self-control, and self-discipline.

Self-Control

"The difference between a successful missionary and an unsuccessful one is that the successful missionary is willing to do things that the unsuccessful missionary will not do."

Why do some missionaries pay the price for success while others do not? Why is it that some will humble themselves, submit to the rigors of missionary work, follow instructions to the letter, and thereby receive a manifestation of the Spirit—while others coast along in mediocrity?

The difference is self-control and self-discipline. Some have it; some do not. It is available to everyone. You become competent at the things you persist in doing. If you persist in acquiring good habits and good traits, self-control becomes an automatic result. To develop better self-control, you should do something every day that is difficult for you to do.

Brigham Young said a number of things about self-control. Among some of his statements are the following:

> No man can ever become a ruler in the Kingdom of God until he can perfectly rule himself. (In *Journal of Discourses,* 9:334)
>
> In this probation, we have evil to contend with, and we must overcome it in ourselves, or we shall never overcome it anywhere else. (In *Journal of Discourses,* 6:100)
>
> Let each person be determined, in the name of the Lord Jesus Christ, to overcome every besetment—to be master of himself, that the spirit which God has put in your tabernacles shall rule. (In *Journal of Discourses,* 8:140)
>
> When my feelings are aroused to anger by the ill-doings of others, I hold them as I would a wild horse, and I gain the victory. (In *Journal of Discourses,* 11:255–56)

President David O. McKay said, "What a man continually thinks about determines his actions in times of opportunity and stress. A man's reaction to his appetites and impulses when they are aroused gives the measure of that man's character. In these reactions are revealed the man's power to govern or his forced servility to yield" (David O. McKay, in

Conference Report, April 1961, 8).

President McKay also said that "spirituality is the consciousness of victory over one's self" (in Conference Report, April 1949, 17). Ralph Waldo Emerson said, "There is no defect except from within. There is really no insurmountable barrier save your own inherent weakness of purpose." Pythagoras said, "No man is free who cannot command himself" (in Sterling W. Sill, Conference Report, October 1963, 82). Seneca said, "Most powerful is he who has himself in his own power." Thomas Burton said, "Conquer thyself. Till thou hast done that, thou art a slave; for it is almost as well to be in subjection to another's appetite as thine own." Roswell Hitchcock said, "The secret of all success is to know how to deny yourself" (in Stephen R. Covey, *Spiritual Roots of Human Relations* [Salt Lake City: Deseret Book, 1970], 37). Elder Neal Maxwell said, "Sometimes the biting of one's tongue can be as important as the gift of tongues" (Neal A. Maxwell, "Put Off the Natural Man, and Come Off Conquerer," *Ensign*, November 1990, 14).

Each one of you must work to gain control of your physical bodies—to place your spiritual selves in control—until you can honestly say, "I am my own master." Then—and only then—can you sincerely and humbly say to the Lord, "I am thy servant."

Self-Evaluation

One of the great things about our weekly planning session is the part that calls for you to evaluate your past week's performance. In planning, one of the first steps is to review the past. When climbing a mountain, it is refreshing to stop and look back to see where you have been. In going through life, it is vital that you occasionally stop and evaluate where you have been and where you are heading. As missionaries, you should make it a practice to regularly check up on yourselves. Here are a number of questions you might ask yourselves as you evaluate your performance:

1. If you were choosing someone you had to trust, would you choose yourself?
2. If you needed someone to really confide in, would you be the one?
3. Would you like to be at your own mercy?
4. Would you compromise on a question of right and wrong?
5. If you found a lost article that no one else knew you had found, would you try to return it, or would you keep it for yourself?
6. Do you talk as well about your fellow missionaries (or members) when they aren't around as you do when they are?
7. Do you make an honest effort to improve your performance?
8. Do you get the job done, or do you loaf along for fear you might do too much?
9. If you were the mission president, would you like to have you for a missionary?
10. Would you honor an unwritten agreement as honestly as if it were written?
11. If you were the bishop of a ward, would you want a missionary like you to be assigned to your ward?
12. If you owned an automobile, would you want it treated the way you treat mission vehicles?
13. If you made a mistake, would you admit it or would you pretend to be right even when you knew you were wrong?

14. Have you left every area of your mission in better condition than when you found it? And your companions?
15. Are you as close to the Lord as you were three months ago? If not, who do you think moved?
16. Do you really follow the programs of the mission, or do you do it the way *you* think it should be done?
17. If you were asked to pick the ten top missionaries in the mission, would you put your name on the list?
18. As you look back over your mission, where would you change things? What are you doing to change them?
19. If you were giving yourself some sound advice, what would it be? If you went to the Lord for advice, what do you think He would tell you?

Look at yourself again, inside and out. Would you want a missionary like you to teach your trusted friends? Are you the kind of person that people like to be around? Would you want to be around you if you had a choice? What are you doing to make yourself a better missionary?

Spirituality

Spirituality is the basis for all missionary success because conversion comes only through the power of the Holy Ghost. Church leaders have given us four musts that each missionary should strive for:

1. He must be worthy to represent the Savior.
2. He must be converted to the gospel and have a knowledge that it is the greatest thing in all the world. He should have a willingness to serve others, to share the gospel, and to go out of his way to help others.
3. He must have inspiration. He must seek divine guidance through prayer. All difficulties are overcome once the missionary senses that he can receive such guidance.
4. He must be humble and repentant.

How does one achieve spirituality? Here are eight things you should do:

1. Memorize and abide by section four in the Doctrine and Covenants.
2. Love your companion and make him a part of all you do. Be with your companion at all times.
3. Pray individually and with your companion.
4. Put out of your thoughts and discussions all references to home, school, girlfriends, worldly things, and premissionary activities.
5. Live all the mission rules and Church standards.
6. Bear testimony frequently.
7. Become acquainted with the Savior through the scriptures.
8. Be happy.

Spirituality can only be achieved through obedience, and as you strive to obtain it, your ability to do right is increased. Only then will you feel what President David O. McKay called spirituality: "The consciousness of victory over self and of communion with the Infinite" (David O. McKay, in Conference Report, April 1949, 17).

Take your callings seriously. Remember that obedience is protection against the adversary and brings strength from the Lord. You don't have to do it—you get to do it. Be the missionary your mother knows you can be. You grow when you do those things you don't want to do. Do everything possible to strengthen your testimony. Above all else, follow the prophet. Do these things, and spirituality will come.

Spirituality

President Harold B. Lee once told new mission presidents, "If a sincere person, being taught by spiritual, enthusiastic elders, is seeking the truth, he will have a witness that it is true."

What is a spiritual missionary? How can you know if you have the Spirit? How can you get the Spirit in your teaching? Here are twenty characteristics of a spiritual missionary:

1. He is eagerly and vigorously involved in the work. He works hard and smart. He is willing to go the extra mile.
2. He has a special spiritual glow and bearing.
3. He has "MMI"—Mormon Missionary Image. He is dignified, conservative, and clean in dress, appearance, and behavior.
4. He is predominantly happy and at peace with himself.
5. He keeps all mission rules—and then some. (Give until it hurts, and then give some more until it feels good.)
6. He has achieved companion harmony.
7. He maintains an optimistic and positive outlook.
8. He meets disappointments and crises with renewed vigor. When the going gets tough, he gets going.
9. When there are infractions and offenses, he does not rationalize but repents.
10. He is obedient, and he happily and willingly follows counsel. The single most important characteristic for a missionary is obedience, according to our leaders.
11. He has a sincere testimony, which he bears often.
12. He prays unceasingly. In addition to private and companion prayer, he keeps a prayer in his heart at all times.
13. He is creative and innovative, and he tries to find better ways to do the work.
14. He is occasionally disappointed but never discouraged.
15. He has a consistent pattern of scripture reading and studying.
16. He supports and sustains the leaders of the Church.

17. He is deeply grateful for the blessings of the Lord and humbly acknowledges that his success comes from the Lord.
18. He meets each day with faith and renewed determination.
19. He knows the discussions so he can teach with confidence and conviction.
20. He shows his love and respect for his parents, relatives, and friends.

Ponder these marks of spirituality, and then honestly and prayerfully compare them with your own performance. Or ask your companion to compare your performance against these twenty characteristics.

Spirituality

President Ezra Taft Benson, in speaking at a special seminar for new mission presidents several years ago, discussed ways in which missionaries could fill successful missions. "The Spirit," he said, "is the most important matter in this glorious work" *(Teachings of Ezra Taft Benson,* 198). The thoughts below are from his talk.

"And the Spirit shall be given you by the prayer of faith; and if ye receive not the Spirit, ye shall not teach" (D&C 42:14).

To be a successful missionary, you must have the Spirit of the Lord. There are three necessary elements to gaining and keeping the Spirit:

1. *The Spirit will not dwell in unclean tabernacles.* Therefore, one of the first things a missionary must do to gain spirituality is to make sure his personal life is in order. The Lord said, "Be ye clean that bear the vessels of the Lord" (D&C 38:42).

2. *Pray sincerely, with real intent, and ask for forgiveness.* The missionary must also pray in faith for the Spirit to bless him and to be with him. The missionary's prayer must be offered with the same desire as the one offered by Enos in the Book of Mormon. Enos 1:4 says, "And my soul hungered; and I kneeled down before my Maker, and I cried unto him in mighty prayer and supplication for mine own soul; and all the day long did I cry unto him; yea, and when the night came I did still raise my voice high that it reached the heavens."

3. *Search the scriptures daily.* The Book of Mormon tells about some of the most successful missionaries who have ever gone forth to preach the gospel. Two of these were Ammon and Aaron, the sons of Mosiah. They were men of God and had spiritually prepared themselves to do the work. From them you have a great example to follow. The prophet Alma described them and their success in the following words from Alma 17:2: "They had waxed strong in the knowledge of the truth; for they

were men of a sound understanding and they had searched the scriptures diligently, that they might know the word of God. But this is not all; they had given themselves to much prayer, and fasting."

Alma also listed the results of their preparedness: "Therefore they had the spirit of prophecy, and the spirit of revelation, and when they taught, they taught with power and authority of God" (Alma 17:3).

Each of you should make President Benson's words a part of you, not only while you are missionaries but also throughout your lives. Spirituality and testimony are inseparably intertwined. One comes from the other, and each one enlarges and strengthens the other. Each one comes from study, prayer, and obedience.

Spirituality

How do you know when you have the Spirit of the Lord with you? Try these comparisons:

When you have the Spirit or when you are being prompted by the Lord:

> You feel calm and happy.
> You feel full of light.
> Your bosom burns within you.
> Nobody could offend you.
> You feel outgoing, eager to be with other people.
> You are glad when others succeed
> You want to make others happy.
> You bring out the best in others.
> You gladly and willingly perform Church duties and ordinances.
> You feel confident in what you do.
> You feel you have control over your appetites.
> You are able to eat and sleep in moderation.
> You feel calm and controlled in your speech.
> You wish you could keep all the Lord's commandments and obey all rules.
> You control thoughts.
> You're glad to be alive!

When you do not have the Spirit or when you are being prompted by Satan:

> You feel unhappy, depressed, confused, and frustrated.
> You feel heavy, full of darkness.
> Your mind is muddled.
> Everything and everyone bothers you.
> You are always defensive.
> You become secretive, sneaky, and evasive.

You want to be alone.

You avoid other people, especially those close to you.

You are envious of what others do and have.

You are critical of others, especially your family and those in authority.

You easily become discouraged.

You don't want to pray.

You find commandments bothersome and restrictive and many rules senseless.

You become a slave to your appetites and emotions.

You feel hesitant, unworthy to perform Church duties and functions.

Your emotions become passionate.

You become overindulgent in eating, sleeping, and thinking improper thoughts.

You tell people off and use strong language.

You wonder if life is really worth it.

Splitting Off

The Church calls it "exchanges." Some missionaries call it "going on splits" or "splitting off." Some call it "joint effort." Whatever it is called, it is the process by which two full-time missionaries divide up and go out in the evenings with Church members, including home teachers, ward missionaries, priesthood quorum leaders, and other members of the Melchizedek Priesthood.

Missionary work is moving ahead in those areas where exchanges occur; it is lagging behind where they are not occurring. One ward missionary, who is going out two nights a week with the elders in his ward, wrote that he had discovered the following benefits from splitting off:

1. "With a ward missionary and a full-time missionary working together, we seem to develop a good contact with the members. The missionaries have the spiritual guidance, while the experience and different background of the ward missionary develops a force that can convince them to do the work."

2. "Even though cars are not necessary or desirable for tracting, we have found that with our cars we can visit those members or referrals that are spread all over our area."

3. "As ward missionaries who work with the full-time missionaries, we are an example to the members that they can do missionary work."

4. "This personal contact with the full-time missionaries helps us as ward missionaries to become committed to our calling."

This ward missionary went on to say, "I have a strong testimony of the value of a team of full-time missionaries and ward missionaries. I can see great benefits already. Make use of it wherever you can. Encourage the ward missionaries to work with you. This is a missionary tool given to us by our prophet, and we cannot and should not treat it lightly."

A missionary wrote to his mission president: "We split off three times this week and took members with us tracting. They were so scared they were hiding behind me. Afterward, one of them said, 'Wow, you ought to take all the members out tracting—that would convert anyone to friend-shipping.'"

Another missionary wrote that going out with his ward mission leader to check referrals was the best missionary experience he had had on his mission. Others have said that the best way to enthuse the members is to take them out with you. Many Church members have written to tell how much they enjoyed exchanges.

In some missions, many missionaries are splitting off four or five nights each week; others are not doing it at all. In view of the emphasis placed on it by the Church and the success of those who are doing it, it probably should be done regularly. Work with your ward mission leader to arrange such exchanges. This is one of the most effective ways to involve members in the missionary effort.

Steps to Use in
Working with Members

The following steps might be used in beginning the work with members. This discussion will be in terms of wards and stakes; if you are working in districts and branches, please substitute the right offices.

1. Work within the framework of priesthood correlation. In other words, work closely with your ward mission leader. Remember that a fundamental principle of missionary work is that the stake president is responsible for all missionary activities within the boundaries of his stake. In turn, he assigns the responsibility to the ward mission leaders (and bishops). Your role as full-time missionaries is to help them get the work done.

2. Meet regularly each week with your ward mission leader. This is vital. You must know at all times what is going on in your ward. He attends the ward priesthood executive committee meeting each week and reports on missionary work in the ward.

3. Either with the ward mission leader or with his permission or introduction, visit each quorum leader in the ward—the elders quorum president and the high priests group leader.

4. With help from the quorum leaders, select several families (from four to eight) in their quorums who might be good in friendshipping nonmembers.

5. After gathering names from the quorum leaders, take the list to the ward mission leader for his approval. The two of you should be prayerful in your consideration of the final list.

6. The ward mission leader should then obtain the bishop's approval of the selected families. (Steps 3, 4, 5, and 6 can all be done together in a single meeting if the bishop and ward mission leader so desire. But don't push this; be willing to do the legwork if needed.

7. Once the families have been prayerfully selected, they must be contacted to enlist their support in the friendshipping program. This first contact will differ from area to area. Some wards will

have the bishop issue a call to the families. Some will have you visit the family the first time with the home teachers. Others will have the quorum leader contact the family. Other wards may want you to make the initial contact and to work with the families. It is usually best to have someone in the ward introduce you to the family.

You should concentrate your friendshipping efforts on those families that are the most promising ones to help in missionary work. All member families are important, but you should be teaching and working with the most promising ones first.

Once the families have been selected and visited, you must begin carefully teaching them how to do friendshipping work and building up their confidence in themselves and you.

Studying

One of your most important decisions is to expand your knowledge of the gospel. With this knowledge will come increased testimony, greater spirituality, more confidence, and expanded self-mastery.

Learn the Ten Commandments for Study. They will help you on your mission and through life—especially at college and in other learning experiences. Here they are:

1. Get the right attitude. This is the first commandment. Develop a taste for reading, learning, the subject you are studying, and the scriptures. Hunger and thirst after the doctrines of the Church. Study because you want to study—not just because your leaders tell you to do it. Pray about it.

2. Think and plan. Get a bird's-eye view of each subject as a whole—an overall view before you get into the details. Whether it is reading the Book of Mormon, learning about the Godhead, or researching the first principles of the gospel, you need to apprehend the general plan before you get into the nitty-gritty.

3. Never waste time. Dawdling is the relentless foe of endeavor. Work intently. Use every free moment for study. Overcome your natural desire for taking a breather.

4. See that conditions are right for study in your apartment. Work out with your companion a cooperative program of mutual help and support. Severely restrict your time for small talk and other distractions. Cut down your telephone time. Try to study in the same place each day, and be sure to have proper lighting and fresh air.

5. Read fast. It is strange but true that the fast reader both understands better and remembers longer than the slowpoke. The reason is that he concentrates.

6. Read ahead. Fulfill your goal for the day, and then do a little more. This is a difficult task for most young people, but few investments pay better dividends.

7. Remember what you learn. The greatest secret to learning is remembering. When you read, make up your mind at once to remember what you are reading. Reading without remembering is useless. Try this: read a page or paragraph, and then see how much you can remember. Psychologists tell us that the average person will forget more than 50 percent of his reading within a half hour.

8. Stick to it. Changing from one thing to another often wastes time. When you sit down to study something, don't let other things interfere. Stay on the subject. Don't let your mind wander.

9. Don't fool yourself. Many missionaries tell me they study a full two hours every day, but their gospel knowledge doesn't show it. They forget the time spent talking to a companion, time on the telephone, daydreaming of home, a minute here and there doing something else. When you study, study. Discipline yourself.

10. Review frequently. Close your book from time to time and ask yourself what you have learned. Ask yourself searching questions. If you cannot recall the answers, read the section again but with greater concentration.

The brain is a giant muscle; the more you exercise it, the more it will develop the strength to better serve you.

S-T-A-R-T

An old Chinese proverb says that "he who takes the first step has covered half the distance." Another one says, "The longest journey begins with the first step." A business survey showed that the two primary reasons for employee failure were (1) lack of ability to get things started, and (2) failure to get things done (persistence).

If you want success, you need to concentrate on getting started. One of the best methods for getting started is called the S-T-A-R-T method:

S—Study the situation
T—Tabulate the possibilities for action.
A—Arrange your plan of action.
R—Recheck the pros and cons.
T—Take the first step.

1. *Study the situation.* This is sometimes called research. Look everything over carefully. Study the background. Talk to people—your priesthood leaders, your missionary leaders, members. Ask questions. In marketing, we call this "the hat trick." When you want to know something, put on your hat and go out and start asking questions. Sometimes the best kind of "hat trick" is to sit down and ask yourself a lot of questions.

2. *Tabulate the possibilities for action.* Once you have done your research and thought of the problems and possible solutions, write down all the possible alternatives. This gives you a chance to see them clearly and firmly.

3. *Arrange your plan of action.* After you have gathered all the facts and written down a list of alternative actions, simplify. Throw out the unimportant ideas and the bad ones. After you have done this, you should narrow your remaining list down to one idea or approach that you think is best. This is the one to concentrate on.

4. *Recheck the pros and cons.* At this point, the temptation is

to start out immediately. But take the time to recheck your thinking. Try it on for size. Talk it out with your companion or with others. Pray about it. This avoids making false starts. When you feel it's right . . .

5. *Take the first step.* Success or failure depends on making this move. After going through the first four steps, this one should be the easiest. Move ahead with confidence. Be a self-starter. And once you start, be persistent!

Success

Discouragement and depression are not reserved just for a few of God's children. At times everyone is discouraged for one reason or another.

What is the best solution for discouragement? That's an easy question to answer: The best antidote for discouragement for a missionary is success.

What is success? Here are some things you might consider:

Success is doing the things you know you should; success is not doing the things you know you shouldn't.

Success is not limited to any one area of your work. It encompasses everything you do: missionary work, your companionship, relationships with parents, relationships with the mission home, relationships with God, relationships with Church members, relationships with your district and zone leaders.

Success is not confined to any one part of your personality but is related to the development of all the parts: body, mind, heart, and spirit. It is making the most of your total self.

Success is focusing the full power of all you are on what you have a burning desire to achieve.

Success is 99 percent mental attitude. It calls for love, joy, optimism, serenity, poise, faith, courage, cheerfulness, imagination, initiative, tolerance, honesty, humility, patience, and enthusiasm.

Success is discovering your best talents, skills, and abilities and applying them where they will make the most effective contribution to your fellow men.

Success is not arriving at the summit of a mountain as a final destination. It is a continuing upward spiral of progress. It is perpetual growth.

Success is having the courage to meet failure without being defeated. It is refusing to let present loss interfere with your long-range goal.

Success is accepting the challenge of the difficult.

The apostle Paul told the Philippians how to achieve success: "This one thing I do, forgetting those things which are behind, and reaching forth unto those things which are before, I press toward the mark" (Philippians 3:13–14).

In the inspiring words of Phillips Brooks, "Do not pray for tasks equal to your powers; pray for powers equal to your tasks. Then the doing of your work shall be no miracle, but *you* shall be the miracle" (*The Best of Words to Live By*, ed. William Nochols [New York: This Week Magazine, 1967], 63).

The Book of Mormon

"I told the brethren that the Book of Mormon was the most correct of any book on earth, and the keystone of our religion, and a man would get nearer to God by abiding by its precepts, than by any other book" (*History of the Church,* 4:461).

This statement by the Prophet Joseph Smith means that the message of the restoration is dependent upon the Book of Mormon. It must be that way. We must stand or fall upon the authenticity of the Book of Mormon.

But what is the Book of Mormon? Many people feel that it replaces the Bible. Others claim that it deifies Joseph Smith. Some profess that it opposes Christianity.

None of these is true. Actually, the Book of Mormon supports and complements the Bible in every way and is an additional witness of Jesus Christ and His divine Sonship. No people on earth have a greater love and understanding of the Bible and the divinity of Jesus Christ than do members of the Church.

Briefly, here is what the Book of Mormon is:

1. The Book of Mormon is an account of three small colonies that left the Near East in Asia and came separately to the Western Hemisphere. The Book of Mormon is silent on whatever else may have transpired in the Americas anciently.

2. The Book of Mormon is a religious record of these three peoples. This religious account is a picture set in an historical frame, but the major interest of the writers is religion, not history.

3. The Book of Mormon is an abridged record. The book of Ether, for example, covers several thousand years of history, yet the story is told in thirty-two pages. Mormon condensed a millennium of Nephite and Lamanite life into less than five hundred pages. Hence, the Book of Mormon is a brief, abridged, religious record of three peoples—the Jaredites, the

269

Lehi colony, and the Mulekites—who came to the Western Hemisphere before the Christian era.

Here is what the Book of Mormon is not:

1. The Book of Mormon is not a history of all pre-Columbian people in America. This book makes no such claim for itself.
2. The Book of Mormon is not a history in the contemporary usage of the term. It is in no sense comparable to a college text in history. A historical work attempts to describe in systematic and comprehensive form all aspects of culture. The Book of Mormon writers give no such balanced account of their people. While there is considerable history in the book, history was not the conscious, primary purpose of its authors.

The Cause

Your mission president has great love and respect for each one his missionaries. He and his companion are grateful for the joy they feel in being able to share this important time of your lives.

This work is the most sacred cause the world has ever known. A cause—any cause—may be important to you, but your role in the cause of the gospel of Jesus Christ is more important than anything you will ever do in mortality.

Someone once said that the most pitiful thing in the world is a person without a cause. Like the man without a country, such a person wanders aimlessly from port to port, knowing no destination, having no goal. Nehru said: "The most important period in my life was the time I was engaged in the struggle. Ultimately, the only true joy for a person is to engage himself in some great cause, in some elementary work, and to give all of his strength and energy to it."

Today, people seem to have difficulty in finding any cause, let alone a great one. It is said that all frontiers are tame, and the seas are all chartered. But despite the permeating complacency of our era, there remain unconquered peaks, new vistas, virgin forests, incomprehensible space. No generation, no society, is without its worthwhile causes. Carrying forth the missionary effort, taking a stand against bigotry or prejudice, and rendering assistance to the less fortunate are all but small examples of the modern-day causes that beckon for your help.

George Bernard Shaw once said that "this is the true joy in life, being used for a purpose recognized by yourself as a mighty one" (in Obert C. Tanner, *Christ's Ideals for Living* [Salt Lake City: Deseret Sunday School Union, 1955], 277). You should heed Shaw's words and commit yourself to the greatest cause the world has ever known—and then throw yourself full force into the thick of the struggle.

Now is the time and here is the place that God wants you to serve. It is your stewardship, and you alone must assume the weight of that responsibility. Your mission president is here to help you in that service and responsibility. You have his faith, his confidence, and his love as you serve him. Do not do anything to disappoint him.

The Meanest Mother

This interesting letter was featured in a national magazine:

I had the meanest mother in the whole world. While other kids ate candy for breakfast, I had to have cereal, eggs, toast. When others had Coke and candy for lunch, I had to eat a sandwich. As you can guess, my supper was different than other kids' also. But at least I wasn't alone in my sufferings. My sister and two brothers that had the same mean mother I did.

My mother insisted upon knowing where we were at all times. You'd think we were on a chain gang. She had to know who our friends were and what we were doing. She insisted [that] if we said we'd be gone an hour—that we could be gone one hour or less—not one hour and one minute. I am nearly ashamed to admit it, but she actually struck us. Not once, but each time we had a mind of our own and did as we pleased. . . . Can you imagine someone actually hitting a child just because he disobeyed? Now you can [begin] to see how mean she really was.

The worst is yet to come. We had to be in bed by 9:00 each night and up early the next morning. We couldn't sleep till noon like our friends. So while they slept—Mother actually had the nerve to break the child-labor law. She made us work. We had to wash dishes, make beds, learn to cook, and all sorts of cruel things. I believe she lay awake at night thinking up mean things to do to us. She always insisted upon our telling the truth and nothing but the truth, even if it killed us—and [sometimes] it nearly did.

By the time we were teenagers, she was much wiser, and our life became even more unbearable. None of this tooting the horn of a car for us to come running. She embarrassed us to no end by making our dates and friends come to the [front] door for us. . . . I forgot to mention [that] while my friends were dating at the mature age of twelve and thirteen, my old-fashioned mother refused to let me date until the age of fifteen or sixteen.

Mother was a complete failure as a mother. . . . None of us has ever been arrested, divorced, or beaten [up] his mate. Each of my brothers served in his time the service of this country. And whom do we blame for the terrible way we turned out? You're right, our mean mother. Look at the things we missed. We never got to march in a protest parade, nor to take part in a riot, burn draft cards, and a million and one other things that our friends did. She forced us to grow up into God-fearing, educated, honest adults.

Using this as a background, I am trying to raise my three children. I stand a little taller and I am filled with pride when my children call me mean. Because, you see, I thank God. He gave me the meanest mother in the whole world. (Bobbie Pingaro, "The Meanest Mother," *Guideposts*)

You may think that sometimes you have the meanest mission president in the whole world as you contemplate the missionary rules from the Brethren and from the mission. But if you will be obedient to your commitments, the people of your area will be blessed. And as your mission president gently but firmly stresses obedience to Church standards and mission rules, remember that he does so in an atmosphere of love and respect for each individual missionary.

The Six B's

In contemplating the work of the ministry in which we are engaged, you should all be living the Six B's of missionary work. Consider carefully their virtues:

1. *Be informed.* All of you have heard about missionaries who stumbled through questions or who were embarrassed because of lack of simple knowledge. Study the scriptures and the standard works. Know the concepts in *Preach My Gospel.* Be informed about the missionary program, the member-involvement program, the area in which you labor, and the leaders of the ward or branch. Keep in perfect correlation with your ward mission leader. Learn to teach by the Spirit, and know and live the mission guidelines and procedures.

2. *Be organized.* Careful planning of your day's activities will save time and mileage. You are given time each night to plan the next day. You are given time each week for your weekly planning session. You are asked to commit yourselves to the goals for the week. You have a planning guide to help you schedule your time, set goals, and record all activities. All of these are provided to help you plan. Plan your work, and work your plan. If you fail to plan, plan to fail.

3. *Be friendly.* This implies genuine concern for those with whom you work—members, investigators, leaders, companions, other missionaries, and contacts. Happiness and joy should radiate from your countenance as you work with people in and out of the Church. Those who see you should feel of your spirit and gladness for the work. This is important. Smile. Be warm.

4. *Be enthusiastic.* Emerson said that "nothing great was ever achieved without enthusiasm" (in *Favorite Quotations from the Collection of Thomas S. Monson*, 162). This work is the greatest force the world has ever known. You should reflect your belief in the work through enthusiastic and diligent devotion.

275

Discouragement is one of Satan's greatest tools, and enthusiasm is one of your greatest weapons against it. Think positively. Act positively. Be enthusiastic.

5. *Be humble.* A humble missionary loses himself in the service of the Lord. He is teachable. He works with an eye single to the glory of God and allows himself to be guided by the Spirit because he lives the commandments to the fullest. "Be thou humble; and the Lord thy God shall lead thee by the hand, and give thee answer to thy prayers" (D&C 112:10). A humble missionary is blessed with the Spirit.

6. *Be prayerful.* Few have recognized the great value and power of sincere prayer. The success of the entire mission depends upon the missionaries establishing communication with our Father in Heaven. Brigham Young said that prayer keeps a man from sin, and sin keeps a man from prayer. The most important time to pray is when we don't feel like it. Pray for guidance. Give thanks for blessings. Love the Lord, and let Him know it.

The Spirit

One mission president said that the question most often asked in his confidential interview with missionaries is, "Why don't I have the Spirit more abundantly?"

After visiting with all of his missionaries concerning their own spirituality (or lack of it), and after reading their reports, this mission president recommended three major ways to gain the Spirit:

1. *Avoid contention.* Joseph Smith said, "Go in all meekness, in sobriety, and preach Jesus Christ and Him crucified; do not contend with others on account of their faith or systems of religion, but pursue a steady course" (*History of the Church,* 2:431–32). Do not contend with members, nonmembers, friends, companions, or other missionaries. Contention of any kind—about doctrines, behavior, government, or ideas—leads to emotions that are contrary to Christ. Contention causes the Spirit to withdraw. President Gordon B. Hinckley has said that we have something extra to offer people of other faiths.

2. *Avoid light-mindedness.* Joseph Smith said, "How vain and trifling have been our spirits, our conferences, our councils, our meetings, our private as well as public conversations—too low, too mean, too vulgar, too condescending for the dignified characters of the called and chosen of God, according to the purposes of His will, from before the foundation of the world" (History of the Church, 3:295–96).

Think back on your own actions during your ministry—your actions with members, your conversations with other missionaries, your talks with companions, your visits in homes. Are you still telling stories that you should have left at home? Are you calling other missionaries at odd hours and disturbing their peace with little acts of nonsense? These actions and others like them are too low, too mean, too vulgar, too condescending for the dignified characters of the called and chosen of God.

3. *Avoid vain aspirations.*

> President [Joseph] Smith arose . . . and [gave] instruc-
> tions respecting the different offices. . . . He spoke of the
> disposition of many men to consider the lower offices in the
> Church dishonorable and to look with jealous eyes upon
> the standing of others who are called to preside over them;
> that it was the folly and nonsense of the human heart for a
> person to be aspiring to other stations than those to which
> they are appointed of God for them to occupy; that it was
> better for individuals to magnify their respective calling, and
> wait patiently till God shall say to them, "Come up higher."
> (*Teachings of the Prophet Joseph Smith*, 223)

The highest calling of a missionary is to be a proselyting elder or
sister. Some elders are called as leaders, but their primary function is still
proselyting. Too many missionaries are striving for worldly recognition.
As Christ said in His Sermon on the Mount, "Do not sound a trumpet
before thee, as the hypocrites do . . . that they may have glory of men.
Verily I say unto you, They have their reward" (Matthew 6:2). Work for
the pure glory of Christ. Do not seek position for position's sake—seek
always to do your best and to magnify your calling that you might be
worthy of leadership if it comes.

To what degree do you have the spirit of contention? Light-
mindedness? Vain aspirations? Are you willing to pay the price and therefore be worthy of the Spirit?

The Three D's

Many years ago there was a musical trio called The Three D's. They made it big in recording and personal appearances. The name of their group was taken from their first names—Dick, Duane, and Dennis. But this message is not about those three D's.

The three D's of this message has to do with the names of three of the most important characteristics a missionary can have: Devotion, Dependability, and Discipline. I hope each one of you will consider carefully the implications of each one of these characteristics in your own life.

DEVOTION

The first great commandment is to "love the Lord thy God with all thy heart, and with all thy soul, and with all thy mind, and with all thy strength: . . . and the second is . . . thou shalt love thy neighbor as thyself" (Mark 12:30–31). Love of God and love of fellow men are basic to your work as missionaries. You should also love life, your country of service, and your work. Devotion and love are at the very center of your lives as you serve others. You must work in harmony with your companions and show love to others in order to teach with the pure spirit of Christ. Only through love can you touch the hearts of your contacts. You must have patience, charity, tolerance, and understanding if you are to truly love others.

DEPENDABILITY

One of the things that you learn about great characters in the standard works is that God has always relied upon those who are dependable. Dependability is not something you put on and off as the occasion arises but something that is an integral part of you. The best example of dependability is God himself. His laws are resolute. He honors his covenants: "I, the Lord, am bound when ye do what I say; but when ye do not what I say, ye have no promise" (D&C 82:10). Be dependable. Do what you say you will do. Keep your word. You cannot be honest with God and dishonest with your fellow men.

DISCIPLINE

The great quest in life is the quest for self-mastery and self-discipline. This includes the ability to so organize yourself that you can follow a planned course of action even though your emotions tell you to do something else. Standing firm in your decisions in the face of temptation gives you greater strength in future decisions. Be master of your own soul and steer your course straight and true rather than be like the rudderless ship that goes where the prevailing winds direct.

Devotion, dependability, and discipline—three great words to live by. They will bring you the promise of untold happiness and success in your labors—and throughout your life—if you will live by them.

The Weather

One mission president recalled a time many years ago when his family was gathered together for prayer. It was a cold, blustery day, and the snow was piling up in large drifts. He was concerned about the children's safety as they went to and from school, and this concern was evident to those in the family as he led them in prayer. As they concluded the prayer and as the children began getting coats and rubber boots on, one of the sons said, "Dad, never judge the day by its weather."

Most missionaries make this mistake—judging the day by its weather, judging a country by its weather, planning their day around the weather, adjusting their missions around the weather, or talking about the weather when they should be talking about the gospel.

The weather is a problem in every mission in the world. Whether missionaries are called to labor in Great Britain, Peru, Mexico, Georgia, Japan, Germany, Finland, Utah, California, the Philippines, New Zealand, or Alaska—all have their own individual problems in coping with changing weather conditions. Some missions have heat, mosquitoes, bugs, snakes, humidity, and other appendages of warmer climates; others have permafrost, the midnight sun, sunless winter days, freezing temperatures, and the discomforts of colder climates.

But life goes on. Millions of people live in climates that are extremely hot or extremely cold. Russia has seven cities within the Arctic Circle with one million or more people living in each one—and carrying on normal lives. Some missionaries never see snow on their missions; others see few days without it.

Do not let the weather dictate your lives. Why fight it? You cannot change the weather, but you can change your attitude toward it. Fighting the weather is much like Don Quixote fighting windmills.

A weather vane changes and shifts with the weather, pointing in one direction with the wind and then changing as the wind shifts. A compass, however, stays true and unchanging in all kinds of weather—no matter what direction the winds shift. You must train yourselves to be more like a compass and less like a weather vane. You must set a course of action and stay with it, no matter how the weather shifts around you.

God asks no man whether he will accept life. That is not the choice. You *must* accept it. The only choice is how. "While the earth remaineth, seedtime and harvest, and cold and heat, and summer and winter, and day and night shall not cease" (Genesis 8:22). Elder Richard L. Evans used to say, "This is life—and it is passing. What are we waiting for?" (Richard L. Evans, "The Spoken Word from Temple Square," *Improvement Era* 50, no. 1 [January 1947]).

The point is that you cannot change the weather. For better or for worse, it should not govern your lives. You should govern your lives. If cold weather or hot weather requires more sacrifice, more dedication, more resoluteness—then you should give it willingly and freely—knowing that the gospel of Jesus Christ must be taken to everyone in every kind of weather.

The Yoke

There are times in every missionary's life when he becomes discouraged with something about the work. There are few missionaries who have not despaired at times because of adversity.

Sometimes it is because an investigator stumbles and falls while trying to overcome a habit; sometimes a Church member will cancel an appointment or turn away from friendshipping work; at times there will be problems at home that seem almost too much to bear; at other times there will be differences of personality between you and your companion; at times you will feel that you are the only one in your area who is really interested in missionary work; at times it will be physical limitations that keep you from the work; and at times the mockery and skepticism of others will make you wonder about the futility of it all. Nearly everyone has had the feeling.

Missionary work is not easy work. "Satan will take every opportunity to discourage a missionary," said President Gordon B. Hinckley in an address to mission presidents. "When these moments come, the yoke they are called to bear may seem heavy and unbearable."

The Lord has given you a key by which you can overcome such problems: "Come unto me, all ye that labour and are heavy laden, and I will give you rest. Take my yoke upon you, and learn of me; for I am meek . . . for my yoke is easy, and my burden is light" (Matthew 11:28–30).

The purpose of a yoke in ancient times was to get oxen pulling evenly together in a united effort. Remember that the Savior has a load to pull— a cause that must move forward. He has asked you to become yoked with Him to move His gospel forward unto all those who will accept His word.

"My yoke is easy, and my burden is light," He said. "Take my yoke upon you." Your work will be light, easy to bear, no matter how difficult it becomes, if your burden is the work of the Savior. Think not of yourself or of the burden; think only of your love for Him and your gratitude for His sacrifice.

Nothing great was ever achieved without effort. The Prophet Joseph Smith struggled with the powers of darkness before his visit from Heavenly Father and Jesus Christ. His entire life was one struggle after another. All of the prophets since that time have had heavy burdens, each one different from the previous one. The history of the Church, both in the decades following the Savior's death and in latter-day persecutions, has been one of sacrifice, sorrow, and burdens.

The Saints have always carried such burdens because they knew they were sharing the yoke with the Master. This must also be our calling as missionaries—perhaps even more now than at other times in our lives.

When you have disappointments, remember that He too carried a heavy burden. If you truly become yoked with Him, you cannot fail. The yoke of Christ is easy and his burden is light.

Teaching

"And he spake many things unto them in parables, saying, Behold, a sower went forth to sow; And when he sowed, some seeds fell by the way side, and the fowls came and devoured them up: Some fell upon stony places, where they had not much earth: and forthwith they sprang up, because they had no deepness of earth: And when the sun was up, they were scorched; and because they had no root, they withered away. And some fell among thorns; and the thorns sprung up, and choked them: But other fell into good ground, and brought forth fruit, some an hundredfold, some sixtyfold, some thirtyfold. Who hath ears to hear, let him hear" (Matthew 13:3–9).

In this great parable, Jesus likened missionary work to the sowing of seeds. Like the sower spoken of by the Savior, you go forth each day sowing seeds in the hearts of both members and nonmembers of the Church. Jesus explained the parable this way:

1. Many of the seeds you sow fall by the wayside and are devoured by the ravens of doubt, skepticism, and sinful living.
2. Others fall in stony hearts that are at first happy to hear the glad tidings, who endure for awhile, but who fall away when tribulation and persecution arise.
3. Many seeds fall among those who hear the word but who reject it because of worldly, material things.
4. But many seeds fall on fertile ground—among those who hear the word and understand it and who pluck the fruit thereof and reap the rewards of everlasting life.

Many of you become discouraged because your seeds are sometimes sown in rocky soil or by the wayside or among the thorns. But in this parable, Jesus promises you that if you will sow your seeds, many will bear fruit. His admonition is that those who have ears to hear should hear the word.

Albert Schweitzer said, "No ray of sunlight is ever lost, but the green which it awakens into existence needs time to sprout, and it is not always granted to the sower to see the harvest. All work that is worth anything is done in faith" (in R. Lanier Britsch and Terrance D. Olson, *Counseling: A Guide to Helping Others* [Salt Lake City: Deseret Book, 1983], 1:118–19).

So it is with you. You must sow in faith, being diligent to sow as many seeds as you can every day. You sow the seeds of the gospel by bearing your testimonies, by teaching the lessons.

Are you satisfied with your performance? Can you give the concepts with confidence and conviction because you know them in your heart? Are you going the extra mile to give lessons every day? The key to baptisms is in consistently teaching quality lessons. If you teach, you will baptize; if you do not teach, you will not baptize.

Do whatever is necessary to reach the goals you have set. Teach, teach, teach. This is your calling. You must hunger and thirst after that opportunity!

Teaching and Sowing

In your mission, you have many of the greatest missionaries in the Church and many of the finest members in the Church. Why don't you have more baptisms than any mission in the Church? Or better retention of converts?

It boils down to teaching. Some missions do better than others in teaching hours per month per missionary. For example, reports from some missions show only a few hours of teaching per month per missionary, while neighboring missions might show more than fifty hours per missionary during that same period of time.

The Church has raised the bar for the calling of missionaries. It has produced a wonderful resource: *Preach My Gospel*. It has standardized the process for learning and teaching concepts rather than requiring the memorization of discussions word for word. And the prophet has called for you to become more spiritually mature, better prepared, and more persuasive as a teacher.

You all know that conversions come through teaching the gospel. If you are not teaching, conversions will not happen. If you are to touch the lives of the wonderful people in your mission, teaching must be put at the top of your list of things to do.

A new spirit of dedication must permeate our missions. It must begin with the missionaries, spread to the priesthood leaders, and then move to the members. You must hunger and thirst for teaching opportunities. As missionaries, you must:

1. Become close to the Lord through prayer, obedience, study, sacrifice, and living humble and spiritual lives. Doing this, you can have the Holy Spirit with you.
2. Concentrate on families. Speak to the head of the family. Look for fathers.
3. Teach the gospel of Jesus Christ as it is. Be completely open and honest. People are searching for quality—for that which has substance and that will add meaning to their lives. Do not

ever cover up or minimize the Word of Wisdom, sexual purity, tithing, or endurance to the end (which means Church activity for the rest of one's life).

4. Bear your testimonies often and openly.

5. Set high goals for teaching the concepts by the Spirit. Commit yourself to them.

Strive to reach new highs for the number of hours you spend teaching the gospel to those of other faiths. District leaders and zone leaders should work with individual missionaries to set goals that will take the gospel to the wonderful people of your mission.

Teaching and Working with Members

General guidelines for working with members and the procedures to use in working with priesthood leaders can help in finding member families with which to work. This discussion is on teaching members how to friendship.

1. *Be prayerful.* Teach and work by the Spirit. The single most important ingredient to success is your spiritual preparation. Don't expect the members to provide the enthusiasm for the work—you must give it. Bear your testimony, and let them know you are excited about the work. Show your enthusiasm for the changes you have seen in the lives of people as they have been converted. Tell success stories about friendshipping.

2. *Use the power of the lessons outlined in* Preach My Gospel. One missionary said that one of the greatest spiritual experiences of his mission came when he was teaching the concepts in the first lesson to a member. The lessons are the greatest single tool you have to get member families converted to friendshipping.

3. *Teach how to hold a family home evening.* Many families are holding active and spiritual home evenings, while many others are floundering. Some will want your help, while others will not. Offer to give a lesson, teach one of the missionary lessons, plan the games, or conduct the entire evening.

4. *Gain the trust and respect of the family.* Get to know them. Learn the names of the children, send birthday cards, write thank-you notes for favors, maintain your ministerial dignity, and keep busy. Be businesslike yet courteous and friendly at all times. Let them know you take your missionary work seriously. Bear your testimony.

5. *Help family members gain more confidence in themselves.* Most families are reluctant to friendship because they don't know how or because they are afraid. As you teach them the discussions, they will gain confidence in you and in

themselves. If they feel they cannot friendship another family by themselves, suggest that another family be invited to help. Strength in numbers will give them more confidence.

6. *Help the family make a plan.* There comes a time when you should encourage the family to make a friendshipping plan.

7. *Keep in touch.* It may take some families a long time before they will be ready to begin friendshipping and even longer before you can begin teaching their friends. Be patient. Don't push or be overly aggressive. Remember that your work is a cooperative adventure with a member family in sharing the gospel. Let them progress at their own speed—every family is different. Don't impose your will on them. Do things for them—save them time so they can spend time friendshipping. Visit them regularly. Give them all of the lessons if they desire.

Joseph Smith said, "After all that has been said, the greatest and most important duty is to preach the gospel" (*History of the Church,* 2:478). Your role is to show members the opportunities that are theirs—and to do it lovingly, understandingly, patiently, and enthusiastically.

Teaching by the Spirit

Too many missionaries have become so intent in grasping the concepts of the lessons and giving the words mechanically that they have forgotten that their first great calling is teaching. Teaching involves much more than merely reciting a group of words. The qualities of a great teacher are: (a) love for the people he is teaching, (b) love of the subject he is teaching, (c) knowledge of his subject, (d) enthusiasm, and (e) ability to convey all of this to those he is teaching.

In teaching, you should compare yourself to the Master Teacher, Jesus Christ. As a teacher and leader, the Savior taught in the following ways:

He served his disciples and taught them to give service.

He companioned with them.

He engaged them in instructive conversation.

He individualized them; each was taught according to his own needs.

He gave them work to do; he challenged them to do something.

He won their confidence. They were at ease with Him.

He asked them questions to stimulate them to think.

He clearly taught them profound eternal truths.

He put responsibility upon them.

He listened to them with patience and understanding.

The following teaching principles may help you become the kind of teacher who will change the lives of those you are teaching:

1. *Learn to give the concepts by the Spirit.* The First Presidency said, "The missionary should feel free to use his own words as prompted by the Spirit" (*Preach My Gospel,* 30). You may depart from the order of the lessons, giving that which you are

inspired to do. They also said that you should speak from the heart. Learn to give the lessons in your own words (keeping the thought of each concept) and in the order you feel is best for your investigators.

2. *Learn to use yourself.* You have your own personality, your own approach. Knowledge of the subject is necessary, but effective teaching also requires that you learn to use yourself in the best way. As you learn about yourself, you become confident; you gain conviction. Your investigators will trust you when you trust yourself.

3. *Look at the other person's point of view.* Sometimes this quality is called empathy. This is the capacity to put yourself in the other person's shoes and to see how things look from his point of view. Would your teaching convince *you?*

4. *Be worthy of and sensitive to the whisperings of the Spirit.* If you have mastered the concepts and are worthy, the promptings will come.

5. *Be sensitive to the needs of your investigators.* Great teachers are concerned about people; poor teachers are concerned with words, dialogues, procedures, statistics, and pride. A great teacher believes in people and what they can become.

6. *Have faith in God, in yourself, and in those you are teaching.* "And the Spirit shall be given unto you by the prayer of faith; and if ye receive not the Spirit ye shall not teach" (D&C 42:14).

Testifying and Challenging

You often hear that you should be missionaries who testify and challenge. Joseph Smith said, "It should be the duty of the elder to stand up boldly for the cause of Christ, and warn the people with one accord to repent and be baptized for the remission of sins, and for the Holy Ghost, always commanding them in the name of the Lord in the spirit of meekness" (*History of the Church,* 2: 263–64).

What does it mean to testify? To testify is to bear record by the power of the Spirit of the truths of the gospel of Jesus Christ. You should testify and teach of the following truths: (1) the divinity of the Lord Jesus Christ, (2) the divine mission of the Prophet Joseph Smith, and (3) the divine purposes of the restored gospel of The Church of Jesus Christ of Latter-day Saints.

What does it mean to challenge? To challenge is to inspire and invite people to repent; to turn away from unrighteousness; to persuade them to read, ponder, pray, and be baptized. People need to be asked. They need to be challenged. They need a goal. Help them set such a goal, and then challenge them to meet it.

The process of testifying and challenging has four principal parts:

1. *Recognize the problem or objections of the investigator.* If he has a problem with the Word of Wisdom or cannot accept a particular doctrine, you must find out what it is.

2. *Teach from the scriptures and from modern prophets.* Once you have isolated his problems or objections (Word of Wisdom, prayer, or whatever), teach the principle and explain why it is important. Use the scriptures.

3. *Testify that what you are teaching is true.* Let him know that you know the principles you have just taught him are true. You are commanded to teach by the Spirit and in so doing you must testify of the truth. If you will bear a strong testimony, the Spirit will bear witness to the person you're teaching.

4. *Issue a challenge to action.* It may be a challenge to study a

specific principle, to attend church, or to live the Word of Wisdom. In making your challenge, you must be positive.

Instead of, "Do you think you might try reading the Book of Mormon since you know it is necessary?" try, "Will you read the Book of Mormon?"

Instead of, "Maybe if you would pray about Joseph, you might find out," try, "I know if you pray and ask Heavenly Father if Joseph Smith was a prophet, you will know too."

Instead of, "Do you think you could quit smoking?" try, "Will you quit smoking today?"

The gospel of Jesus Christ is best taught through sincere, personal testimony. A challenge presented with a sincere testimony will lead a person to action. If you will learn and apply these principles, you will find success in your labors.

Thoughts #1

"For as he thinketh in his heart, so is he" (Proverbs 23:7).

Most of you understand the principle given by the Lord to "let virtue garnish thy thoughts unceasingly" (D&C 121:45). You know how important it is to control your thoughts. You know that actions are preceded by thoughts. You know that you must strive to purify your thoughts. You know that those who can control their thoughts can control themselves. You know that the great quest in life is the quest for self-discipline and self-control.

One of the most common questions is, "How can I control my thoughts?" How do you keep your mind free from immoral, carnal, sensual thoughts?

Unclean thoughts are always around you, waiting to get into your minds. In this day and age—when pornography and sensuality are everywhere—you must fight even harder to keep out their unholy influences. It has been said that we cannot keep birds from flying over our heads, but we can keep them from nesting in our hair. We cannot keep strangers from knocking on our doors, but we can keep from inviting them in and entertaining them. Similarly, you cannot keep thoughts from coming into your mind, but you can—and must—get them out again immediately. The more you harbor them, play upon them, entertain them, think about them—the more difficult it is to get rid of them.

The brain is a marvelous and unique storage bank. It works like a giant muscle: the more you use and exercise it, the stronger it becomes. The more you train it to reject or eject unclean thoughts, the more capable it becomes. You must therefore exercise the brain regularly in rejecting unclean thoughts.

The brain also seems to work in ruts or creases. Once a crease has been formed, other thoughts seem to drift into this crease. This might be likened to a ski hill on which many skiers have worn creases or ruts into the slopes by constant use. As a skier tries to cross one of these ruts, he is pulled into it as he goes downhill. Once he gets caught in one of them, it is difficult to change his course or to get out of the rut until he reaches the bottom. If the rut is going the wrong way, skiers must carefully build new creases or new ruts to go in the direction they want to go. Your thoughts follow this pattern. Once something triggers a thought or a memory, you are prone to follow along that rut until it takes you farther and farther down the hill toward destruction. The secret is to build new creases in your brain—creases that are holy, uplifting, and righteous rather than debasing, destructive, and immoral.

You do this by replacing evil thoughts with good thoughts. You cannot have two separate thoughts in your mind at the same time. Using this principle, you must get rid of the evil thought by replacing it with a virtuous thought. This habit must be formed by doing it over and over again until it becomes an automatic reflex in your thought patterns—as soon as an evil thought comes into your mind, your system must automatically turn to a spiritual or uplifting thought to force out the evil thought. This can become a built-in habit and reflex.

President Gordon B. Hinckley said, "Mental control must be stronger than physical appetites. . . . Each of us, with discipline and effort, has the capacity to control our thoughts and our actions" ("Reverence and Morality," *Ensign*, May 1987, 47). You have the capacity. What you need is the discipline.

Thoughts #2

It is important—vital—to replace unclean thoughts with virtuous thoughts. You can force out evil thoughts by placing in the mind virtuous and wholesome thoughts that will take their place.

It takes a powerful thought to do this. When you try to force out a thought as powerful and as consuming as a sensual thought, your new thought must be something important and meaningful to you. It must, in a sense, overwhelm the unclean thought. A struggle will usually take place, and you will need a heavyweight thought to overcome the one with which you are struggling.

Each one of you must develop for yourself those thoughts that are important enough to create new creases in your mind to replace the ruts that you sometimes have. Here are a few ideas:

1. President Boyd K. Packer suggests that sometimes your favorite Church hymns will be sufficient to erase other thoughts from your mind. He suggests that you sing the words of the hymn out loud and ponder the words as you sing them. This will start you off on a string of thoughts that will take you far away from your unclean thoughts (Boyd K. Packer, "Inspiring Music—Worthy Thoughts," *Ensign,* January 1974, 25).

2. Another method is to turn to your favorite scriptures. Read, ponder, and pray as you study them. Some missionaries see how many scriptures they can recite from memory. Others see how many concepts from the lessons they can remember.

3. Some have recommended an intense look at the chapters in *Preach My Gospel* to study and be reminded of the principles taught there. A particular subject may have sufficient interest to occupy your full thoughts and interests.

4. Thoughts of mothers, fathers, grandparents, sweethearts or other dear ones are often sufficient to crowd out the thoughts of evil. As you contemplate the goodness of such close ones, the negative feelings of the adversary leave you.

5. Many people replace bad thoughts with thoughts of the Savior—his goodness, his ministry, his unselfishness, his sacrifice, and his teachings. If you have sincerely studied His life and teachings, this will be a powerful influence that will move all unclean thoughts out of your mind. Thinking about Christ and remembering him brings His Spirit into your life.

6. One mission president's method was to turn to the Prophet Joseph Smith and his great strengths and sacrifices. His courage, stalwartness, undeviating testimony in the face of adversity, trials and tribulations, goodness to his associates, unselfishness, and great humility have always been examples this mission president has admired. As he thinks about the Prophet's experiences, his mind is overwhelmed with Joseph's greatness. His thoughts are filled with his teachings, his leadership, his total dedication to the cause of the gospel. There is no room left in his mind for other things.

Whether your method includes one of these or something of your own making, remember that replacement is the answer. While replacing bad thoughts with good thoughts, pray to your Heavenly Father for the strength to overcome. Commit yourself to Him that you will keep your thoughts virtuous and holy, for as He has said, "Look unto me in every thought" (D&C 6:36).

Time

There is an intriguing statue in Chicago that portrays time as standing still while mankind passes by. The concept is that time is always there—endless and inexhaustible—while man comes, uses, and passes on. Like a magic fountain that never runs out of water, time is there for those who want to partake of it.

But there is something wrong with this concept. For you, time is not endless and inexhaustible. Nothing you can do will stop the clock from inexorably going on, minute after minute and hour after hour, until your time runs out.

The supply of time is truly a daily miracle. God has given you each day—whether you be good or bad, industrious or lazy, rich or poor, mighty or weak. It is yours, and no one receives more or less than another. The use you make of it determines your success or failure, your joy or sorrow, your status in life and in the life to come.

You cannot buy more time. You cannot borrow time from the future to use today. Tomorrow is kept for you by a benevolent Heavenly Father, and the time already spent cannot be recovered. Everything depends upon how you use the twenty-four hours given to you each day. If you have time, anything is possible; without it, nothing is possible.

Elder Neal A. Maxwell said, "Time, unlike some material things, cannot be recycled" (*Neal A. Maxwell Quote Book*, ed. Cory H. Maxwell [Salt Lake City: Bookcraft, 1997], 348). He also said, "How we spend our time . . . is as good a measure of us as how we spend our money" (347). Benjamin Franklin said that if you love life you should not squander time. "Time," he said, "is the stuff life is made of" (in *Teachings of Ezra Taft Benson*, 383). Thoreau states that we "cannot kill time without injuring eternity" (*Waldon* [Boston: Beacon press, 1997]).

How are you using the time given you each day by your Father in Heaven? When you leave your apartment, do you always know where you are going and for what purpose? Do you crisscross your path unnecessarily? Do you spend two hours at a member's home when fifteen minutes would serve your purpose and make your future visits more welcome? Do you use the tools provided for the wise use and management of your time—your daily planner and area books? Do you and your companion carefully plan each day so as to get the most value out of each hour and minute? Can you effectively manage your time? Do you? Bernard Baruch said, "The man who can manage his time can manage anything."

Budget your time even more carefully than you budget your money. You can always get more money, but you can never get more time. Remember that the future is that time when you will wish that you had done what you aren't doing now!

Time—how precious it is, yet how much is wanted by all. Resolve with your companions that you will plan more wisely, think more carefully, work more diligently, and act more exemplary.

President Gordon B. Hinckley said to missionaries, "You have a great work to do, and if you don't do it, who will? Don't waste your time, please. You are here to do the work of the Lord. He needs your help. On your narrow shoulders rests this work" (*Teachings of Gordon B. Hinckley*, 363).

To Forgive

A hardened Japanese soldier was captured by the U.S. Marines during the battle for Corregidor during World War II. Full of hatred for his captors, he vowed revenge for those of his countrymen who had died in battle. He was placed in various prison camps, but everywhere he was sent, he caused trouble.

One day a fellow prisoner of war handed him a copy of the Bible. Having nothing else to do, he began to read it and became particularly interested in the trial of Jesus. When he read in Luke the words Jesus spoke while on the cross, "Father, forgive them; for they know not what they do," (Luke 23:34) he was stunned. He became converted to Christianity, was released from prison at the end of the war, and lived out his life in the United States among the people whom he had once hated.

One of the greatest qualities you can develop is that of forgiveness. George Herbert said, "He that cannot forgive others breaks the bridge over which he himself must pass if he would ever reach heaven, for everyone has need to be forgiven" (in *Favorite Quotations from the Collection of Thomas S. Monson*, 203). The Apostle Paul said, "And be ye kind one to another, tenderhearted, forgiving one another, even as God for Christ's sake hath forgiven you" (Ephesians 4:32). The Lord has commanded you to forgive one another: "Ye ought to forgive one another; for he that forgiveth not his brother his trespasses standeth condemned before the Lord; for there remaineth in him the greater sin" (D&C 64:9).

When a person is wronged in some way, his natural inclination is to fight back, to get even. Although this reaction is human, it is almost always in error. It is not Christ's way.

There is a story told about a Hungarian refugee who fled to America after the Hungarian uprising in 1956. He was a strong believer in freedom for his country. He had fought Russian tanks in Budapest.

When he arrived in the United States, he had no money, no job, and no friends, but he was well educated. He spoke and wrote several languages and had been a successful young lawyer in Hungary. It finally occurred to him that perhaps his knowledge of languages might be an asset to an import-export company. He selected one such company and wrote a letter to the owner. Two weeks later he received an answer. Among other things, the answer from the company said that even if they did need someone, they wouldn't hire him because he couldn't write proper English.

His hurt soon turned to anger, and he wrote a scathing reply that was calculated to rip to shreds the man who wrote the letter. But his anger began to diminish before he mailed the letter. He remembered that "in wrath, remember mercy" (Habakkuk 3:2). He decided that maybe the man was right; maybe he did need further study. He tore up the letter and wrote another. He apologized for his previous letter, explained his situation, and thanked the writer for pointing out his weaknesses. Two days later he received a telephone call to invite him to an interview. Later he became president of the company—succeeding the very man who had written the letter that so angered him.

If you seek retribution against those who have wronged you, if you think bad thoughts about a companion, if you become angry with someone who is not doing as you think he should, remember the admonition of the Lord: "I, the Lord, will forgive whom I will forgive, but of you it is required to forgive all men" (D&C 64:10).

Transgressions

A man was once excommunicated from the Church. He was a wealthy man with many worldly possessions, such as a boat, an airplane, several cars, a luxurious home, and a high monthly income. With tears in his eyes, he said, "I would give all I own and all that I will ever own if I could have back my membership in the Church."

One mission president was working on a Church matter concerning a man who had been excommunicated several years before. All of his papers for rebaptism had been sent to the First Presidency, including letters of recommendation from his former bishop and stake president and other required materials. Later, this mission president received a letter from the First Presidency that indicated that the time was not yet right for this man to come back into the Church.

These experiences prompt me to again review the hazards of moral transgressions. The sexual drive within you is one of the great blessings of God. Like so many of His blessings, however, Satan has twisted it to make it one of his strongest weapons of destruction. Like fire, water, or nuclear energy, your physical desires can bring you happiness and joy if used properly and wisely. If allowed to run wild or if used improperly, they can destroy you just as surely as fire, water, or nuclear energy. It would be good for each missionary to witness a disciplinary council for a fellow missionary—to feel and see the anguish and heartache of those involved and to talk to the missionary's parents and feel of their sorrow and disappointment.

In nearly every case of moral transgression by a missionary, the problems began when he began treating lightly the missionary rules. Any mission president, stake president, or bishop will tell you that he has never known of a missionary who committed fornication without first violating other missionary standards.

This is Satan's way. He lures you into breaking small rules and then helps you rationalize and justify your actions. Then larger transgressions occur, along with the appropriate justification. Next comes criticism of the rules and of those who are called to enforce them. Then, in some way, comes the feeling that "everybody does it," and somewhere along the line comes the illusion that these infractions would not come to light—that no one will find out about them.

President Kimball said, "You might be able for a time to deceive your associates and leaders. But you cannot lie to yourself nor to your Lord, for in spite of all the rationalization, you know deep in your heart what you are. You may be able to convince your mind that it is not so wrong, but, down deep in your heart, you will always be uneasy and unhappy and know that your sin is vicious and base. Remember, there are no rooms with such tight windows or with blinds so heavy but that the Lord and his angels know what is going on. There are no corners so dark, canyons or hills or deserts so remote, but that every word and act and thought is known and is recorded."

Repent of any past problems or transgressions and thereby arm yourselves against temptation. "Be ye clean that bear the vessels of the Lord," the Savior said (D&C 133:5). Seldom does a person show greater courage and faith than when he is humble and repentant. Following the steps of repentance will bring forgiveness, peace of mind, and matchless joy.

Transgressions

A mission president related the following: "My heart is heavy as I address the missionaries this week. The painful experience of excommunication is always difficult. To see a missionary excommunicated from the Church is even more excruciating and sorrowful. One of our elders was excommunicated by a disciplinary council this week for violations of the moral code of the Church.

"I wish each missionary could be a part of the interviews and of a mission court to feel and see the anguish and heartache of those involved—and could talk to the parents and feel of their despair, sorrow, and disappointment.

"These experiences prompt me again to review with you the hazards of moral transgressions. The sexual drive within us is one of the great blessings of God; like so many of His blessings, however, Satan has twisted it to make it one of his strongest weapons of destruction. Like fire, water, or nuclear energy, the blessings of our physical desires can bring us happiness and joy if used properly and wisely; if allowed to run wild or if used improperly, they can destroy us just as surely as fire, water, or nuclear energy can destroy us if used improperly or allowed to get out of hand.

"In nearly every case of moral transgression by a missionary, the problems began when he or she began treating lightly the missionary rules. In my experience with missionaries here and as a bishop and stake president at home, I have never known of a missionary who committed fornication without first of all violating other missionary standards over a period of time. That was also true in this case.

"This is Satan's way. He lures you into breaking small rules and then helps you rationalize and justify your actions. Then larger transgressions occur, along with the appropriate justification. Next comes criticism of the rules and of those who are called to enforce them. Then in some way comes the feeling that everybody does it, and somewhere along the line comes the illusion that these infractions will not come to light—that no one will find out about them."

President Gordon B. Hinckley has recounted the time he went to President McKay to plead the cause of a missionary, saying to the prophet, "He did it on an impulse." President McKay said, "His mind was dwelling on these things before he transgressed. The thought was father to the deed. There would not have been that impulse if he had previously controlled his thoughts" (Gordon B. Hinckley, "Be Ye Clean," *Ensign*, May 1996, 48).

President Hinckley said to missionaries, "Clever are the designs of the adversary. Be careful. You want to go home in honor. Don't step into tragedy. Transgression never was happiness. Sin never was happiness. Evil never was happiness" (*Teachings of Gordon B. Hinckley*, 358).

Repent of any past problems or transgressions, and thereby arm yourselves against temptation. "Be ye clean that bear the vessels of the Lord," the Savior said (D&C 133:5). Seldom does a person show greater courage and faith than when he is humbly repentant. Following the steps of repentance will bring forgiveness, peace of mind, and matchless joy.

Trouble

There was a member of the Church whose employment required him to look for problems. His job was to visit the various offices and plants of his company and find trouble. He became very good at it. In fact, he became vice president of his company because he was adept at finding problems. He could visit a plant, look at their production schedule, walk through the assembly lines, spend a few minutes looking at the records, and then spot slowdowns, bottlenecks, inefficiency, unqualified personnel, and other problems.

Unfortunately, he carried his nose for trouble into his personal life. He became critical of his wife and family. He began to find fault with his community, state, and country. He nitpicked Church procedures and the way the bishop ran the ward. He complained about the way the neighbors raised their children. Finally, he became disenchanted with the way God ran the world. Life became bitter as he spent more and more time finding problems and less and less time finding solutions.

At the time of his death a few years ago, he was making progress on the long, slow road back. He retired from his company early, became active in the Church, and began training himself to find the good in things. He developed a positive attitude toward others. In short, he discovered the error of his ways and began making a conscious, determined effort to find good in all people and all things. A poet once wrote:

> Do not trouble trouble till trouble troubles you;
> Do not look for trouble, let trouble look for you.
> Do not hurry worry—by worrying, it comes;
> To flurry is to worry, 'twill miss you if you're "mum."
> Then do not trouble trouble, till trouble troubles you;
> You'll only double trouble, and trouble others, too.

It is often easier to find fault with others than it is to find good in them. It is easier to criticize a program than it is to follow it or support it. But there would be less faultfinding if all faultfinders had to come from the ranks of the faultless. Thomas Fuller said, "Search others for their virtues, and thyself for vices" ("In the Wake of the Church," *Contributor* 4 [May 1883], 307).

He who is critical toward himself will often be charitable toward others. He who looks for faults in others will usually be blind to his own shortcomings. He who is looking for solutions will not be burdened down with problems.

Develop a positive attitude—one that will find good in all things. By doing this, you will find friends, satisfaction, happiness, and joy. You will be constructive rather than destructive. You will be a builder rather than a destroyer, and you will help rather than hinder. Anyone can grumble, criticize, or censure. Faultfinding is as easy as it is dangerous.

There may be merit in questioning, doubting, and looking for a better way, but first of all, develop the firm foundation of a positive attitude. Then, and only then, should you step out onto the thin ice of criticism, negativism, and questioning.

True Grit

One of the essential elements in successful missionary work is "true grit"—sometimes called by such names as firmness, resolution, courage, fortitude, spirit, determination, internal strength, perseverance, and diligence.

Whatever it is, it is the best there is in a person. It is that fine, sturdy quality that whispers in your ear in moments of discouragement: "Hang on, don't give up, you can make it if you keep trying." It usually isn't talent that ensures success—it is the power to labor energetically and perseveringly.

When you stumble or fall in your pursuits, it isn't because of your lack of ability; it is because of laziness, discouragement, impatience, superficiality, or lack of confidence. True grit will overcome all of these.

Laziness blinds the creative juices within you, destroys resourcefulness, and undermines the spirit to succeed. It despises effort. It is utterly lacking in any positive qualities. It is when your get-up-and-go has got up and gone. Determination overcomes laziness. True grit helps you overcome your weaknesses.

Discouragement is nourished by past events—living in yesterdays. Yesterday is gone, tomorrow hasn't come, so today's discouragement should be forgotten tomorrow. Remember only enough of past mistakes to learn from them. Will Rogers said, "Don't let yesterday use up too much of today." True grit helps you forget yesterdays.

Lack of confidence is also caused by past events. Use your forgetter. Approach every new task, every new companion, every new area, and every new threshold with confidence of success. True grit helps you have confidence in the future.

Impatience is the opposite of perseverance. It is always in a hurry. Impatience says, "Life is too short," "Step on the gas," "What do I care?" "Full speed ahead," and "Roll over anybody who gets in my way." Impatience is one of the great causes of failure because an impatient person doesn't have time to love others. Take time to enjoy what you are doing—to enjoy others. Avoid contention and recognize the feelings of others. True grit helps you to love life and to love others.

Superficiality is often called the "soap bubble of life." The superficial person inflates himself with an idea, colors it with all the colors of the rainbow, and then—pop!—it disappears. Superficiality—soap bubbles— contain nothing of an enduring solidarity. Bubbles are transitory pleasures. Many missionaries live in a dream world where they fancy themselves doing all kinds of impossible things. When their bubbles pop, they have nothing left to stand on. Build your labors on a solid basis of work and preparation. True grit helps you make your wishes come true.

Robert Collier said, "True grit is the power to say 'no' to what seems like a multitude of angels when they could counsel you away from downright loyalty to your instant duty." You get to the top—you find success—because of the strength that grows out of meeting resistance. True grit helps you stick with a task until it is done.

The Lord said, "If they humble themselves before me, and have faith in me, then will I make weak things become strong unto them" (Ether 12:27).

Trunkiness

As you contemplate goals for the coming weeks, here is a suggestion that will help your mission greatly: do not get trunky, and help others to avoid it.

Ever since missionaries began entering the field, some of them, in the closing stages of their missions, have developed that well-known malady labeled "trunkiness." You smile at it, poke fun at it, kid others about it, make jokes about it. Yet, it is a serious indication of a missionary's true attitude and feeling.

Trunkiness is something you must correct early in your life. Otherwise, it will plague you in every calling and assignment you ever receive.

Many people tend to put their eggs in one basket—the basket of the future. Think of how often you have said, "When I get off my mission . . ." or "When I get through college . . ." or "When I get my car paid off . . ." or "When spring comes . . ." or "When I get a new job . . ."

This attitude of living in the future is devastating. The future depends upon how you use the present. Dale Carnegie said, "One of the most tragic things I know about human nature is that all of us tend to put off living. We are all dreaming of some magical rose garden over the horizon instead of enjoying the roses that are blooming outside our windows today." Today's efforts are the foundation stones upon which we build the opportunities of tomorrow.

Nathaniel Hawthorne said that by "postponing the reality of life, one has no present and gradually ceases to have a future." Henry Thoreau said: "Pluck the fruit of each day as it passes, and store it safely."

The main complaint of many missionaries who are being released is the relentless pressure of other missionaries talking about going home: "Only five more weeks?" "How many days left?" "What's the date?" "Are you getting trunky?"

It is not a laughing matter. An elder's most productive time on his mission should be the last six months. By this time he has gained the experiences and abilities to make him an outstanding missionary. But the worries and concern of going home—plus the constant reminders by well-meaning missionaries and Church members—combine to drag him down.

It is a serious problem. All missionaries need to make those last six months the very best and most effective. You can do it by working together. Never mention a date. Keep your own date confidential. Don't ask about the release date of other missionaries.

One elder kept his release date so confidential that his own companion did not know it until the final day. This elder was determined that not one day of his mission would be lost to trunkiness.

Your total commitment to this principle will result in raising the morale and effectiveness of the mission in which you are serving and will make your own mission more rewarding.

Trust

President Gordon B. Hinckley said, "Missionary work is a work of love and trust, and it has to be done on that basis" (*Teachings of Gordon B. Hinckley*, 374). President David O. McKay frequently said, "It is better to be trusted than loved" (in Victor L. Ludlow, *Principles and Practices of the Restored Gospel* [Salt Lake City: Deseret Book, 1992], 425).

Missionaries need to be trusted by members, priesthood leaders, investigators, and fellow missionaries. Most important, however, they need to be trusted by God.

How does God learn to trust you? Only by experience. Here are seven ways to gain the trust of your Heavenly Father:

1. *Have faith.* Have faith in God, faith in Church leaders and the prophet, faith in prayer, people, mission programs, and yourself. Know that the kingdom is here in its fulness and that Satan is here to deceive you. Grasp the iron rod.

2. *Be obedient.* God cannot work through an unworthy vessel. "I, the Lord, am bound when ye do what I say; but when ye do not what I say, ye have no promise" (D&C 82:10). Samuel said to Saul, "To obey is better than sacrifice" (1 Samuel 15: 22). God no longer trusted Saul, and he was denied the kingship.

3. *Be dedicated.* Be unwavering in your commitment to the work. "For he that wavereth is like a wave of the sea driven with the wind and tossed. For let not that man think that he shall receive any thing of the Lord" (James 1:6–7). Be loyal to your calling as a minister of the gospel. "And if your eye be single to my glory, your whole bodies shall be filled with light, and there shall be no darkness in you; and that body which is filled with light comprehendeth all things" (D&C 88:67).

4. *Get knowledge.* Follow the study plan outlined in *Preach My Gospel.* Learn and love the scriptures. Teach regularly to members and investigators. Remember this basic principle: The more you learn, the more you are capable of learning. The Lord

expects His missionaries to be prepared to teach His gospel. "If ye are prepared ye shall not fear" (D&C 38:30).

5. *Learn to love.* Love God, love your investigators, love the members, love your companion, love yourself. Be patient and tolerant of others. If you are offended by someone, forgive them. "Let thy bowels also be full of charity towards all men . . . and let virtue garnish thy thoughts unceasingly" (D&C 121:45). President Hinckley said, "Love of God is basic. It is the very foundation of true worship. It puts heart and soul and spirit into our lives. It leads to love for all" (*Teachings of Gordon B. Hinckley*, 318–19).

6. *Set high goals and standards.* The final step upward is the result of many steps in the right direction, and the final step downward is the result of many steps in that direction. Set high goals for yourself, both in your missionary efforts and in your personal life.

7. *Be enthusiastic.* Have a positive mental attitude. Go the extra mile. You are engaged in the greatest cause the world has ever known—recognize it and be enthusiastic about it.

There is no greater feeling in the world than to be trusted by God. Do all you can to get and maintain this trust.

Winning

Most major league baseball pitchers keep a little black book in which they note weaknesses of opposing batters. Vernon Law, a pitching star of the Pittsburgh Pirates for many years and now a retired member of the BYU physical education staff, kept a notebook—but with far different notations.

When asked one day by a baseball reporter for a look in his notebook, Vern was a little embarrassed because of his lack of data about his worldly opposition. He felt that his greatest problem was not in other people—opposing batters and other ballplayers—but in himself. Although he had information in his book about opposing hitters, he also had listed on every page at least one reminder to himself that success came not from outwitting others but in controlling himself.

Look over the following observations made in Vern's little black book, and see how they apply to your work as a missionary:

1. You'll never become a .300 hitter unless you take your bat off your shoulder.
2. When you start to slide into base—*slide.* He who changes his mind halfway through may exchange a good leg for a broken one.
3. A winner never quits, and a quitter never wins.
4. Experience is a hard teacher because she gives the test first, and the lesson afterward.
5. Nobody ever became a ballplayer by walking after the ball.
6. If you don't play to win, why keep score?
7. There is no "I" in "team."
8. Those who are busy rowing the boat don't have time to rock it.
9. Some people are so busy learning the tricks of the trade that they never learn the trade.
10. Don't throw the ball before you have it.
11. When you're through learning, you're through.

It's interesting to see how each one of Vern's observations applies to missionaries as well as to big league pitchers. It's also interesting to look over each one of these statements and to think about how they apply to the great stalwarts of God—the Savior, Joseph Smith, Moses, Abraham, Ammon, Alma, Wilford Woodruff, Gordon B. Hinckley, and many other prophets and leaders. Add these statements to your own little black book and resolve to be a stalwart in the kingdom.

Worry

A. J. Marshall said, "If you don't have to do anything about the problem, it's silly to worry about it; if you intend to solve it, worry isn't necessary." This means that you shouldn't worry about things you cannot change, and you should stop worrying and get to work on things you can change.

However, if you are like everyone else, you probably have a slight tendency to worry more than is necessary. If so, the following guidelines may help you:

1. *Keep your perspective.* When you sense that you may be making a mountain out of a molehill, ask yourself how big this problem will look in six months.
2. *Don't fear mistakes.* Remember, you can only be free from error if you never do anything. Learn from your mistakes, but don't repeat them.
3. *Take a positive attitude.* Thinking that you can is half the battle.
4. *Expect some disappointment.* You can't win 'em all. Even if you are perfect, the umpires sometimes are not.
5. *Make decisions.* Indecisiveness is the root of many problems.
6. *Pinpoint your worries.* Worries thrive best when you refuse to acknowledge them. Analyze what you are worrying about. Isolate the problems so you can solve them.
7. *Talk out your problems.* Talk with your companion or one of your leaders. Don't seek sympathy; seek solutions.
8. *Make a change.* Remove yourself from the situation. You may get new insight on how to cope with the problem by turning your interests temporarily to something else. Back away from the problem to get a good look at it. Sometimes you are so close to the tree that you can't see the forest, or so deep in the forest that you can't see the tree.
9. *Remember that you are not alone.* Others have had problems similar to or even worse than yours, and many have learned to

deal with their problems. Therefore, you know it can be done because others have done it.

10. "Faith without works is dead" (James 2:26). Even faith needs action to make it work. Worry will dissolve as you get to work on the problem.

See if you can remember what you were so worried about last year at this time. If you can't, then this should convince you to stop worrying about worries.

About the Author

Dr. Raymond E. Beckham is a retired faculty member and administrator of Brigham Young University. He has been a member of the Church Melchizedek Priesthood Committee, the Church Adult Curriculum Committee, the Church Home Teaching Committee, and the Church Olympic Coordinating Committee. He has served as a bishop, stake president, mission president, temple sealer, a member of a temple presidency, and a regional representative of the Twelve.

He served eight years as a full-time volunteer in the Public Affairs Department of the Church. In community service, he was president of the Utah National Parks Council of the Boy Scouts of America, chairman of a Red Cross chapter, president of the Provo Downtown Alliance, and a member of United Way and many other community organizations. He has been awarded the BYU Presidential Medal, the Rotary Club's Service-above-Self Award, the Red Cross Clara Barton Award, the BYU Alumni Association Distinguished Service Award, Provo's Outstanding Citizen

Award, and scouting's Silver Beaver.

He is the father of five children, nineteen grandchildren, and five great-grandchildren. After his wife, IdaLee Jackson, passed away, he married Janette Callister Hales, former general president of Young Women. She and her late husband, Robert H. Hales, have five children and fourteen grandchildren.